THE HIRSCHFELD ARCHIVES

In the series Sexuality Studies,
edited by Janice Irvine *and* Regina Kunzel

ALSO IN THIS SERIES:

Ryan Murphy, *Deregulating Desire: Flight Attendant Activism, Family Politics, and Workplace Justice*

Heike Bauer, *Sexology and Translation: Cultural and Scientific Encounters across the Modern World*

Lynette Chua, *Mobilizing Gay Singapore: Rights and Resistance in an Authoritarian State*

Thomas A. Foster, *Sex and the Founding Fathers: The American Quest for a Relatable Past*

Colin R. Johnson, *Just Queer Folks: Gender and Sexuality in Rural America*

Lisa Sigel, *Making Modern Love: Sexual Narratives and Identities in Interwar Britain*

THE HIRSCHFELD ARCHIVES

Violence, Death, and Modern Queer Culture

HEIKE BAUER

TEMPLE UNIVERSITY PRESS
Philadelphia • Rome • Tokyo

TEMPLE UNIVERSITY PRESS
Philadelphia, Pennsylvania 19122
www.temple.edu/tempress

Copyright © 2017 by Temple University—Of The Commonwealth System
　of Higher Education
All rights reserved
Published 2017

Library of Congress Cataloging-in-Publication Data

Names: Bauer, Heike, author.
Title: The Hirschfeld archives : violence, death, and modern queer culture / Heike Bauer.
Description: Philadelphia : Temple University Press, 2017. | Series: Sexuality studies |
　Includes bibliographical references and index.
Identifiers: LCCN 2016049922| ISBN 9781439914328 (hardback) |
　ISBN 9781439914335 (paper)
Subjects: LCSH: Sexual minorities—Violence against. | Institut für Sexualwissenschaft—
　Archives. | BISAC: HISTORY / Modern / 20th Century. | SOCIAL SCIENCE /
　Gay Studies.
Classification: LCC HQ73 .B38 2017 | DDC 306.76—dc23 LC record available at
　https://lccn.loc.gov/2016049922

∞ The paper used in this publication meets the requirements of the American National
Standard for Information Sciences—Permanence of Paper for Printed Library Materials,
ANSI Z39.48-1992

Printed in the United States of America

9 8 7 6 5 4 3 2 1

In memory of

my grandmother, Amalie Kirstein,

and my great-aunt Anna Zimmer,

strong, beloved women

Contents

	Acknowledgments	ix
	Introduction	1
1	Sexual Rights in a World of Wrongs: Reframing the Emergence of Homosexual Rights Activism in Colonial Contexts	13
2	Death, Suicide, and Modern Homosexual Culture	37
3	Normal Cruelty: Child Beatings and Sexual Violence	57
4	From Fragile Solidarities to Burnt Sexual Subjects: At the Institute of Sexual Science	78
5	Lives That Are Spoken For: Queer in Exile	102
	Coda	125
	Notes	135
	Bibliography	183
	Index	211

Acknowledgments

I have accrued many debts in the course of this research: to the people who read and commented on parts of the book; the colleagues with whom I had the good fortune to collaborate and share ideas; and the scholars, librarians, and archivists who went out of their way to give me access to materials that were difficult to obtain. I am grateful for the support of the many librarians and archivists who have assisted my research at the British Library in London; Harvard Law Library; Cambridge University Library; Oxford University Library; the Deutsches Literaturarchiv Marbach, Germany; the Deutsches Institut für Japanstudien in Tokyo; Humboldt University Library of Berlin; and the National Library of Wales in Aberystwyth. In particular, thanks are due to Ralf Dose from the Magnus-Hirschfeld-Gesellschaft in Berlin; Margaret Phillips from Berkeley Library, University of California; Shawn C. Wilson from the Kinsey Institute Archives; and Barbara Wolff from the Hebrew University of Jerusalem, who all went out of their way to assist my research. Thanks also go to the librarians and archivists from the Wellcome Library, especially Lesley Hall, who shared her own research insights. Roc Ren from the National Library of China assisted my search for an edition of the *Peking Daily News*, which seems to have mysteriously disappeared or been blocked from access. Lisa Vecoli from the Jean-Nickolaus Tretter Collection at the University of Minnesota helped with my research on Magnus Hirschfeld's legacy and revealed another mystery to me, which I discuss more fully in the Introduction. I am grateful to Stephan Likosky, who kindly granted permission to reprint the postcard of cross-dressing soldiers from his private collection, and to Jeremy Mason and Ashley Robins for their assistance with the image of Oscar Wilde on his deathbed. The research was made possible by generous funding from the Arts and Humanities Research Council (AHRC); the Wellcome Trust; the Leslie Center for the Humanities at Dartmouth College; the Birkbeck Institute for Social Research (BISR) and Birkbeck Gender and Sexuality (BiGS); and the Department of English and Humanities and the School of Arts, Birkbeck College, University of London.

While completing the book, I had the good fortune of being able to share my work with many brilliant colleagues. Jana Funke, Andrea Josipovich, Liat Kozma, Anna Katharina Schaffner, and Katie Sutton all read draft chapters, and I am extremely grateful for their astute criticism and the generous words that kept me going. Special thanks are also due to Patricia Watt, who cast her eagle eye over the manuscript. Some of the preliminary ideas and research presented in the book were first developed in articles and chapters I previously published, including "'Race,' Normativity and the History of Sexuality: The Case of Magnus Hirschfeld's *Racism* and Early-Twentieth-Century Sexology," *Psychology and Sexuality* 1, no. 3 (2010): 239–249; "Sexology Backward: Hirschfeld, Kinsey and the Reshaping of Sex Research in the 1950s," in *Queer 1950s: Rethinking Sexuality in the Postwar Years*, ed. Heike Bauer and Matt Cook (Basingstoke, UK: Palgrave Macmillan, 2012), 133–149; "Burning Sexual Subjects: Books, Homophobia and the Nazi Destruction of the Institute of Sexual Sciences in Berlin," in *Book Destruction from the Medieval to the Contemporary*, ed. Gill Partington and Adam Smyth (Basingstoke, UK: Palgrave Macmillan, 2014), 17–33; "Suicidal Subjects: Translation and the Affective Foundations of Magnus Hirschfeld's Sexology," in *Sexology and Translation: Cultural and Scientific Encounters across the Modern World, 1880–1930*, ed. Heike Bauer (Philadelphia: Temple University Press, 2015), 233–252; and "Staging Untranslatability: Magnus Hirschfeld Encounters Philadelphia," in *Un/Translatables: New Maps for Germanic Literatures*, ed. Bethany Wiggin and Catriona MacLeod (Evanston, IL: Northwestern University Press, 2016), 193–202. In developing these publications, I have benefited especially from the feedback of Matt Cook, Peter Cryle, Lisa Downing, Catriona MacLeod, Gill Partington, Adam Smyth, and Bethany Wiggin. Much of the research is in some way linked to papers I presented as part of conferences, symposia, and workshops. I express my thanks to the colleagues who invited me to share my ideas, including Nadje Al-Ali, Serena Bassi, Sean Brady, Robert Craig, Kate Fisher, Veronika Fuechtner, Robert Gillett, Douglas Haynes, Ann Heilmann, Lise Jaillant, Esther Leslie, Ina Linge, Elena Loizidou, David Midgley, Sylvia Mieszkowski, Sharon Oudit, Tuija Pulkinnen, Hadley Renkin, Sasha Roseneil, Antu Soreinen, and Elizabeth Stephens.

Thanks also go to Howard Chiang, Laura Doan, Jennifer Fraser, Natalia Gerodotti, Ting Guo, Birgit Lang, Churnjeet Mahn, Geertje Mak, Ofer Nur, Leon Rocha, Liying Sun, Michiko Suzuki, and Chris Waters.

The anonymous readers as well as the series editors at Temple University Press, Regina Kunzel and Janice Irvine, have animated my thinking and helped me clarify my ideas. My editor, Sara Cohen, and the team at Temple University Press have guided the project to completion. As always, I am first and foremost grateful for the love and support of Diane Watt.

THE HIRSCHFELD ARCHIVES

Introduction

Magnus Hirschfeld's Institute of Sexual Science plays a central role in season 2 of Jill Soloway's *Transparent* (2015), the Amazon series following the lives of the Pfefferman family from the time the now retired father, Mort, starts living openly as a woman, Maura. Set mainly in an affluent, predominantly white twenty-first-century Los Angeles, season 2 of *Transparent* frequently flashes back to life at Hirschfeld's Berlin institute in 1933. These backward glances, which are prompted by one Pfefferman daughter's exploration of her Jewish identity, affectively link Maura's turmoils to the life of her transgender aunt, Gittel, who had chosen to remain at the institute when the rest of the family left for America. While the details of what ultimately happened to Gittel never come to light in this season of the series, we last see her alive during the Nazi attack on Hirschfeld's institute, which took place on Saturday, May 6, 1933, in the cold light of day. *Transparent* renders these traumatic events as a dreamlike sequence that depicts how the serene play of a salon of beautiful queer and transgender people is harshly disrupted by Nazi men who burst through the door and brutally drag away the young people—Gittel included—while the institute director, Hirschfeld, is forced to look on helplessly. The sequence is a loose interpretation of events, not least because the historical Hirschfeld had long fled into exile by the time his institute was destroyed. By inserting an imagined character, Maura's aunt Gittel, into the surviving accounts, *Transparent* draws attention to the significance of the many unknown and unknowable figures in queer history whose lives have left no imprint on the official historical record but whose existence continues to haunt the present. The aesthetic staging of the raid on the institute in the dream-turned-nightmare spaces of trauma and (post) memory is a reminder that modern queer and transgender existence has been forged out of, and against, violence and suffering. At the same time, however, the exaggerated whiteness of the characters—many of the salon's performers are covered in white body paint—problematizes the status of queer victimhood by raising questions about the location of emerging modern sexual and transgender rights activism in central European nations such as Germany, which were built on the bodies of colonized subjects. Despite playing fast and loose with historicity, *Transparent* captures some of the fundamental truths of queer history: that the lives of people whose bodies and desires do not conform to binary social norms and expectations have been subjected to violence across time; that the victims of such violence are often imagined as white; that the intertwined histories of sexual, gender, and racial oppression and their affective reach, can be difficult to bring into view; and that Hirschfeld's life and work remain of importance to those who seek to explore these questions today.

The Hirschfeld Archives examines the violence of queer existence in the first part of the twentieth century. It pays attention to the victims of homophobic attack and gender violence but also to how the emerging homosexual rights activism was itself imbricated in everyday racism and colonial violence from around 1900 to the 1930s. During this time the new vocabulary of sex—words such as *homosexuality* and *lesbianism*, which had been coined in nineteenth-century cultural and scientific discourses in Europe—came into more widespread use, and the idea that humans are sexual beings who are somehow defined by their sexual object choice started to gain traction.[1] The book is prompted by the realization that while this history has received much attention, including in relation to the many people who have been attacked and sometimes lost their lives because their bodies and desires, real and imagined, did not match social norms and expectations, we know surprisingly little about the impact of such violence on the emergence of a more collective sense of modern queer existence. Spending time with ordinary victims whose lives have barely left an imprint in the historical archive, I want to try to bring into view how the emergence of homosexual rights discourses around 1900 was framed—and remains haunted—by not only antiqueer attacks but also colonial violence, racial oppression, and the unequal contribution of power within a society that denied full citizenship on grounds of gender. My claims are built around the work and reception of Magnus Hirschfeld, an influential sexologist who is best known today for his homosexual rights activism, foundational studies of transvestism, and opening of the world's first Institute of

Sexual Science in Berlin in 1919. The book is, however, not a biography. Instead, it excavates Hirschfeld's dispersed accounts of same-sex life and death before World War II—including published and unpublished books, articles, and diaries, as well as films, photographs, and other visual materials—to scrutinize how violence, including death, shaped modern queer culture. I turn to Hirschfeld's lesser known and overlooked writings on homosexual suicide, war, racism, sexual violence, and corporal punishment, presenting little-known, and sometimes speculative, evidence that documents the difficult, often precarious lives of ordinary people whose bodies and desires did not fit the sexual norms of their time. At the same time, I also ask what these writings can tell us about the historical situatedness of modern sexuality: Did a parochial focus on homosexuality at times obscure gender-based and colonial violence? By exploring Hirschfeld's complex and sometimes paradoxical work and reception, then, the book attends not only to how violence constitutes the archive in terms of what is destroyed and what remains across time. Examining the violence felt and experienced by people whose lives have barely left an imprint in the archives of queer and mainstream histories, it also pays attention to the gendered and racialized limits of empathy and apprehension that shaped the emergence of modern queer culture in the West and continue to haunt gay rights politics today.

This Archive Is (Not) Empty

Hirschfeld gathered what was arguably the first full-scale archive of sexual science.[2] With his colleagues at the Institute of Sexual Science in Berlin, he accumulated a large library containing books, journals, objects, and visual material as well as clinical notes, questionnaires, and other documents relating to the work of the institute itself. Hirschfeld thus played an active part in the institution of sexual knowledge. The doors to his archive were open to both scientific and lay visitors from around the world. They included doctors, scientists, and campaigners, who sometimes partook in the institute's research and clinical work, but also queer and transgender people who met, and occasionally lived, at the institute. The institute came to a sudden end when in May 1933 Nazi henchmen raided it and removed parts of the library for public burning. Chapter 4 examines these events in detail. Here I briefly discuss what happened to Hirschfeld's estate after his death, introducing the archives that underpin this book and reflecting more broadly on the issues at stake in historical archive formation.

The Nazis did not manage to destroy all Hirschfeld's papers and publications. They are today gathered in major collections in Berlin, London, and Indiana, as well as scattered across other libraries around the world. Some of

Hirschfeld's private papers and books were saved by his partner Tao Li. After Hirschfeld's death Tao Li settled for a while in Switzerland and then left Zurich for Hong Kong in the early 1960s, when his whereabouts became unknown. In 2002, however, Ralf Dose from the Magnus Hirschfeld Society in Berlin read in an online forum a message that had been posted there in 1994 by a certain Adam Smith, who was looking for members of the families of Magnus Hirschfeld and Tao Li.[3] Smith, it turned out, had been living in the same apartment building as Tao Li in Vancouver, British Columbia. While he did not know the man, he came across Tao Li's belongings by chance because they had been cleared out after his death and left in the communal bin area. It was here that Smith found a suitcase full of Tao Li's papers. Realizing that they might be of interest, he advertised their existence online and then held on to them until he was eventually contacted by Dose in 2002. Dose bought the materials from Tao Li's estate with the support of the Hirschfeld Society, the Munich forum for Homosexuality and History, and the Jean-Nickolaus Tretter Collection of the University of Minnesota. These events are now well documented. In a further twist to the story, I found that when I tried to locate the materials in Minnesota they were not listed in the library catalogue. The librarian, Lisa Vecoli, told me that the boxes from Germany had arrived empty. There is little doubt that the materials were shipped by the Hirschfeld Society, but it is unclear how they were emptied in transit and why. The only certainty at this stage is that part of Hirschfeld's—and Tao Li's—estate is once more lost. Amy L. Stone and Jaime Cantrell have likened archives to the closet, arguing that both are "queer spaces; they contain, organize, and render (il)legitimate certain aspects of LGBT life."[4] The complex history of Hirschfeld's material legacy furthermore indicates that archives are subject to circumstance, the keeper of strange knowledges, which can be shaped by serendipity and unexplained events as much as by traceable personal and financial investments or the agendas of the institutions that make it their task to select materials to keep or destroy.

The title of this book—*The Hirschfeld Archives*—takes its name not from a physical collection of texts but rather from my own queer gathering of examples from Hirschfeld's work and reception of the negation of queer existence, 1900–1930s, and the apprehensive blind spots of the emerging homosexual rights movement. The title indexes my theoretical debts to recent feminist, queer, transgender, and critical race scholarship on archives and archiving, which has shown that archival practices are bound up with fundamental questions about power, resistance, and the legitimatization or erasure of certain lives and deaths.[5] The archive as metaphor, method, and material space links bodies to discourses and subjectivities to the social. Negation here is not always manifest as a gap in the historical record. Anjali Arondekar, for example, in her work on sexuality and the colonial archive, points out that she works with an "exhaustingly plentiful" official record that "run[s] counter to our expectations of archives as lost, erased and/or disappeared."[6] In Hirschfeld's case, it is certainly true to say that despite the attacks on his work, a large body of materials survives, which provides detailed insights into his life and work. At the same time, however, Hirschfeld's often parochial focus on documenting the denial of same-sex existence indexes the kind of archival bias that lets certain subjects slip off the historical record.

The Hirschfeld Archives engages in archiving by gathering evidence from neglected sources and reading against the grain of official ones. It follows Daniel Marshall, Kevin P. Murphy, and Zeb Tortorici, who have argued that "archives [are] stages for the appearance of life,"[7] where, we might add, cultural texts function, in Ann Cvetkovich's memorable words, as "repositories of feelings and emotions, which are encoded not only in the content of the texts themselves but in the practices that surround their production and reception."[8] The book retrieves stories of queer suffering from Hirschfeld's writings and places them in dialogue with accounts of his own violent reception to reveal some of the sociopolitical contingencies that caused women and men to kill themselves or mutilate their bodies because their desires seemed to fundamentally deny their existence. It further tracks the violence that framed the emergence of homosexual rights activism by considering Hirschfeld's silences for the insights they provide into the structural and everyday inequalities that shaped modern homosexual rights discourse.

I have deliberately sought out Hirschfeld's lesser known and overlooked writings and their contexts, reading them against his more familiar studies of homosexuality and transvestism (a term he coined) with the intention of documenting something of the precariousness of modern queer life alongside the limits of queer apprehension in relation to other forms of injustice, especially colonial violence and the deeply entrenched social habits and practices of marginalizing women. If this method does not formally follow Jack Halberstam into a "silly archive" that is cobbled together from popular culture, my engagement with sexological literature, newspaper reports, literary and visual representations, and biographical and autobiographical accounts nevertheless shares Halberstam's suspicion of "disciplinary correctness," meaning the rigid adherence to particular disciplinary conventions, that all too often "confirms what is already known according to approved methods of knowing."[9] A degree of deliberate disciplinary slipperiness befits the book's concern with the paradoxically overinvested yet forever-evasive queer subject. By paying attention to the traumatic shaping of queerness in modernity, I do not seek to fix the queer subject, rehearsing often problematic narratives of victimhood that deny queers of the past an existence that is not marked by injury. Instead I focus on queer traumas because they constitute what Ann Cvetkovich has called "experiences of politically situated social violence [that forge] overt connections between politics and the emotions."[10] The accounts of violent acts and practices I have gathered here problematize the intersections between the individual and emerging collective forms of identification and activism in the early twentieth century, revealing that queerness was bound up in complex ways in the racialized (re)production of modern gender and social norms.

Violence and the Queer Angel of History

That violence is part of modern queer culture has been documented in some detail in studies of what Michel Foucault has called the "correlative" emergence of sexology and sexuality in the nineteenth century.[11] It was then that medical doctors, lawyers, criminologists, and social scientists first turned sustained attention to matters of sex, initially at least as part of efforts to identify and categorize (male) sexual offenders, especially those men who were suspected of sexual acts with other men, which was a crime in many European countries and in North America until well into the postwar years. While critics have sometimes located the emergence of sexual categories such as homosexuality specifically in this scientific realm, understanding them as problematic products of the disciplining of sex in the medical and legal institutions through which the state exercises power over its subjects,[12] the contributions of literary scholars and cultural historians to the history of sexuality as a field have loosened the disciplinary grip on sex to show that modern sexuality and sexual identifications are part of a more complex process of social renegotiation, which is most overt in but by no means exclusive to the ties between sexual acts and identities.[13] We today know, for example, that cultural production as much as medico-legal intrusions influenced subjects' development of a sense of self and brought it in relation to others via categories of sexual pleasure and desire and that such allegiances were forged out of imaginative, material, and affective encounters across time as well as the experiences of living in specific places and spaces.[14] Furthermore, studies of the intersecting histories of sexuality and violence[15] and the growing body of work on different national and global histories of sexuality[16] have extended the critical focus beyond questions of sexual identity to expose, in Regina Kunzel's words, "the fretful labor involved in the making of modern sexuality and its distinctive fictions."[17]

If violence, as Nancy Scheper-Hughes and Philippe Bourgeois have argued, "can never be understood solely in terms of its physicality," physical attacks are nevertheless often what alert us to the hidden "social and cultural dimensions [that give] violence its power and meaning."[18] It was an attack on Hirschfeld that first led me to articulate some of the questions that prompt this project. During a visit to Munich in October 1920, at the height of his fame, the sexologist was ambushed on the street by right-wing thugs who viciously beat him and left him for dead in a gutter.[19] The impression of Hirschfeld's death must have been convincing, because international newspapers soon afterward published obituaries, with the English-speaking press announcing the death of what the *New York Times* called "the well-known expert on sexual science."[20] Three days later, the newspaper was forced to publish a correction, explaining that the "noted German physiologist" was alive after all but that he had fallen victim to "a beating given him by some Anti-Semites because he was a Jew."[21] In Germany meanwhile, right-wing newspapers openly bemoaned the news that Hirschfeld, whom one paper called "this shameless and horrible poisoner of our people," had not come to "his well-deserved end."[22] While Hirschfeld claimed to have embraced the "opportunity of reading his own obituary," there is little doubt that the verbal attacks compounded his physical injuries.[23] The events indicate the precariousness of Hirschfeld's situation in Germany, where, rather than pursuing his attackers, prosecutors charged him "with the distribution of obscene material, mainly dealing with homosexuality."[24] The assault on Hirschfeld in Munich marks the rising antisemitism that would escalate so horrendously when the Nazi Party came to power in 1933, and it also indicates how deep-seated antihomosexual sentiments denied justice to a victim of violence.

In some ways the violence against Hirschfeld adds further evidence to the catalogue of injuries that mark queer history, a history "littered," in Heather Love's memorable phrase, "with the corpses of gender and sexual deviants."[25] It also speaks to the growing body of scholarship on public feelings and their archives, especially those projects that focus on the "bad feelings" that gather around negative experience.[26] Scholars such as Sara Ahmed, Judith Butler, Heather Love, and Ann Cvetkovich, despite their distinct concerns, all understand negative feelings, in the words of Elizabeth Stephens, as "shared and communal experiences, rather than personal or private sensations."[27] In these projects negativity is understood variously in terms of the discursive negation of certain lives (Butler); the phenomenological impact of sexism, racism, and resistance (Ahmed); as a refusal of the forward-looking, affirmative recuperation of the queer past (Love); and as part of ordinary, everyday life that indexes the affective reach of power (Cvetkovich).[28] By documenting feelings and affective states, my project archives racist, gender-based, and antiqueer violence, including in terms of how, in Cvetkovich's words, such violence is "forgotten or covered over by the amnesiac powers of national culture."[29] It in turn examines the violence in and around Hirschfeld's work to bring it back into memory and consider how it might haunt twenty-first-century homosexual rights activism in sometimes unexpected ways.

The dead and the wounded are difficult subjects in transformative criticism, which struggles with the fact that "its dreams for the future," in Love's words, "are founded on a history of suffering, stigma, and violence."[30] Some critics seek to bury the hurt of the queer past, focusing instead on the legal and social gains and achievements that have collectively improved queer existence. Many Hirschfeld scholars, for instance, emphasize Hirschfeld's contributions to "the gay liberation movement," casting him in the role of a "pioneer" of "sexual freedom."[31] Yet such straightforward progress narratives fail to capture the complexities of a queer past whose grand narratives of oppression and liberatory struggle intersect with countless personal and fictional life stories, confused cultural fantasies, and fragmentary evidence of intimate relationships that sometimes support and sometimes undermine our understanding of their historical context. Acknowledging the affective pull of the difficult queer past, Elizabeth Freeman has argued that we need to "laboriously rework [pain] into pleasure."[32] Carla Freccero, in contrast, welcomes the ghosts, arguing for a spectral approach to queer history that "reworks teleological narratives of reproductive futurity" by allowing the ghosts of historical and fantastic subjects to haunt us and demand justice.[33] Both Freeman's injunction to find pleasure and Freccero's reparative wish fulfillment can be elusive, however. For while queer history, like other traumatic histories, is undoubtedly a haunted subject, its subjects often refuse to submit to recuperative pleasures and remain lost in mundane or unresolved miseries, as Love argues in *Feeling Backward*. Moreover, and this point is often neglected, the past is populated not only by the victims of antiqueer attack but also by those awkward queer subjects whose place in affirmative or redemptive histories is brought into question by cruelties they have committed, aligning themselves with oppressive politics or simply remaining silent on, and apparently unmoved by, the violence and injustices of their time.

Hirschfeld himself was not merely a victim of antihomosexual and antisemitic persecution; nor was he simply a defender of those who suffered because their bodies and desires made them subjects of attack. It is certainly true that he was concerned with the difficulties of lives marked as different, as indicated in particular by his discussions of homosexual suicide. But Hirschfeld was also implicated in discriminatory practices, most obviously in relation to eugenics. Despite his later work on racism, published posthumously in 1938, he was in favor of the efforts of racial hygienists and eugenicists because like many scientists and political activists around 1900 he believed that these sciences could improve the health of the nation.[34] Paying little direct attention to the effects of German colonial expansion, Hirschfeld also occasionally brushed over what we would today call abuse, often marginalizing women despite his self-proclaimed feminism. Compared to many of his contemporaries Hirschfeld certainly was one of the more radical reformers who made significant structural and political contributions to the well-being of people whose desires and gender expressions were denied or ostracized. His silences are nevertheless also important, because they indicate how sexual rights activism, despite its transformative aims, remained bound up in the everyday injustices of modern German society.

The agency of the historical subject can be difficult to establish. Yet if we accept that silences, gaps, and omissions, as much as concrete evidence, tell a story about past lives and the norms and power relations that shaped them, then it is imperative that we account for unspoken acquiescence alongside overt forms of resistance. Scholarship on the histories of homosexuality in particular, which is founded on, albeit no longer limited to, the recuperation of dead white men, has had to expand and must continue to expand its analytical focus to examine the gendered, raced, and classed privilege that underpins the emergence of homosexuality as a category of collective identification. I conjure the figure of the queer angel of history to capture the complexities of the queer past and explain my concern both with the victims of antiqueer violence and the blind spots of emerging homosexual rights discourse in relation to other forms of oppression and injustice. Unlike the open-eyed figure of historical progress so famously summoned in Walter Benjamin's reading of Paul Klee's *Angelus Novus*, the queer angel of history has its sight obscured by the grit of experience. While the angel of history, according to Benjamin, is speedily propelled away from an inevitably receding past, its queer counterpart is pulled hither and thither by an affective "temporal drag," to borrow Freeman's phrase, that throws a spanner in the linear works of historical time.[35] On the cover of this book is Paul Klee's painting *One Who Understands* (1934). It features an abstracted face that is both drawn from and segmented by a series of lines. According to the description in the Metropolitan Museum of Art catalogue, the lines "divide the picture like a cracked windowpane," giving the impression that the subject is both part of and witness to shattering historical experience, simultaneously formed and fragmented by it.[36] The image captures well my conception of a queer angel of history. A reminder that "motions do not always go forward," the queer angel of history is compelled by the paradoxical disjuncture between the sociopolitical gains that have improved queer lives collectively and the experiences of violence that nevertheless continue to mark the felt realities of queerness across time.[37]

By conjuring the queer angel of history, I signal that queer history requires what I think of as the tasks of slow theory: accounting for the felt relationship between past and present; exploring the intersections between subjectivity, emotional life, and the public spheres of law, science, and society; and recognizing the significance of cultural production for shaping lives and archives. Slowness here refers to the lingering impact of past traumas that continue to shape, and sometimes haunt, queer lives across time. In my analysis of Hirschfeld's work, the queer angel of history marks the complex, felt links between violence and queer existence. While Hirschfeld's work documents antiqueer attacks and their impact, close attention to the gaps and silences in his writings reveals that his narrow focus on affirming homosexuality forged a particular kind of righteous cause that privileged attention to its own victims in a way that sometimes obscured or failed to recognize other forms of violence. I use the term *queer* here to describe the collective identifications that started to gather around sexual desires from the later nineteenth century onward, especially the desires and gender expressions that ran against binary conventions. This use is indebted to debates about intersectionality, which have brought into focus, in Kimberlé Crenshaw's words, "the tension [of identity politics] with dominant conceptions of social justice," and to the more recent critiques of the livability of lives whose bodies and desires do not match social norms and expectations.[38] Yet I am mindful of the analytical limits of *queer* when applied as an umbrella term that uses sexuality to cover gender and obscure the specificities and complexities of transgender and intersex lives.[39] In the book I focus primarily on the emergence of male homosexual rights activism, using the vocabularies of homosexuality and lesbianism (and sometimes other early twentieth-century cognates), transgender (including its early twentieth-century forms of transvestism and transsexuality), and intersex when I discuss these specific histories. In addition, however, I deploy *queer* to denote something of the sharedness of experience—however historically, socioculturally, and somatically contingent and emotionally inflected—that comes with living lives that are figured as being against accepted norms, and I think *queer*, as Judith Butler puts it, as "part of the weave of a broadening struggle" for livability and justice.[40]

Queer Oblivion

A central concern of the book is the apparent obliviousness of Hirschfeld to certain kinds of gendered and racial injustice. The word *oblivious*, most commonly understood today as a state of unawareness, is derived from the Latin *obliviosus*, meaning "forgetful" but also "producing forgetfulness," a tension between passive and active states that speaks to my concerns with the possibilities of apprehending violence. *Obliviousness* is linked etymologically to *oblivion*, a word that can mean, for instance, "freedom from care and worry" but also "forgetfulness resulting from inattention or carelessness; heedlessness; disregard" and the "intentional overlooking of an offence." A linked but separate definition understands *oblivion* as "the state or condition of being forgotten," "obscurity," "nothingness," "void," and "death."[41] These conflicting meanings oscillate between the engaged and the subjected, the jubilant and the miserable in ways that speak to my focus on the exigencies of queer existence across time. While oblivion can be understood in terms of the negation of queer existence—the denial, obscuring, and deliberate forgetting of queer lives—that has been one of the hallmarks of heteronormative history, it also captures the blind spots of emerging homosexual activism: the violence ignored or sidelined in attempts to affirm and celebrate queer culture.

The five chapters that make up the main part of the book present new research on the violent norms and discourses that shaped queer modernity and the lives of the people who were their subjects. Chapter 1, which introduces Hirschfeld's career, reframes the emergence of modern homosexual rights discourse in colonial context to ask whose suffering was apprehensible, and on what terms, in early twentieth-century public and sexual discourses. Chapter 2 reveals that the emotional prompts for Hirschfeld's work came from a series of sad, and sometimes devastating, interpersonal encounters with suicidal women and men. Examining how queer suicides and the death of arguably the most famous modern homosexual, Oscar Wilde, were received by the women and men who identified in some way with this suffering, the chapter demonstrates that death affectively shaped modern homosexual culture. Chapter 3 then shifts the focus to questions of physical violence. It explores Hirschfeld's little-known writings on abuse and the treatment of offenders to reveal how a degree of intimate violence was normalized in modern society. In Chapter 4 I turn attention to life at the Institute of Sexual Science, examining the complex relationship between sexual science and the emerging queer and transgender subcultures before demonstrating that the attack on the institute was shaped by deeply engrained homophobic norms that dictated how the Nazi men handled the attack. Chapter 5 explores Hirschfeld's final years in exile to scrutinize the subtler processes by which lives are denied. Hirschfeld escaped Nazi persecution by embarking on a journey that would take him across North America, Asia, and the Middle East. The published account of his travels, together with the surviving evidence of how he was received, for instance, in North America, India, and the Middle East, offer intriguing insights into the existence of global sexual reform networks before World War II even as this material also demonstrates that Hirschfeld allowed only certain voices into his narrative. The book concludes with a Coda that explores Hirschfeld's postwar legacy and how his work might provide, if not necessarily straightforward *lessons* for contemporary same-sex rights activism, then nevertheless a *historical proxy* for twenty-first-century debates about the gendered and racialized binds of sexual politics. Hirschfeld's silences, as much as the times when he talks over the voices of others, are reminders that it is important to remain alert to the dangers of single-issue politics, emphasizing that sexual rights efforts must be part of the wider struggle for social justice.

By examining Hirschfeld's work and reception, the study attends to the discursive denials, structural exclusions, and symbolic attacks that gathered around same-sex sexuality in the first three decades of the twentieth century. These more theoretical considerations are animated by a concern with the everyday realities and felt experiences of women and men whose lives were subjected to attack because they did not conform to particular social expectations about how a person should look or feel or be. Turning attention to the violence experienced, critiqued, and ignored by Hirschfeld brings into view the complicated ways that the discursive and lived realities of same-sex sexuality were linked emotionally as well as culturally and politically. *The Hirschfeld Archives* brings fragments of queer experience into proximity with each other to reveal some of the fragile threads that held together queer lives and that sometimes unraveled in the face of persecution or denial but also form part of a larger web of oppression that cannot be sufficiently accounted for by a focus on homosexual rights and liberation alone.

1

Sexual Rights in a World of Wrongs

Reframing the Emergence of Homosexual Rights Activism in Colonial Contexts

Magnus Hirschfeld, best known for his sexual theories and activism, completed one of the first modern studies of racism. Titled *Racism*, the work, which was prompted by Hirschfeld's own persecution by the Nazi regime, was written during the last years of his life and published posthumously in English translation in 1938.[1] *Racism*'s protoconstructivist critique of the production of racist ideas no doubt helped form the critical consensus that Hirschfeld, like other sexual activists on the left, "shared a distaste for the imperial project."[2] Yet while the book may be partly a belated response to Hirschfeld's own experience of the rise and fall of the German Empire, it also raises questions about how exactly he responded to the German colonial venture and why it took him so long to apprehend the existence and implications of racism. This chapter takes *Racism* as its prompt for reframing Hirschfeld's work in the context of the racist debates and colonial violence that formed its historical backdrop. Opening with an analysis of *Racism*, the chapter examines Hirschfeld's fairly fragmented writings on race, as well as his silences in the face of racial injustice and colonial oppression. While silence is a difficult critical subject, fragmentary accounts and narrative gaps reveal what Sara Ahmed in a different context has called "the partiality of absence" that informs how objects come in and out of view.[3] Building on the insights of Ahmed and scholars of sexuality, colonialism, and scientific racism such as Siobhan Somerville, I pay attention to both Hirschfeld's writings on race and the points on which he remained silent to bring into view the racial subjects excluded, submerged, and marginalized in his sexual rights activism.[4] I here reckon with the archives of sexology not merely as records of changing attitudes to sex but as evidence of how modern sexuality is part of what Ann Cvetkovich has called an "archive of ordinary racism" that documents how deep histories of oppression have fashioned "an environment steeped with racialized violence," shaping everyone's experience yet typically going unnoticed or being dismissed by those who are not subjected to racism.[5] One aim of the chapter, then, is to ensure that Hirschfeld's colonialist and jingoistic writings are not glossed over in assessments of the more radical sexual politics for which he is most famous today. Its broader concern, however, is to explore how racism and colonial violence framed—and haunted—the emergence of modern homosexual rights politics.[6]

The Sexuality of Racism

While scholars have shown that the emergence of modern homosexuality, via its debts to scientific racism, is implicated in the production of racialized bodies and subjects; that race tends to be policed most violently in relation to sex; and that intimacy remains a difficult subject in histories that are so profoundly shaped by the unequal flow of power between colonizers and the people subjected to colonial rule, we still know relatively little about how early homosexual rights activists such as Hirschfeld responded to the colonial violence and everyday racism that framed their life and work.[7] While Hirschfeld wrote about a wide range of issues, including, as this book shows, suicide, war, and corporal punishment, he typically angled the focus of any of his discussions toward affirming homosexuality. This is also true for his book-length study *Rassismus* (Racism), which was written in the early 1930s, when Hirschfeld had already left Germany to escape Nazi persecution. Completed not long before his death in French exile in 1935, the book was first published in 1938 in an English translation by the socialist couple Eden and Cedar Paul, who had visited Hirschfeld in France.[8] It was one of the first works to use the term *racism* in an English context.[9] Hirschfeld's motivations for writing *Racism* were clear. He argued that he had decided to examine "the racial theory which underlies the doctrine of race war" for the very reason that he himself "numbered among the many thousand who have fallen victim to the practical realization of this theory."[10] These words, noting Hirschfeld's personal investment in the topic, firmly identify *Racism* as a response to Nazi ideology and its implementation. A number of scholars have argued that it was the practices and principles of German colonialism that paved the way for the rise of Nazism.[11] Hirschfeld's historicization of Nazism in contrast traces the roots of racist thinking in Germany to the ideas and scientific developments of the German Enlightenment. Providing an overview of racial thinking in German culture and science from Enlightenment discipline formations to Nazi ideology, he focuses in particular on how ideas about race have been constructed and transmitted in the country. Somewhat curiously perhaps, given his own experiences, he barely touches on antisemitism, figuring racism instead in terms of spurious theories about skin color. Explaining that he was taught in school that humanity is divided according to Friedrich Blumenbach's color-coded taxonomy into five distinct "races"— black, white, yellow, red, and brown—Hirschfeld suggests that the teaching of this classification is partly how scientific speculation is vernacularized as a universal truth. Such truths in turn underpin Western assumptions about modernity, which conflate ideas about civilization (or its perceived lack) and skin color to make claims for the existence of racial hierarchies that inevitably privilege whites and that are more often than not—as in the case of German Nazism—used to further a politics of national expansion and supremacy.[12]

Hirschfeld's understanding of the construction and naturalization of racial categories led him to proclaim that "if it were practicable we should certainly do well to eradicate the use of the word 'race' as far as subdivisions of human species are concerned; or, if we do use it in this way, to put it in quote-marks to show that it is questionable."[13] There is a hesitation in this sentence—*if it were practicable*—that gestures toward the realization that racism cannot simply be unsaid. Suggesting that in place of "race," cultural and social categories should be used when articulating differences between groups of people, Hirschfeld goes on to introduce the notion of "social mimicry" as a replacement for what he identifies as the misguided focus on racial types. He defines social mimicry as what is "sometimes called custom or convention, sometimes decency or morality, sometimes *esprit de corps* or tradition; sometimes routine; sometimes solidarity; while sometimes . . . it struts as etiquette, or is boasted of as good form."[14] The idea of social mimicry echoes Hirschfeld's earlier writings on what he calls "sexual mimicry," a term he uses to describe what happens when people hide their same-sex desires to conform to, and fit it in with, binary social norms.[15] He first used the expression in an early work, *Naturgesetze der Liebe* (Natural laws of love), which is indebted to Charles Darwin's ideas on the evolutionary adaptation of species to the environment. Reappropriating Darwin's observations, Hirschfeld here argues that pressures to conform led many people to "mime" an acceptable social façade, hiding their sexual desires because of shame and fear.[16] While *sexual mimicry* draws attention, then, to the victims of heteronormative expectation, Hirschfeld deploys *social mimicry* as a term without agents. Switching from a critique of the color-coded racism that occupied the post-Enlightenment German imagination to a more general discussion about what we might call group formation, Hirschfeld's discussion here loses track of the specific workings of racism and the people who are subjected to it.

Racism quickly moves from its critique of race to a more essentialist argument about sexuality. The shift in focus is signaled by Hirschfeld's claim that "the uniform aspect of homosexuality in all races and under all skies [is] a convincing proof of its biological causation" and that "in this matter, beyond question, the sexual type conquers the racial type."[17] While Hirschfeld had previously rejected essentialist arguments about race, he here returns to the idea of a "racial type" when staking out his argument that the "sexual type"—or what he elsewhere calls "pansexuality"—supersedes social, cultural, and geographical contingencies.[18] Given that Hirschfeld argued for the de-essentalization of race, why was he so keen to naturalize sexuality? The apparent contradiction is at least partly explained when *Racism* turns to what within early sexological literature is a rare mention of heterosexuality, a term coined after the emergence of homosexuality, which remained largely untheorized.[19] Hirschfeld writes:

> Heterosexuals regard themselves as "normal" because they are in the majority, and [they] have an instinctive dislike for homosexuals and their ways—a dislike that is fostered by the suggestive influence of education—hypocritically including to pretend that homosexual practices cannot have arisen spontaneously in their own happy land and among their own fortunately endowed "race."[20]

The passage problematizes the normalizing of heterosexuality even if the claim that the heterosexual majority develops an "instinctive dislike for homosexuals" seems to imply a biological cause for homophobia.[21]

Hirschfeld's observation that homosexuality is always considered *against* heterosexuality anticipates later work on the implication of modern science in the production of what Georges Canguilhem has called the "ideological illusion" of the validity of norms, which come into existence only *after* the conceptualization of the perceived abnormality.[22] Hirschfeld's astute critique of how homosexuality is constructed as an abnormality within the nation suggests that sexual debates are racialized. However, the subject of racism soon slips off the analytical radar as Hirschfeld's focus turns instead to staking a claim for the essential naturalness of same-sex sexuality. According to Judith Butler, "only once we have suffered . . . violence [are we] compelled, ethically, to ask how we will respond to violent injury."[23] *Racism* indicates that while Hirschfeld's own suffering from the Nazi escalation of antisemitism prompted his critique of the subject, his prevailing concern with the affirmation of same-sex sexuality continued to limit his apprehension of the full extent of racial violence. By turning from racism to homophobia, Hirschfeld obscured their intersections, foregrounding sexual matters rather than maintaining a focus on racial oppression.

Colonial Career(ing) in the German Empire

The discursive slippages and displacements in *Racism* are in line with Sara Ahmed's observation that racism is supported and reproduced in a way that "is not noticeable" to those who are part of the privileged flow until it is pointed out to them.[24] They prompt questions about how Hirschfeld himself might have benefited from the colonial exploitations that form the historical backdrop to his professional life, drawing attention to the significance of his writings on race and colonialism but also, perhaps especially so, to when he remained silent in the face of racial violence. Hirschfeld came of age, professionally, during Germany's official reign as a colonial power from 1889 to 1919.[25] German colonialism has only relatively recently received sustained critical attention, partly because it lasted for a relatively brief period compared to the long histories of, say, the British, Dutch, French, or Spanish Empires.[26] The lateness of German colonial expansion is tied to the formation of the German state, which came into existence only in 1871, when two dozen or so independent states joined political forces. In 1884 the hitherto dispersed mercantile and missionary ventures of the new nation were harnessed to establish a series of colonies and so-called protectorates (*Schutzgebiete*) in West and East Africa, the Pacific, and parts of China. The "protection" was for German businesses and settlers rather than the colonized subjects, who were subjected to new laws, regulations, and violent oppression. While Hirschfeld did not directly participate in the colonial expansion effort, his career benefited from investments in the sciences, including medical research, that accompanied the German determination to gain new territories.

Career is a useful term to capture the mixture of agency and contingency that shaped Hirschfeld's work, allowing us to contextualize it in relation to the exigencies of colonial modernity. The meaning of *career* has its origins in the language of horse racing. It was transformed over the course of the nineteenth century, when it increasingly came to be associated with a person's progress through life, eventually settling in the early twentieth century on the meaning still in use today: "a course of professional life or employment, which affords opportunity for progress or advancement in the world."[27] The modern sense of the noun *career*, and especially its association with progress, reflects the scientific positivism of the later nineteenth century. Its association with "opportunity" in turn speaks to the opening up of new colonial workspaces—such as roles as administrators, missionaries, and nurses—and the formation of new businesses and academic subdisciplines, which were dedicated to processing goods and people and to producing knowledge that would benefit individual wealth even while strengthening the colonial nation. Furthermore, the verb *to career*, which is associated with speed and movement and turning this way and that, aptly describes both the proliferation of scientific specialisms dedicated to mapping and measuring the colonial world and Hirschfeld's own diverse professional interests, which intersected with these new specialisms in numerous ways.

Hirschfeld initially studied literature and languages before embarking on a medical career in the 1880s. In 1892 he graduated from what was then the Friedrich-Wilhelms-Universität in Berlin—one of Germany's oldest universities, today known as Humboldt University—with a doctorate in medicine, specializing in illnesses of the nervous system following influenza.[28] He was following in the footsteps of his father, Herrmann, who too had a doctoral degree from the Friedrich-Wilhelms-Universität, where he had studied in the recently established but soon world-famous medical program under Rudolf Virchow, one of the country's first public health advocates.[29] Hirschfeld, also taught by Virchow, took up his father's interest in public hygiene. Paul Weindling has argued that the German "sexual reformers [such as Hirschfeld] had a similar background to racial hygienists in that as neurologists and venereologists they were on the margins of the medical profession."[30] Hirschfeld's medical beginnings indicate the cross-influence between these different fields.[31] His doctoral thesis, concerned with the effects rather than the epidemiology of influenza, discussed a catalogue of influenza symptoms still familiar today, such as headache, fever, and nausea, examining them primarily in relation to what he called their *"Nervenaffectionen"* (nervous effects), including psychological issues such as depression, suicidal thinking, and hysteria, in a soldier afflicted with influenza.[32] The research was highly topical. It responded directly to the flu pandemic that had swept through Europe between 1889 and 1892. The pandemic, which became known as the Russian flu, after its country of origin, spread around the world via the new transport networks that crisscrossed the modern world.[33] According to Hirschfeld the pandemic had "put all the cultured nations into the enormous grip of the East,"[34] a turn of phrase that reveals his debts to contemporary debates about the impact and feared contamination of (German) civilization through encounters with people from the borders of Europe or beyond, debates that gained momentum during the colonial expansion of the German Empire.[35] Hirschfeld's doctoral thesis at first glance seems only tenuously linked to the German colonial project, but it was clearly framed in relation to the imperial and scientific discourses that gathered in its wake.[36] The influence of these debates can be traced to Hirschfeld's later work. He openly supported eugenics, for example, if not for "racial refinement," then as a way of improving health via selective reproduction,[37] and returned to questions about the acclimatization of colonizers to the weather and (perceived and real) endemic diseases of the tropical regions as late as the 1930s, when he speculated about the suitability of the bodies of "the white man" and "the white woman" to life in the tropics.[38]

The clinical subjects for Hirschfeld's doctoral research were drawn directly from the medical department of one of the most influential institutions in the German Empire, the Royal Prussian Ministry of War.[39] The role of the soldiers in Hirschfeld's dissertation research, which marks the beginning of a lifelong professional interest in working with soldiers, indicates one way that medical research directly benefited from the investment in military strength that marked the early decades of the Wilhelmine Empire.[40] Furthermore, as Robert Deam Tobin has shown, Hirschfeld came into direct contact with colonial settlers, such as in 1906 when he provided a written medical assessment of a certain Viktor van Alten, an ex-soldier who had settled as a farmer in German southwest Africa and was tried there under Paragraph 175 of the German Penal Code for "unnatural indecency."[41] Hirschfeld diagnosed the man as homosexual, arguing, however, that he should not be tried for his sexual misconduct because neurasthenia diminished his responsibility.[42] If his early research as a medical student had already shown, then, to borrow Bradley Naranch's words, that "when it comes to colonialism, there are no marginal players and no protected places entirely free of impact," Hirschfeld's involvement in the van Alten case illustrates that he directly participated in the legal process that upheld German colonial rule.[43]

Sexual Sameness and Racial Indifference on Display

Shannon Sullivan has argued that "whiteness" operates in a typically concealed fashion, partly because white self-formation is often accompanied by an unscrutinized attachment to the institutions that uphold such oppression and partly because "the unconscious habits of racial privilege . . . actively thwart the conscious process of critical reflection on them."[44] Hirschfeld's own encounters with racism support this point. Not long after graduation he traveled to the United States, where he encountered a spectacular display of colonial power: the 1893 Chicago World's Fair (also known as the World's Columbian Exhibition), which commemorated the four-hundred-year anniversary of Christopher Columbus's "discovery" of the "New World." The fair was in many ways typical of the racial displays that started to proliferate in nineteenth-century Europe and North America.[45] What distinguished it from other similar events is that the exhibition came under sustained attack from activists such as Frederick Douglass, who pointed out that the "white city"—so called because of the color of the buildings in which it was housed—also employed a "white politics" because it excluded people of color from the exhibition committee and instead limited their participation to menial labor.[46] Douglass and other activists such as Ida B. Wells, who had initially supported the exhibition for its potential to "celebrate the contributions . . . of Afro-Americans," protested its racial representation, which in Douglass's words aimed to "exhibit the Negro as a repulsive savage."[47] Douglass here referred to displays such as the Dahomean village, a reconstruction of a West African village complete with human inhabitants, which literally put colonized bodies on display, exploiting and perpetuating stereotypes about primitive culture. Elsewhere, World's Fair–related cartoons peddled racist ideas, typically adapting the language and imagery of evolutionary theory to support their claims about distinctive primitive and civilized societies. There is no need for this study to recirculate these images in the twenty-first century. Suffice it to say that cartoons such as "Mr. Orang Utang," which suggested that an ape could take charge of a Dahomey village, circulated far beyond the World's Fair exhibition space, helping turn racial spectacle into everyday discourse. "Mr. Orang Utang" appeared in *Puck*, a popular satirical publication that had originally been written in German for a relatively small number of immigrants.[48] By the time of Hirschfeld's visit to the Chicago fair, *Puck* had long since changed to English, attracting a wide readership from across the United States. Its publication of "Mr. Orang Utang" indexes the widespread dissemination of racist cartoons, which had begun to circulate in the 1860s and typically conflated "Negro" subjects with apes—even if, as Zakkiyah Jackson has argued, the apparently dehumanizing racist representations and discourses were fueled by the knowledge of the humanity of the enslaved.[49] This racist visual genre had gained momentum in British, American, and German contexts with the publication of Charles Darwin's *On the Origin of Species*, in the wake of which cartoons such as "Monkeyana," depicting an ape carrying a board bearing William Hackworth's abolitionist slogan "Am I not a man and a brother?," were widely popularized.[50] At the same time, however, the voices of abolitionist and antiracism campaigners such as Douglass and Wells, who challenged not just legal and social discrimination but also the popular racism that propped up such practices, were increasingly, and widely, heard. Given the popularity of the abolitionist movement in the United States, Hirschfeld's silence on the debates about the Chicago World's Fair is all the more noticeable. It indicates both his own detachment from the abolitionist and antiracism struggle and the more insidious privilege of whiteness, which normalized and made invisible to him the racism of the Chicago World's Fair and American society more widely.

It was during Hirschfeld's travels around Chicago and other parts of the Midwest that his sexological career began to take shape. With the help of his older brother Immanuel, who worked as a physician in Milwaukee, Hirschfeld delivered during his time in America some of his first public lectures on how to live a "natural" life, and he began to stake out his argument that homosexuality is a naturally occurring, global phenomenon.[51] Immersing himself in Chicago's same-sex culture, he described, for instance, the homosexual graffiti in the city, arguing that similar graffiti could also be found "in exactly the same manner" in Tangier, Rio de Janeiro, and Tokyo.[52] Hirschfeld mentioned the anarchic art of graffiti to support his argument about the universal existence of homosexuality, a concern that preoccupied him at the time.[53] The allusion to homosexual graffiti contrasts with Hirschfeld's silence on the racist cartoons that circulated in Chicago during his visit. It draws attention to the formal differences between graffiti and newspaper cartoons, differences that reflect the distinct conditions of visibility for homosexuality and racism. While the anarchic art form of graffiti marks how homosexual subcultures began to claim public space in their own, semisecret code, the racist newspaper cartoons spoke for their subjects, framing black lives in terms that supported race-based inequality. Hirschfeld, who was part of the homosexual subcultures of the time, clearly responded to the queer graffiti but seemed to have remained unaffected by both his encounters with racism and the antiracism struggle in Chicago. Given that he attended the Chicago World's Fair as a newspaper reporter[54] and that at the time of Hirschfeld's first American travels, as Fatima El-Tayeb has pointed out, "an astonishing number of German articles and books dealt with blacks in the U.S.," his silence on the racial issues that preoccupied the country stands out.[55]

It would take until 1929 before Hirschfeld commented—briefly—on American racism. Noting in a commentary on capital punishment that "in the States, white and black are measured differently," Hirschfeld mentioned the frequency by which black men receive the death penalty when convicted of raping white women, while white men who rape black women were typically merely fined.[56] He leaves this observation to stand without further explanation. It seems unlikely, therefore, that Hirschfeld's realization of American racism is a belated response to his earlier visit to Chicago. Instead, the brief observation, which is the only comment he makes about the different treatment of blacks and whites in America, is directly tied to Hirschfeld's concern at the time with the treatment of sexual offenders. The brevity of the comment suggests that Hirschfeld continued to remain detached from the American black liberation struggle even in the late 1920s, when reviews of the art and politics of the Harlem Renaissance filled the pages of many major German newspapers.[57]

Colonial Normality

The Chicago World's Fair would not have been the first time that Hirschfeld encountered racial displays. Ethnic displays were a hugely popular form of mass entertainment during the Wilhelmine Empire and most of the Weimar Republic when so-called *Völkerschauen* (displays of peoples) proliferated.[58] Hirschfeld returned from his travels to witness another colonial spectacle, the Grosse Berliner Gewerbeaustellung (Great Industrial Exhibition of Berlin). This event took place from May 1 to October 15, 1896, and marks a formative moment in Berlin's—and German—colonial history. In a country where the sense of national identity was still new—Jennifer Kopf has pointed out that organizers focused on celebrating more specifically Berlin rather than, as with other world fairs, the nation—framing the capital city as a global center was an important assertion of power.[59] At the same time, however, such colonial fairs also reflected and (re)produced social anxieties. Walter Benjamin, who famously called the world fairs "sites of pilgrimage to the commodity fetish," has read the Berlin fair as an indicator of the alienation and attendant commodity fetishism that defines modernity.[60] Alongside technological innovations—many of them directly or indirectly linked to colonial ventures—the influx of goods from the colonies transformed everyday life around the turn of the nineteenth century. While the consumption of commodities such as soap and sugar literally brought colonial exploitation to bear on to the bodies of the colonizers, the attendant rise of what David Ciarlo has called the "advertising empire" further changed public culture, as representations of exotic people, lands, and goods became part of everyday life.[61]

The mundane presence and everyday uses of colonial wares obscured the violence of their production and helped establish, in Wulf Hund's words, "the conditions of possibility for the acquisition of racist symbolic capital by the general public."[62] Hund's argument that racist advertising was crucial to the construction of an "imagined racial community" also sheds new light on racial exhibits at fairs such as the one that took place in Berlin in 1896.[63] The event included native village exhibits featuring people from Germany's new colonies in East and West Africa and New Guinea.[64] Roslyn Poignant, who has traced the histories of people who crossed the world to be exhibited at such fairs, argues that some women and men voluntarily joined the colonial exhibits or the company of explorers and scientists who would arrange for them to be displayed at fairs and sometimes in circuses.[65] Yet as Sadiah Qureshi has shown, the voluntary nature of their engagement is problematic.[66] For while there exists evidence that becoming part of such human display groups could open up for the performers new possibilities for shaping their lives outside the norms and traditional restrictions imposed on them in the societies of their birth, it is clear that the terms of display were restrictive and dictated by the organizers. Furthermore, while the format of displays varied, ranging from strictly fencing off the performers from their audiences to performers and audience mingling, it is accurate to say that the exhibits emphasized the "primitive" otherness of the subjects on display, including through the very act of exhibiting them.[67]

Völkerschauen such as the one in Berlin in 1896 made visible colonized bodies in particular ways.[68] Newspaper reports from the time make clear that the presence of black women and, especially, black men brought to the fore anxieties about sexuality and gender. For instance, an article published in the *Deutsche Kolonialzeitung* (German colonial newspaper) some time after the fair recalls the "shameful memories of the colonial exhibition in Berlin in 1896,"[69] shameful, according to the paper, because the exhibition turned Berlin into a place "where white women and girls . . . ran after Negroes from Cameroon and other colonies."[70] Bearing in mind Hund's argument about the role of colonial *goods* in the forging of a modern German national identity, it is perhaps not surprising that the presence of these black *bodies* destabilized the rules of colonial consumption, fueling anxious fantasies about black virility and sexual allure. Newspapers represented and fueled sensationalist fears about racial hygiene and mixing, fears that would lead to the introduction of special legislation for so-called *Mischehen* (mixed marriages) in 1912.[71] Hirschfeld's major work, *Die Homosexualität des Mannes und des Weibes* (The homosexuality of man and woman), which was published in 1914 but had been many years in the making, shows that his thinking was influenced by these debates. It encompasses, for instance, a discussion of "sexual ethnography," which followed the colonial world map as it explored sexual habits and phenomena in "Germanic and Anglo-Saxon nations and their colonies" as well as the "Romanic nations and their colonies" and included a table that schematized antihomosexuality legislation across the German, British, and French Empires. In it Hirschfeld claimed that homosexuals were of benefit to "racial hygiene" because they tended not to marry. He argued that if homosexuals were forced into marriage, their offspring would likely be "mentally deficient," a statement that might have come from Hirschfeld's efforts to dissociate homosexuals from debates about marriage but that challenged his affirmative portrayal of homosexuality.[72] Furthermore, the eugenicist suggestion that the sexual "mixing" of heterosexuals and homosexuals would be detrimental to the German "race" sits uncomfortably close to the debates about "mixed marriages" and the problem of "racial mixing," debates that commanded much public attention when Hirschfeld was working on his ideas.[73]

Robert Deam Tobin, in his analysis of "the German discovery of sex," argues that "while progressives in the field of sexuality, like Hirschfeld, tended not to be invested in colonialism per se, their reliance on a scientific worldview that saw sexual categories as similar to racial ones put them in an oddly overlapping relationship with racist colonialists."[74] He goes on to illustrate his point, not by examining Hirschfeld's work but by analyzing a popular novel set in Samoa, one of Germany's colonies. The critical shift reflects the difficulty of dealing with the colonial omissions in Hirschfeld's work. Yet tempting as it is to look elsewhere for an explanation of how sexologists such as Hirschfeld experienced colonialism and how racial thinking fed into their work, attention to the synchronicity of Hirschfeld's early work with German colonial expansion not only helps demarcate the racial limits of his sexual politics but also reveals some of the pernicious implications of white privilege, which seem to have left Hirschfeld largely unconcerned by the racist norms and practices that inveigled their way into everyday life in the Wilhelmine Empire.

Imperial Entanglements: From the Petition to Abolish Paragraph 175 to Homosexual Paranoia

Despite Hirschfeld's early silences on racism, there is tangible evidence of the links between sexual and colonial politics around 1900. For a better understanding of how the emerging homosexual rights movement was entangled in the imperial machinations of the time, it is useful to take a fresh look at Hirschfeld's early contributions to sexual rights activism, which not only emerged proximal to colonial debates but intersected with them in a number of ways. Hirschfeld's career was set in motion with the publication of a short pamphlet, *Sappho und Sokrates* (1896), under the pseudonym Th. Ramien.[75] In it, using his medical training, he attempted to provide a scientific theory of sexuality, explaining it in relation to embryonic and hormonal developments and providing plenty of scientific graphs to support the arguments. Its publication marks the beginning of a fruitful professional relationship between Hirschfeld and the publisher Max Spohr, who became hugely influential in shaping the—by no means uniform—homosexual rights activism.[76] In 1899 Hirschfeld and Spohr launched the *Jahrbuch für sexuelle Zwischenstufen* (Yearbook for sexual intermediaries), the first journal dedicated to same-sex sexuality, which became the mouthpiece for the recently founded Wissenschaftlich-humanitäres Kommitee (WhK; Scientific Humanitarian Committee), the first sexual rights organization. The WhK had been inaugurated in 1897 during a small private meeting between, among others, Hirschfeld, Spohr, and the colonial administrator Franz Josef von Bülow, who had recently returned from German-occupied southwest Africa and who complained in his memoirs that the colonial administration had acted "too passively toward the natives," thus hindering the success of the settlers.[77] While the WhK thus involved people who had directly taken part in the German colonization of southwest Africa, the *Jahrbuch* reproduced some of the scientific racism of the time when it published anthropological studies of "pederasty and tribadism" among *Naturvölkern* (primitive peoples) to support its argument that same-sex sexuality was a naturally occurring phenomenon in the distinct group of *Kulturvölker* (civilized peoples).[78]

In 1898, the year that the Reichstag, the German parliament, passed the first of the Naval Laws establishing the country's navy, Hirschfeld first[79] came to wider public attention through his spearheading of a petition to revoke Paragraph 175 of the German Penal Code.[80] The petition was introduced for discussion in the Reichstag by August Bebel, a member of the Social Democratic Party (the only party to refuse to support the Naval Laws) and one of Hirschfeld's friends from university. While Hirschfeld too was a member of a socialist association for physicians, he engaged in only a limited way with socialist party politics.[81] The attempt to get Paragraph 175 revoked was unsuccessful, leading to an equally unsuccessful attempt to criminalize sex between women.[82] Yet its coincidence with the Naval Laws nevertheless indicates that homosexual emancipation gained political currency precisely at the point when the Wilhelmine Empire increased its colonial expansion efforts. This argument is supported by Hirschfeld's involvement in the Harden trials, a political scandal that made homosexuality a focus of popular debate in Germany for the first time.[83] The Harden trials—also known as the Eulenburg affair after the diplomat Prince Philipp of Eulenburg, who was accused by the journalist Maximilian Harden of having an affair with the military commander of Berlin, Kuno von Moltke—occurred partly in response to a perceived colonial weakening of Kaiser Wilhelm, the German emperor, in the early 1900s.[84] In spring 1905 Kaiser Wilhelm had announced his plans not to fight the French over Morocco, declaring that German colonial efforts would focus instead on the South Pacific, where several colonies had already been established. This decision prompted questions about the kaiser's strength, which culminated in Harden publishing a series of articles that alleged homosexuality in the emperor's inner circle. Sued for defamation, Harden asked Hirschfeld to act as medical expert for his defense when the case came to court. These events brought Hirschfeld to public attention in and beyond the German Empire, where his defense of homosexuality was generally negatively received. For instance, as part of the backlash, a political caricature was circulated in 1907 that challenged his status as a medical expert by depicting him instead as a political agitator drumming up support for abolition of Paragraph 175 (Figure 1.1).[85] German, French, and British newspapers from across the political spectrum attacked Hirschfeld's homosexual rights efforts, frequently in antisemitic terms, claiming, for example, that his "abnormal propensities" should be distanced from "mainstream" medicine,[86] that his Jewishness rendered him unfit for citizenship,[87] and even going as far as to insist that "we must make an end of people like Dr Hirschfeld."[88]

While Hirschfeld did not address directly the antisemitism, he noted that the attacks against him in the wake of the Harden trial, a scandal that had started out as a response to the perceived weakening of Germany's colonial might, "brought the laborious achievements [of the fledgling homosexual rights movement] once more into question."[89] Hirschfeld noticed the rise of what Eve Kosofsky Sedgwick would later call "homosexual panic," a term she borrowed from the psychiatrist Edward Kempf, which describes "the most private, psychologized form in which many twentieth-century western men experience their vulnerability to the social pressure of homophobic blackmail."[90] According to Hirschfeld "it was after the Moltke-Harden scandal

Figure 1.1 A 1907 political cartoon depicting sex-researcher Magnus Hirschfeld, "Hero of the Day," drumming up support for the abolition of Paragraph 175 of the German Penal Code, which criminalized homosexuality. The banner reads, "Away with Paragraph 175!" The caption reads, "The foremost champion of the third sex!" U.S. Holocaust Memorial Museum Photo Archives.

that such delusions cropped up like mushrooms" in Germany.⁹¹ In an article about "sexual hypochondria and scrupulousness" written not long after the events, Hirschfeld claimed to have observed an increase in paranoia in both people who feared that they would be suspected of homosexual practices and those who accused others of such behavior.⁹² He argued that he now "frequently observed among married people [who came to his clinic] the delusion that either wife or husband is homosexual."⁹³ As an example, Hirschfeld cited the case of a "workingwoman" who asked him for advice because her husband was convinced that she had "homosexual tendencies." When meeting with the husband, Hirschfeld was told that the man's suspicions about his wife's sexuality had been confirmed "when a young woman on meeting his wife had moved the tip of her tongue between her lips."⁹⁴ It is not clear where the idea that tongue-flicking signifies lesbianism comes from, but in the early 1890s the French writer Léo Taxil, in a work on fin de siècle "corruption," was already claiming that the "elegant lesbians" of Paris identified each other "by the quick movement of the tongue and the lips."⁹⁵ According to Taxil, "This is the conventional sign adopted by tribades to say: 'I am for woman,'" meaning sexually attracted to women.⁹⁶ In the case of Hirschfeld's patient, it was not the wife herself who was accused of signaling with her tongue. Instead her husband claimed that the gesture of a stranger provided evidence that the wife was homosexual.⁹⁷ While the account itself reveals little about the colonial contexts in which it was produced, Hirschfeld's involvement in the Harden trials and his observations on its aftermath show that the emergence of this particular kind of homosexual paranoia was directly linked to the imperial scandal.

Homophobia and the Herero Genocide

The Harden trials inspired Hirschfeld to publish a study, *Sexualpsychologie und Volkspsychologie* (Sexual psychology and national psychology), which analyzed in more detail what we today call homophobia. In it he claimed that his own experiences of attack had prompted him to study how hatred against groups of people is instilled in the wider public. According to the study, antihomosexual attitudes are generated by "mass suggestion," or the production and perpetuation of antihomosexuality discourse in the media.⁹⁸ *Sexualpsychologie und Volkspsychologie* coincided with sociologists such as Georg Simmel beginning to analyze the psychology of the masses, especially in relation to urban life. Hirschfeld's book, which cites his defamation by the press as an example of how such negative suggestion is executed, expanded the sociological scholarship to include a critique of antihomosexual attitudes. Derived from Hirschfeld's own experiences of attacks against homosexuality, the book in some ways anticipates the postwar conceptualization of homophobia by the psychologist George Weinberg. Weinberg challenged the idea that homosexuality was a social problem, arguing instead that antihomosexual prejudice caused deep psychological issues, including a phobia "of being in close quarters with homosexuals—and, in the case of homosexuals themselves, self-loathing."[99] Critics have rightly problematized Weinberg's concept, some of them complicating it, for instance, by relating it to questions about the policing of gender boundaries, while others have rejected it for its focus on health and obscuring of the specifics of other kinds of violence.[100] Yet in relation to Hirschfeld's work, homophobia serves as a useful umbrella term for describing attacks against people on the grounds of their assumed sexual preference, a definition that fits Hirschfeld's understanding of the psychology of antihomosexual persecution.

But *Sexualpsychologie und Volkspsychologie* reveals more than Hirschfeld's developing understanding of antihomosexual attack as a collective, psychosocial phenomenon. Amid the discussion of his experience of persecution and of the widespread suffering caused by homophobic attack is a short remark that indicates Hirschfeld's awareness of colonialism. As a regular medical advisor to prisoners and those accused of—mostly sexual—crimes, Hirschfeld mentions that he had visited an inmate in the "colonial prison" in the northern German town of Neumünster, tasked with diagnosing whether the man suffered "severe nervous disturbances caused by a combination of malaria, blackwater fever, and congenital sexual anomaly."[101] Hirschfeld does not relate what diagnosis he made, but he notes that the prisoner himself blamed his ill health on an unnamed criminal act he had by his own admission committed during the "Hereroaufstand" (Herero uprising) in southwest Africa.[102] The Herero uprising is an especially brutal event in German colonial rule that is often described as the first genocide of the twentieth century, anticipating or, according to some historians, even directly paving the way for the atrocities of the Nazi regime.[103] A brutal war was unleashed to suppress a revolt in 1904 of the Herero and Nama people against German settlers. After drawn-out battles, the German colonial army gained the upper hand in 1908. But rather than treating the enemy according to the rules of warfare, the German commander, Lothar von Trotha, announced a war of annihilation, ordering that the surviving Herero and Nama were to be kept away from water sources and left to die in the desert. The women, men, and children who survived this ordeal were then imprisoned in a concentration camp on an island off the colonial town of Luederitz. Known as Shark Island, it was a place of immense suffering. Prisoners were subjected to forced labor, medical experiments, disease, random violence, and killings. German newspapers, which followed the war in detail, printed biased reports that focused on the deaths of German settlers and soldiers. Emphasizing the "bestial cruelty" of the Herero, the reporting added fuel to racist fears of the dangerous, animal-like primitivism of the indigenous people, developing public discourses that were used to stake claims for intensified colonial power in the area.[104]

In addition to such psychological manipulation of racist attitudes, the genocide would also take on a somewhat less widely publicized material presence in German science. The bodies of many dead Herero and Nama women, men, and children were transferred to Germany where they became human research objects. In 1908 Eugen Fischer, who would later gain infamy as a Nazi anatomist, visited the camp on Shark Island and experimented on the prisoners, which led him to formulate a spurious but influential theory about white European supremacy. He ordered the bodies of some dead Herero and Nama men to be mutilated by German soldiers, who in turn tasked some of the indigenous women with stripping the flesh of their dead. The skulls and some skeletons were then sent to back to Germany for use in scientific research at institutions such as the Institute for Pathology in Berlin and the city's Charité hospital, which is where Hirschfeld had completed his medical training a decade earlier. It is unclear how widespread knowledge of the traffic in these bodies was at the time, but evidently a substantial number of people were involved in the killing and subsequent claiming, transporting, storing, and abuse of the bodies. It would take until 2011 before the remains were returned to what is now Namibia.

Colonial soldiers such as the traumatized prisoner visited by Hirschfeld brought a psychic presence of the suffering caused back to the German Empire. That such traumatic events haunt the nations that commit them has been well documented.[105] The German prisoner clearly seems to have been haunted by his role in the events. Hirschfeld, in contrast, apparently had nothing to say about the atrocities committed on indigenous people in the name of the German Empire. Given, as Tobin's research has revealed, that Hirschfeld was linked directly to events in German southwest Africa via his involvement in the court case of Viktor van Alten, his silence when faced with the violence against the Herero and Nama people is all the more striking, suggesting that the colonial atrocities remained out of view as he focused on homosexual matters.[106]

Colonial Tribadism

Despite Hirschfeld's silences on the colonial atrocities committed in German southwest Africa, it is perhaps no coincidence that in the early 1910s he seems to have begun to distance his work on the global aspects of same-sex sexuality from the work of certain anthropologists. Within anthropological as well as some sexological discourses of the time, primitive sexuality had been a focus of attention, especially in relation to debates about gender, excessive sensuality, and the somatic expressions of primitiveness. Hirschfeld took issue with the work of the anthropologists Herrmann Heinrich Ploss, Max Bartels, and Paul Bartels, who in 1885 published a three-volume study titled *Das Weib: Die Frau in der Natur- und Völkerkunde*. It was translated into English in 1935 under the expanded title *Woman: An Historical, Gynaecological and Anthropological Compendium*.[107] The work is typical in many ways of the scientific racism of the time, illustrating how women's bodies became a focus of racialized debates about sexuality. Ploss, Bartels, and Bartels argued, for example, that tribadism among Hottentot women was the result of a physical characteristic they called *Hottentottenschürze*, a term that described their belief that Hottentot women were typically born with enlarged labia. They claimed that this alleged physical distinction was the reason for Hottentot tribade practices. In *Die Homosexualität des Mannes und des Weibes* Hirschfeld argued instead that bodies throughout the world shared similar physical features and desires. Observing that male homosexuality and female tribadism were to be found in equal measure in the English and "the native African indigenous population," Hirschfeld responded to Ploss, Bartels, and Bartels's claim by arguing for the existence of homosexuality around the world.[108] For instance, in a chapter on homosexuality in Germanic and Anglo-Saxon countries and their colonies, he claimed, "The differences appear minimal compared to what is shared" by homosexual men and women.[109] He argued that every human develops in "intermediate sexual stages." This notion was premised, in Anna Katharina Schaffner's words, on the "ontogenetic bisexuality of the embryo," which might then grow via developmental disturbances into a whole range of different kinds of sexual intermediaries.[110] Hirschfeld's argument that "sex" might exist on a spectrum rather than in binary form ran counter to claims about racial hierarchies.

However, Hirschfeld's focus on biology, which apparently conceived of all people on equal terms, was itself problematic because it focused overly on sexual practices and tended to decontextualize the lives of the subjects of his inquiry. For instance, when Hirschfeld cited the frequency of tribadism among Hausa women as evidence of the universal existence of same-sex sexuality, he here uncritically reproduced Ploss, Bartels, and Bartels's observation that before English colonial rule these women would have been punished by death if found to have engaged in same-sex acts.[111] Hirschfeld's collection of private papers contains evidence of a more nuanced understanding of the role of colonized women. An anonymous short review acknowledges the impact of colonial rule, citing the example of women in Algeria, who are "subjected to colonial circumstance" and whose lives are hence distinct from the concerns of the French and German women's movement.¹¹² Hirschfeld's discussion of tribadism among the Hausa, in contrast, is less circumspect, as it reproduces imperialist claims that colonialism is a progressive influence. This argument anticipates later debates about the role played by sexual rights discourses in cultural imperialism and political and military attacks against regions that are seen to fail certain sexual rights standards. Hirschfeld lent credibility to Ploss, Bartels, and Bartels's claims by citing his own source of information on Hausa life, a man called "Mischlich." This presumably refers to Adam Mischlich, a leading expert on the Hausa language who had started out as a missionary in West Africa but soon took up a post as "imperial district leader" in Togo.¹¹³ Hirschfeld thus aligns himself with the views of a man who in his professional role directly profited from the expansion of the Wilhelmine Empire, suggesting that he took for granted the structures that enabled his countrywomen and countrymen to study and comment on the bodies of the colonized.¹¹⁴

Imperial Leanings during World War I and Jingoistic Defense of Queer Soldiers

Arguably, Hirschfeld's most overtly procolonial outburst occurred during the early months of World War I. In 1915 he published a pamphlet, *Warum Hassen uns die Völker?* (Why do other nations hate us?). Returning to the subject of collective hatred, he here argued for the superiority of Germany, claiming that it was the country's success as a colonial nation that had prompted its envious neighbors to start the war. *Warum Hassen uns die Völker?* not only redeploys the language of homosexual struggle in support of the German war effort but also paints a highly prejudiced, positive image of German colonialism.

The pamphlet claims that the war was started because of the *affektbetonte* (affective) response of Germany's neighbors to the success of the German Empire:

> As ... the unified new Germany gained power and increasing importance in the world, its astonished old European neighbors considered this change and elevation not without care but affectively. ... Because the nations could not love the parvenu ..., they hated it.¹¹⁵

This passage explicitly and positively equates German colonialism with a new "importance in the world," representing it as a source of wealth whose sole negative aspect was that it caused envy in other nations. *Warum Hassen uns die Völker?* returns to the idea of mass suggestion, this time, however, explicitly to critique what Hirschfeld calls the hatred for Germany in England, France, Russia, and Italy. Hirschfeld's conception of hate here is perhaps most clearly aligned with Sigmund Freud's argument that hate is a libidinal wish to destroy an object of love, an argument that underpins critiques of homophobia considering it a form of repressed homosexuality.[116] At the same time, it reveals Hirschfeld's own self-identification as a subject of colonial Germany, which he represents as the repressed love object of other imperial nations. Arguing that anti-German rhetoric in these countries laid the foundations for the war, he criticizes the misrepresentation of Germans as "'vandals,' 'wild hordes,' 'traveling animals,' or, in the words of an American newspaper, 'the Apaches among the nations.'"[117] Hirschfeld uses quotation marks to distance himself from what he represented as racist anti-German language yet fails to comment on the racism against Apaches.

Couched in the terminologies of capitalism and psychoanalysis, *Warum Hassen uns die Völker?* provides an analysis of the causes of World War I that squarely places blame outside Germany. In particular, Hirschfeld is critical of England, one of Germany's strongest colonial rivals, which challenged German rule in East Africa. He argues that England is responsible for starting the war because the country suffered from "envy of the development and size of the young German Empire."[118] Commentators in England received Hirschfeld's comments somewhat mockingly, not least because they associated his work with homosexuality. The *Manchester Courier*, for example, published a review of *Warum Hassen uns die Völker?* titled "The Hatred of the Hun." Claiming that the "eminent pathologist [Dr Magnus Hirschfeld] did not think that the [anti-German] hatred was the result of any particular line of conduct pursued by Germans," the article homes in on Hirschfeld's references to queer literary culture to discredit his views. "Dr Hirschfeld pointed to the treatment extended to Shelley, Byron and Wilde," writes the anonymous author, "as evidence that the British were the most hopeless obscurants in the world, and therefore the most hopeless haters."[119] If Hirschfeld's literary references are a reminder that his anti-English sentiments had been shored up initially by the trial of Oscar Wilde (discussed in Chapter 2)—and that his English critics were quick to turn against his homosexual allegiances—they also show how Hirschfeld used homosexual persecution in England to fuel nationalism and colonial rivalry.

The jingoistic tone of *Warum Hassen uns die Völker?* has puzzled critics such as Charlotte Wolff, who calls it a "perversion of the values [Hirschfeld] had always stood for."[120] Yet the pamphlet clearly suggests that Hirschfeld identified as a subject of the German Empire, an empire that was now under threat. World War I started just over six weeks after Hirschfeld's fiftieth birthday, long after he had established himself as a leading defender of homosexual rights. The birthday was celebrated widely, including via a special journal issue published by the WhK (the sexual rights organization), which suggests that its members saw certain similarities in the battle for homosexual rights and Germany's war effort. The issue opened with a poem by Sophie Hoechstetter, the poet, writer, feminist, and lesbian activist, who praised Hirschfeld's achievements in the language of military battles. Writing about his "fight" against "stupidity, cruelty, and ignorance," Hoechstetter notes that Hirschfeld had not only "fought without human fear and hatred" but "never abandoned anyone."[121] Hoechstetter captures well how Hirschfeld and his circle conceptualized their activism: as a heroic struggle for human rights—*Menschenrecht*—that was marked by "danger" and "attack."[122] This rhetoric and the real experiences of violence that underpin it provide context for Hirschfeld's initial response to the war. For while his romanticization of Germans as "a people who love peace and work [and] loathe meanness and cruelty"[123] suggests that he, like many other intellectuals of the time, was simply swept up in the extreme patriotism of the German war effort, Hoechstetter's tribute is a reminder that Hirschfeld's response to the war typically came from a place of defense of homosexuality.[124]

Hirschfeld's nationalistic attitudes were connected in real terms to the role he played in the homosexual subcultures of the time. Elena Mancini has examined in detail how Hirschfeld "helped thousands of homosexual men and women, transvestites and heterosexual women to enter the war by instructing them on how to pass as a 'normal' soldier."[125] Furthermore, she notes that he supported soldiers whose homosexuality was discovered and who were subjected to punishment by the army because of it. In Figure 1.2 a postcard shows a group of German soldiers, some of whom are cross-dressed while others remain in uniform. The handwritten note reads "lancers of our regiment in the field." While the context in which the image was produced is today unknown, the photograph nevertheless signals the existence of a queer military culture, whose well-being during World War I was a major concern for Hirschfeld and other members of the homosexual reform movement. Under Hirschfeld's leadership, for example, the WhK published records of bravery and heroic acts by homosexual soldiers. Hirschfeld himself, as Gilles Tréhel has pointed out, was especially interested in supporting the women who had cross-dressed as men to be able to fight in the war.[126] These activities do not explain, let alone justify, Hirschfeld's celebration of colonialism in his pro-German war pamphlet. They indicate, however, that at the start of the war, his German identity and efforts to enable homosexual women and men and people whose gender did not conform to binary norms to join the German army were connected in a way that made them complicit in the perpetuation of jingoistic, procolonial discourse.

Figure 1.2 World War I card depicting German soldiers. Courtesy of Stephan Likosky.

Hirschfeld revised his nationalistic prowar views shortly after writing *Warum Hassen uns die Völker?* when he published a study titled *Kriegspychologisches* (The psychology of war) in 1916. He emphasized the trauma caused by war, noting that nobody wanted to take responsibility for it because the horrors of war are so "superhuman in size."[127] Unlike the previous work, *Kriegspychologisches* was well received in the Anglophone world. A New Zealand newspaper observed, for instance, that Hirschfeld's empathic antiwar stance positively marked "the distance which has been travelled since Haeckel, Harnack, Ostwald and others lauded war to the skies as the reawakener and regenerator of the national soul."[128] Applauding Hirschfeld's argument that "it is not enough that the war ends with peace; it must end with reconciliation," the paper picked up on a major change in Hirschfeld's views: his move from nationalism to internationalism.[129] This changing position was in line with the general development of leftist and sexual reform politics of the time, which, faced with the traumatic horrors of the war, increasingly emphasized the importance of internationalism and pacifism. Hirschfeld later returned to the events of World War I in *Die Sittengeschichte des Weltkriegs* (1930), edited with Andreas Gaspar, which was translated in an abridged form into English as *The Sexual History of the World War* in 1934.[130] Here he emphatically distanced himself from the war, describing it as an "interregnum of the social order."[131] *Die Sittengeschichte*, one of Hirschfeld's best-known works other than those on the history of sexuality, was published at a time when the Nazis had already gained considerable power in Germany. Including case studies and other accounts of the diverse contributions made by cross-dressers and homosexual women and men to the war, it outlined Hirschfeld's pacifist position, founded on the argument that war should not be considered an inevitable part of human nature. Linked chronologically to *Racism*, *Die Sittengeschichte* reinforces that Hirschfeld's apprehension of violence and persecution was shaped by his own experience of, and to some extent his identification with, the rise and fall of the German Empire.

Haunted Rights

It can be difficult to untangle the different strands of oppression and privilege that shape queer existence, not least because homosexuality first entered public discourse in the West via the contrary, yet oddly intertwined, efforts of medico-forensic scientists, cultural elites, and political agitators. While this history has been examined primarily in terms of its impact on the lives of people whose bodies and desires did not conform to binary norms, the political efforts of early activists such as Hirschfeld indicate that the emerging homosexual rights discourses cannot be separated from the racial injustice and colonial violence of the modern period. Or to say this differently, if one view is that the emancipation of gay women and men should be celebrated for its liberatory social and cultural impact, then it is equally important to remember that the early homosexual rights struggle was not a fight for wider social equality per se. Laurie Marhoefer, in a recent reappraisal of homosexual politics in the Weimar Republic, notes "the dilemma of homosexual emancipation," which according to her arises from homosexual rights gains being contingent on "thwart[ing] more radical strains of activism [and] the renunciation by homosexuals and transsexuals of an assertive public presence [even] though they carved out a limited subcultural presence."[132] This chapter shows that the first claims for homosexual rights were largely built over, rather than against, the racism of the time.[133] By reading Hirschfeld's writings not for the familiar celebratory narratives about his theoretical and political achievements in relation to gender and sexuality but for their often less immediately tangible colonial underpinnings, I have brought into view some of the "invisible ties," in Ann Laura Stoler's words, between sexuality and race in Hirschfeld's work.[134] This analysis provides a historical perspective to twenty-first-century debates about what happens when, in the words of

Jasbir Puar, "(some) homosexual bodies [are marked] worthy of protection by nation-states."[135] It reveals that around 1900, homosexual rights were already conceived of in relation to debates about national and imperial strength—if not by the state that still persecuted its homosexual subjects, then by the activists who fought for recognition as citizens. Framing Hirschfeld's contribution to modern homosexual rights discourse in terms of its proximity to German colonial rule captures some of the ways racist and colonial violence came to bear on modern homosexual rights activism, haunting the queer struggle for justice and livability.

2

Death, Suicide, and Modern Homosexual Culture

While colonial violence provided the broader framework for Hirschfeld's work, the emotional prompts for it came from a series of sad, and sometimes devastating, interpersonal encounters. Hirschfeld claimed that he was compelled as a young doctor to specialize in sexology when one of his patients committed suicide and left him a legacy of documents that testified to the anguish the young man had felt because of his desire for other men. Hirschfeld gathered a number of today little-known writings on homosexual death and suicide. Made up of dispersed and sometimes fragmented narratives, they show not only that in the early twentieth century queer women and men sometimes felt the precariousness of their own existence but that the witnessing of the suffering of others also affected their sense of collective belonging.[1] Examining this material, the chapter is not concerned with the notoriously difficult and often problematic psychology of suicide or the diagnostic aim of trying to establish why some people kill themselves while others in comparable situations continue living. Instead, inspired by Ann Cvetkovich's work on the cultural and political reach of trauma beyond the strictly psychoanalytic, I turn attention to the suicidal aspects of modern queer culture to track the individual and collective impact of persecution and social denial.[2] I argue that queer suicide and violent deaths are part of a traumatic collective experience, markers of the potentially lethal force of heteronormative ideals and expectations but also complex sites of shared identification and resistance. By gathering Hirschfeld's accounts of lives that ended tragically or prematurely, I build an archive of queer death including suicide to trace some of the emotional threads that held together queer existence at the turn of the nineteenth century and that sometimes unraveled in the face of real and imagined rejection. These accounts reveal not only that the denial of homosexuality profoundly shaped the lives of many individuals who felt "different from the others" but also that individual suffering contributed to the shaping of a collective sense of homosexual identity.[3]

Ordinary Subjects

Suicide plays a troubled, and sometimes iconic role, in modern history. Analyses of the self-inflicted deaths of famous figures such as Virginia Woolf and Walter Benjamin show the many, often opposing, ways in which suicide has been understood and historicized either, as in the case of Woolf, in relation to mental illness, or as in the case of Benjamin, as the result of devastating political circumstance.[4] Taking a different approach, Jose Muñoz has explored the radical utopian potential of queer suicide. His analysis focuses on the famous, self-consciously staged "exit from life" of dancer Fred Herko in Greenwich Village in 1964.[5] Herko killed himself in front of an audience of friends who unwittingly became witnesses to his final dance and last exit—a jump through the window of a fifth-floor apartment. Muñoz reads Herko's suicide as a "queer act" and radical performance, not only because of the careful choreography of the death but also because of its "linger[ing] imprint": the "different lines of thought, aesthetics, and political reverberations trailing from this doomed young artist."[6] Muñoz's arguments about suicide as a signifier of the utopian potential of queer failure, and about the collective impact of Herko's death more specifically, are bolstered by historical eyewitness accounts of the event and Herko's material legacy, an archive of texts and ephemera. Such a deep historical footprint is, if not unusual, then restricted to famous lives or those whose legacy has been preserved in a way that is accessible beyond their immediate circle of family and friends. In contrast, my concern here is with the lives—and deaths—of ordinary women and men whose existence has left little trace in the historical archive because they were not famous and did not get caught up in cultural or political events, scandals, or other such circumstance that typically produces a historical footprint.

Sexological writings—Hirschfeld's included—are full of anecdotal narratives about such elusive ordinary lives, but the dearth of contextual records makes them difficult subjects for queer history. This became clear to me when my esteemed colleague the historian Reiner Herrn, who has undertaken much painstaking research on Hirschfeld and his Institute of Sexual Science, suggested to me that because of the lack of contextual evidence we might assume that Hirschfeld invented the account of the patient suicide to lend credibility to his fledgling sexological practice.[7] But if there is no tangible historical evidence to verify Hirschfeld's narrative, there equally is no evidence to prove that his account is a mere invention. Why, then, should we not take it seriously? Feminist, queer, and critical race scholars and historians of class and disability have, after all, long recognized that evidence is not everything in analyses of the past and that attention to fragmentary accounts and the gaps in narrative and visual representation can alert us to the existence of subjects excluded from the conventional historical archive because their lives left little tangible trace. With this in mind, I set about looking for other suicide accounts in Hirschfeld's work and found that he was deeply concerned with documenting the existence of queer women and men who killed themselves or felt suicidal.

Given the prevalence of antiqueer stereotypes and attitudes even today, it may seem critically counterintuitive to focus on an archive of death and suffering. My insistence here not on celebrating queer culture but on lingering with the dead and the injured clearly sits uneasily in affirmative histories, which focus on recuperating positive evidence from the queer past. I want to acknowledge the political value of, and critical pleasure in, pursuing affirmative historical research, not least because of the influence it has had on my own queer becoming.[8] Yet affirmation alone, as Heather Love has pointed out, cannot account for the full range of feelings and experiences that shape queer existence.[9] The narratives about doomed existence gathered by Hirschfeld offer glimpses at the relationship between discourse and everyday existence and at what it might have felt like to live an ordinary queer life before World War II, a time when same-sex subcultures had began to flourish but positive public representations of homosexuality remained rare and social attitudes predominantly negative. By excavating Hirschfeld's overlooked writings on suicide—and concluding with a section on the impact of Oscar Wilde's death on the men who identified with his suffering—the chapter complicates accounts of modern queer culture formation. It shows that the persecution, social denial, and deaths of individual women and men whose bodies and desires did not fit social norms and expectations caused collective shockwaves, contributing to the emergence of a precarious sense collective queer existence.

The Suicide Archive

Hirschfeld switched from general medical practice to sexology after "the suicide of a young officer who shot himself on the eve of his marriage, bequeathing . . . Hirschfeld many of his notes and drawings."[10] He repeatedly returned to this traumatic event in his writings, to both validate his sexology and let speak the voice of a "*Selbstmörder*."[11] The German word *Selbstmörder* has no single English equivalent, translating literally as "someone who murders himself" (a woman would be a *Selbstmörderin*), thus overtly casting the person in criminal terms. Andreas Bähr has argued that the modern introduction of the Latin term *suicide* alongside the older *self-murder* marks a gradual historical shift from criminalizing to pathologizing self-killing.[12] Yet suicide, not unlike homosexuality, remained stigmatized as it moved from the courtroom to the clinic. Countries as politically diverse as the United States, England, Russia, and the German nations all had antisuicide laws that posthumously punished the person—for instance, by annulling the dead person's will.[13] In addition, Judeo-Christian religions treated harshly those who had committed the sin of suicide, often denying the dead person conventional burial rites.[14] While over the course of the nineteenth century some of these laws were repealed—the German Penal Code of 1871 decriminalized unassisted suicide—and while religious attitudes softened, this did little to change social attitudes. In one of the earliest histories of modern suicide, the English observer Henry Romilly Fedden noted that when "the comforts of Victorianism overlay the primitive horror of suicide and blunt the precise dogmatic teaching of the Church it [was] no longer the thing in itself that create[d] the scare, so much as what other people [thought] of it . . . [because] loss of fortune [was] substituted with the scourge of gossip."[15] Fedden's observation anticipates the tone of the suicide letter written by Hirschfeld's patient. The letter emphasizes the man's fear of social disapproval, explaining that he will kill himself because he lacks the "strength" to tell his parents the "truth" and stop a marriage "against which nothing could be said in and of itself."[16] Hoping that his parents will never learn about "that which nearly strangled my heart," the man avoids giving "that" a name, indicating his unspeakable sense of shame.[17]

The suicide letter shows how the expectation of marriage and family together can reinforce heterosexual norms in a way that makes queer life both unspeakable and unlivable. Hirschfeld's own choice of words suggests that he did not consider the young man's suicide a voluntary act. For while *Selbstmörder* was already the common German term by the time of this particular death, it existed alongside *Freitod*, literally "free death," an older concept that gained renewed popularity around the turn of the nineteenth century through Friedrich Nietzsche's work.[18] Nietzsche celebrated "the free death, which occurs because I want it," arguing that the ability to choose death is one of the characteristic features of the superman.[19] Hirschfeld was familiar with Nietzsche's work, considering him one of the thinkers "who at least theoretically fully understood homosexual love."[20] This makes it all the more significant that he ignored the more heroic, romantic notion of the freely chosen death, describing the patient suicide instead in terms of *Selbstmord*, a choice of word associated with shame, taboo, and social ostracization.

Yet if, for the man, naming his feelings was an unspeakable act, his suicide note nevertheless also conveys awareness that there are others who are like him. Entreating Hirschfeld to listen to the "outcry of a desolate man," the *Selbstmörder's* final words implore his physician to dedicate his life to the homosexual cause: "The thought that you [Hirschfeld] could contribute to [a future] when the German fatherland will think of *us* in more just terms," he writes, "sweetens my hour of death."[21] The plural "us" and the forward-looking plea for action alert us to the fact that suicide is a final act only for the person who dies. Katrina Jaworski has argued that "in relation to suicide, death is not power's limit, since norms, meanings and assumptions and the processes that are part of making sense of suicide will constitute knowledge before, during and after the act of taking one's life."[22] For Jaworski, this realization is closely tied to the difficult question of agency, which in her reading is overshadowed by the fact that "dead or alive, it may not be possible to be free of the operations of power."[23] The suicide letter transfers the man's own failed hopes onto Hirschfeld via an ambiguous demand for justice "for us" in the "fatherland." The word *us* evokes both a larger group of people and a closeness between Hirschfeld and the man. By his own account, Hirschfeld was treating the young officer for severe depression around the time of this death. We cannot know for certain if the closeness evoked by the young officer refers to an actual friendship between him and his doctor. However, this seems unlikely given the overall tone of the letter and its formal address ("Sie"). Ultimately, the psychic, emotional, and social pressures that led to the young officer's suicide are unknowable to us, in the same way that there is no hard evidence that the man's posthumous opening up to Hirschfeld is linked to a recognition that Hirschfeld himself was attracted to men. Yet if the truth of events appears elusive partly because we must rely entirely on Hirschfeld's narration, the account nevertheless reveals the conditions that might contribute to the end of a homosexual life around 1900. It constitutes, in Cvetkovich's terms, a repository "of feelings and emotions, which are encoded not only in the content of the texts themselves but in practices that surround their production and reception."[24] The poignancy of the story lies in the young man literally bestowing on Hirschfeld a material record of the fears and unfulfilled desires that he was unable to discuss in their face-to-face meetings, a move that self-consciously turns the life that was unspeakable for him into one of the emotional prompts for Hirschfeld's subsequent professional practice.

Professional Haunting

The narrative of the young officer's suicide gained a relatively prominent role in Hirschfeld's vast oeuvre because he included it in autobiographical reflections published over the course of his life. He made use of the story to legitimize his sexological practice, aiming to give it an emotional credibility and political urgency that would distinguish his work from that of his colleagues. An account of events published in 1922–1923 in the homosexual journal *Die Freundschaft* (The friendship), shows that Hirschfeld used the suicide narrative in an attempt to gain professional credibility in the competing factions of early twentieth-century homosexual culture. He mentions the suicide in an article about the history of the Wissenschaftlich-humanitäres Kommitee (WhK; Scientific Humanitarian Committee), which was directed specifically at a homosexual audience and sought to promote Hirschfeld's many reform activities. The WhK was cofounded by Hirschfeld in May 1897, shortly before Oscar Wilde's release from prison, to increase public knowledge about and acceptance of homosexuality. Its best-known campaign was the petition for the revocation of Paragraph 175 of the German Penal Code. The WhK also played a key role in the publication of new sexuality research, competing and overlapping with other journals in complicated ways. For instance, Sigmund Freud explained in a letter to Carl Jung in 1908 that an article of his had appeared in the new *Zeitschrift für Sexualwissenschaft* (Journal of sexual science) after "a bit of skullduggery on the part of the editors [who had] originally solicited the piece for the *Jahrbuch für sexuelle Zwischenstufen* [Yearbook for sexual intermediaries]." He continues, "I was not told until several months later that it was to be published in the *Zeitschrift für Sexualwissenschaft* which was just being founded. I asked for a guarantee that this new organ was not to be a chronicle of the [WhK] in which case I preferred to withdraw my contribution, but received no answer."[25] Freud's words indicate the sometimes rapidly shifting allegiances of the early sex researchers. While he had originally submitted his work to the *Jahrbuch*, knowing that it was closely aligned with the WhK, Freud soon turned his back on the WhK in a row over Hirschfeld's use of a questionnaire to assess homosexual life. Freud's article, meanwhile, was passed from the editors of the *Jahrbuch* to the editors of the newly founded *Zeitschrift*, probably because of the quarrel, who then contacted Freud with their editorial queries.

The episode, which is barely more than a footnote in the history of sex research, nevertheless illustrates how a complex web of professional disputes and personal rivalries shaped the sexual sciences. By the time Hirschfeld wrote his short history of the WhK in 1922, the organization had undergone further transformations as it became closely associated with the broader activities of the Institute of Sexual Science. The institute, founded by Hirschfeld in 1919, had a significant popular reach, drawing in large audiences through initiatives such as the Marriage Consultation Department—closely tied in to the institute's eugenics work—and Questionnaire Evenings, which gave members of the public the opportunity anonymously to deposit questions about sex. A member of the institute would then answer these questions in a public talk.[26] Despite its popular success, the institute competed with other homosexual organizations. The WhK's greatest rival in Berlin's homosexual subculture, for example, was the Gemeinschaft der Eigenen (Community of the Autonomous).[27] Led by Adolf Brand and Benedict Friedländer, it was heavily influenced by the anarchist writings of John Henry Mackay.[28] Founded in 1903, the Gemeinschaft der Eigenen supported Hirschfeld's fight for the abolition of antihomosexuality legislation but rejected both Hirschfeld's leadership and his theorization of sexual intermediaries.[29] Instead, Brand and Friedländer adapted the masculine ideals of Hellenic revivalism, which had gained such popularity in nineteenth-century England, by combining them with the physical pursuits of outdoor culture and an affirmative focus on homosexual virility that stood in stark contrast to Hirschfeld's ideas about the infinite variations of gender and sexuality. In 1906 Friedländer founded a splinter group of the WhK, which became known as the Bund für männliche Kultur (League for Manly Culture). He committed suicide a couple of years later, apparently in response to the suffering caused by a long-standing intestinal illness.[30]

In contrast to Brand and Friedländer's ideal of strong masculine homosexuality, Hirschfeld's understanding of homosexual existence was influenced by the traumatic suicide of his patient. His (re)telling of the story indicates how cultural conventions work themselves into the representation of traumatic memory. Cathy Caruth has argued that it is difficult to listen and respond "to traumatic stories in a way that does not lose their impact, reduce them to clichés or turn them all into versions of the same story."[31] Hirschfeld's repeated accounts of the suicide of his patient reached beyond the realm of the well-rehearsed anecdote even as they were shaped by narrative conventions. Hirschfeld's final mention of the suicide occurs in one of the last pieces he wrote, his "Autobiographical Sketch," published posthumously in 1936.[32] Unlike the 1922 account in *Die Freundschaft*, this later piece was written in English. The two accounts tell slightly different stories about the suicide. According to Hirschfeld's 1922 version, the man died "unmittelbar *nach* seiner Hochzeit" (immediately *after* his wedding).[33] There is something particularly poignant about the young man going through the rituals of a wedding before committing suicide, especially because this chain of events goes against the conventional conception of wedding nerves, which locate the moment of crisis *before* the wedding.[34] When Hirschfeld returns to the event at the end of his life the conventional time frame is restored; he writes that the man killed himself on the "eve of his marriage."[35] Given the absence of other sources we cannot know the actual time of the death, but the temporal slippage in Hirschfeld's accounts alerts us to the ease with which cliché attaches itself to the narration of traumatic events.

Hirschfeld wrote "Autobiographical Sketch" for the *Encyclopedia Sexualis* (1936), a compendium of key themes and figures in the sexual sciences edited by an American physician and historian of medicine, Victor Robinson. Robinson had a particular interest in the stories that shaped scientific development, an interest that defined how he approached and wrote history. His subsequent *The Story of Medicine* (1943), for instance—a book that, it should be noted, makes no mention of Hirschfeld or homosexuality—begins with the imaginative assertion that "the first cry of pain through the primitive jungle was the first call for a physician."[36] If Robinson's conventional narrative about the civilizing impact of medicine is anything to go by, it seems plausible that his editorship played a role in the conventionalized temporality of Hirschfeld's English-language account of the suicide. Furthermore, Hirschfeld's own memory of the details of the event might have faded over time. Yet the fact remains that he repeatedly returned to the suicide over the course of three decades, suggesting that this tragic death retained a traumatic presence in Hirschfeld's life, haunting his professional practice.

Statistical Ends

Where, then, does this single death more broadly fit into Hirschfeld's work and the history of sexuality? For some critics the question of whose life counts in the narratives modern society tells about itself can inevitably be answered by referring to what they consider the decisive impact of nineteenth-century sciences on the regulation and expression of intimacy, desire, and the vagaries of identity. Karma Lochrie, for instance, takes for granted what she calls "the installation of norms first in statistical science and second in sexology."[37] She argues that the emergence of these sciences marks a fundamental distinction between "normal" modernity and a premodernity, which "is neither hopelessly utopian nor inveterately heteronormative."[38] According to Lochrie's interpretation of Georges Canguilhem's work on the invention of scientific norms and Michel Foucault's discursive history of sexuality and modernity, statistics and sexology are the harbingers of medico-scientific reductiveness, legal persecution, and related social norms that bring an end to the anormality she accords to premodernity. It is of course not difficult to find evidence of the damage caused by the process of disciplining sex—including in terms of its problematic conceptual and scientific legacies and the physical and psychic suffering caused by practitioners who actively tried to "cure" their homosexual or transgendered patients—and it is vital that we take account of this damage.[39] Yet I am uneasy about histories such as Lochrie's, which hinge on a clearly identifiable modern invention of sexual norms. The attribution of seismic structural shifts in power to one or two scientific developments problematically smooths over many of the edges that delineate the emergence of modern sexuality, a process that sharpened queer lives across time and space.

Hirschfeld's complex role as a sexologist is a case in point. While he singled out the transformative power on his work of the suicide of the young German officer, he also notes in his account of the event in 1922 that he had received countless other "Abschiedsbriefe" (farewell letters) in the intervening years.[40] If these words create a certain distance between Hirschfeld and the young officer whose death here slips into the realm of statistics, Hirschfeld's evocation of the large number of queer suicides hardly expresses detached scientific concern. Rather, the tragic deaths motivated Hirschfeld's political work, prompting him to collate statistics that would raise awareness of the suffering of homosexuals as a group of people, a group not normally included in the burgeoning scientific literature on suicide around 1900.

The subject of suicide first began to garner sustained scientific interest in the late nineteenth century. In Berlin, psychiatrists started to collect an archive of case studies of women and men who killed themselves. Furthermore, a new kind of social research turned attention to the topic. Émile Durkheim, whose large-scale study *Le Suicide* is considered a founding text of modern sociology, famously focused on suicide as a measure of social circumstance. Containing findings from a comparative study of the suicide rates of Catholics and Protestants, *Le Suicide* was first published in 1897, around the same time that Hirschfeld published his first, short pamphlet, *Sappho und Sokrates*.[41] Durkheim's classification of four different types of suicide according to social factors is considered an important methodological step in modern social research.[42] Ian Marsh and others who have traced the shifting historical conceptions of suicide and its etiologies show, however, that Durkheim's rejection of pathological models of suicide was not unique. Over the course of the nineteenth century, philosophers and thinkers increasingly turned attention to the social causes of suicide.[43] Karl Marx, for instance, had already noted in 1846 that suicide constitutes "one of the thousand and one symptoms of the general social struggle ever fought out on new ground."[44] It is not my concern here to track the complex cultural history of suicide or critique the methods by which it has been studied and treated by medical practitioners, psychologists, and lawmakers. Instead I want to pick up on a queer absence in nineteenth-century debates about suicide: before Hirschfeld began to count homosexual suicides—and despite the explosion of discourses around sex at the time—the "act whose author is also the sufferer" was rarely considered in relation to homosexuality.[45]

The discursive absence of homosexuality in mainstream discussions of suicide reinforces how easily heteronormative assumptions work themselves into the fabric of social research. Marx and Friedrich Engels, for instance, who so famously sought to challenge the gendered as well as classed boundaries of modern society, expressed strong antihomosexual sentiments that indicate the limits of their radical politics.[46] In a letter to Marx, written June 22, 1869, Engels observed that

> the paederasts are beginning to count themselves and discover that they are a power in the state. Only power was lacking, but according to this source [pamphlets by Karl Heinrich Ulrichs], it apparently already exists in secret. . . . *Guerre aux cons, paix aus trous-de-cul* [war on cunts, peace for arseholes] will now be the slogan. It is a piece of luck that we, personally, are too old to fear that when this party wins, we shall have to pay physical tribute to the victors. But the younger generation![47]

Employing a derogatory older sexual vocabulary to discredit the emerging emancipatory efforts of men who love and desire other men, Engels here turns to a foreign language—French—to articulate what is otherwise unspeakable to him. The outburst was prompted by Engels's encounter with the work of the lawyer and homosexual rights activist Karl Heinrich Ulrichs, who in the lead up to the unification of the German states was campaigning for the adoption of an antidiscriminatory penal code in the new nation.[48] Ulrichs developed a new term, *urningism*, which conceptualized love between men in affirmative terms, and popularized the idea that same-sex desire was a form of gender inversion, drawing on the work of Plato in particular to emphasize that male same-sex love has a long and positive cultural history. The existence of female same-sex sexuality was for Ulrichs largely a theoretical exercise, something to be included in his new sexual taxonomy on the basis of likely occurrence rather than personal knowledge. The male focus of Ulrichs and Engels is a reminder of the historical marginalization of women from the political and public spheres. Both Ulrichs's activism for and Engels's outrage against "paederasts" beginning to "count themselves" suggests that numbers, if not statistics, held powerful sway in the debates about sexuality and politics. Engels's derogatory language furthermore shows that what we would now call homophobia was forcefully articulated long before the concept of homosexual identity was widely recognized.

Hirschfeld's attempt to draw statistical attention to homosexual suicide can be understood as a protest against the denial of homosexuality in death as well as life. It challenges the negation of women and men whose sexuality discounted their existence socially and politically. "Without doubt a large number of homosexuals feel prompted by their sexual particularity to voluntarily end their life," writes Hirschfeld in his magnum opus *Die Homosexualität des Mannes und des Weibes* (The homosexuality of men and women), which was published in 1914.[49] While he acknowledges that one of the reasons for suicide is the universal problematic of "unrequited love," he is at pains to point out that homosexual suicide should not be seen as a voluntary act but as the product of social rejection and legal persecution, caused by feelings of upset about the negative status of homosexuality and its persecution and a pronounced fear of blackmail and scandal.[50] In a discussion of *Doppelselbstmorde* (double suicides), for example, Hirschfeld points out that such self-inflicted deaths are relatively common among female and male urnings, arguing that these "couples who kill themselves together . . . prefer togetherness in death to loneliness in life, unity in dying to a socially and legally enforced separation in life."[51] Given the emphasis placed by Hirschfeld on the social and legal causes of homosexual suicide, his statistical work on the issue can be understood as an attempt to intervene in what he considered the double attack on homosexuality in life as well as death.

When Walter Benjamin looked back to the economic crises of 1840, he noted that it was during this time that "the idea of suicide became familiar to the working masses" who "despair[ed] of earning a livelihood."[52] He observed that suicide gained a degree of cultural capital at the time, as indicated by the popular circulation of a lithograph depicting a suicidal unemployed English worker whose fate, according to Benjamin, provided inspiration to many others who, finding themselves in similarly hopeless financial straits, followed suit. Hirschfeld in turn suggested that homosexuality can create feelings of hopelessness, emphasizing that "homosexuals don't suffer because of their homosexuality but because of the false judgment passed on them by themselves and others."[53] For Hirschfeld, then, homosexual suicide was not the result of an inherent homosexual defect but the product of attacks against women and men whose desires did not fit heterosexual norms and expectations.

Penal Death

Paragraph 175 of the German Penal Code punished sexual acts between men with imprisonment and the optional revocation of civil rights. In Prussia, the death penalty for sodomy had been abolished in 1794, but this did not mean that the penal system no longer contributed to the deaths of men imprisoned for sex with other men. Hirschfeld's account of what he calls the "unnecessary" suicide of a fifty-five-year-old man from Baden in southern Germany shows just how cruelly the prison system could conspire in fostering a potentially deadly sense of social rejection. The man, who had been arrested for homosexual conduct while on holiday in Berlin, hanged himself in his cell a few days after sending notification of his arrest to Hirschfeld—who was known to offer support in such circumstances—and to his family and employer. The prison delayed sending the letters for five days, a time span that proved too long for the man, who killed himself believing that "outside nobody wanted to know him any longer."[54] According to Hirschfeld, the death was particularly tragic because the man's sense of rejection turned out to have been unfounded: in addition to Hirschfeld's support, the man's family and employer sent supportive letters, the latter emphasizing that the man would be able to return to his job "even if he was found guilty."[55] In other words, while the man clearly suffered from legal persecution, his sense of social rejection turned out to have been imagined rather than real, enforced by a punitive prison system that interrupted vital communications.

Hirschfeld also mentions that he often encountered on the bodies of his patients "Suizidialnarben" (scars left by suicide attempts).[56] The image of suicidal scarring not only bears witness to the damage caused by social norms but indicates how such damage touched Hirschfeld's sexological practice. It suggests that the body in the clinic is not only, as Foucault would have it, the docile product of disciplinary power but also a repository of experience, which sometimes imprints itself onto the skin, making legible what language fails to articulate. With this in mind, the data collected by Hirschfeld on homosexual suicide can be seen as an attempt to make visible the queer scar tissue that marks modern homosexuality. By counting homosexual suicides within a statistical framework, Hirschfeld emphasized the collective shape of the individual suffering. This archive documents the deadly effects of homosexual persecution and how social ostracization could make queer lives feel unlivable.

Gender Bias

Hirschfeld's intervention in social research and debates about suicide has its own, gendered, blind spots. While he discussed both homosexual and lesbian suicides, his focus was clearly on men who kill themselves. To some extent, the gender imbalance reflects that Hirschfeld drew heavily on personal experience in his work. As a cross-dresser, he had many connections with people whose gender did not match the one assigned at birth or who were intersex, as discussed in Chapter 4. But writing in 1914, his focus was clearly on male homosexuals; he claims to have known personally over half of the one hundred men who had killed themselves in recent years. According to his analysis of the ten thousand or so responses to his psychobiological questionnaire, Hirschfeld estimated that around three in every one hundred urnings successfully commit suicide, that about a quarter of all homosexuals attempt suicide, and that the remaining three-quarters have suicidal thoughts at some point in their lives.[57] In short, according to Hirschfeld, homosexual existence is at least *felt* to be unlivable at some point. If this paints a grim picture, Hirschfeld also mentions that the numbers are not necessarily accurate. He cites the work of a Dutch physician who had undertaken a similar survey and arrived at slightly lower numbers.[58] His figures are further compromised by their being based largely on accounts of visitors to the institute, many of whom had come to seek help in dealing with feelings of isolation, rejection, and despair. But the statistical accuracy of this data or the methodology that framed the investigation is not the main point of interest here. More significant is that Hirschfeld spoke publicly about the fact that homosexuality could seem unlivable because it lacked rights, acceptance, and in the case of lesbianism—as Hirschfeld's own work shows—visibility.

Examples of women taking their lives appear in a section dealing with "Doppelselbstmord" (double suicide) and "unglückliche Liebe" (unhappy love).[59] Here Hirschfeld mentions the unsuccessful double-suicide attempt of two young female factory workers whose relationship was threatened by the interference of their parents and the successful suicides of two married woman who shot each other, leaving a note with the request "Please do not search for the reason behind this deed."[60] Hirschfeld's gendered evidence base indicates how closely the analysis of suicide remained tied to conventional debates about masculinity and femininity, as well as sexuality and citizenship. For example, Hirschfeld does not reflect on the fact that while lesbianism, unlike male homosexuality, might not have been criminalized, the social taboo of love between women and the pressures on women to conform to heterosexual norms created difficult living conditions for lesbians—to the extent that some women felt unable to continue their lives in this context. While Hirschfeld acknowledged the social factors of lesbian suicide, his focus on issues of unfulfilled love and tragic relationship does not address in any detail the circumstances that doomed the lives of these women. Adrienne Rich has argued that "the destruction of records and memorabilia and letters documenting the realities of lesbian existence must be taken very seriously as a means of keeping heterosexuality compulsory for women, since what has been kept from our knowledge is joy, sexuality, courage, and community, as well as guilt, self-betrayal and pain."[61] There is no evidence that Hirschfeld actively destroyed lesbian archives, and it is worth reiterating that he wrote about both female and male same-sex sexuality. Yet his relatively limited analysis and superficial treatment of lesbian suicide nevertheless illustrates what Rich has identified as the historical deprival of lesbian "political existence through 'inclusion' as female versions of male homosexuality."[62] The silences on the deaths of trans and intersex people further limit Hirschfeld's suicide work. They reflect a long history of gendered exclusions and marginalization, which seeped into affirmative debates about homosexuality and shaped scientific research, as well as political interventions.

A Verbal Arsenal

Hirschfeld's gendered silences are all the more remarkable because one of his main concerns was precisely the challenge of what he considered the potentially fatal unspeakability of homosexual life as well as death. He contributed, for example, to the silent film *Anders als die Andern* (Different from the others), released in German cinemas in 1919, which treated in a sympathetic manner the blackmail of homosexuals.[63] The film opens with the main character, Paul Körner (played by Conrad Veidt, later famous for his roles in the 1920 films *The Cabinet of Dr Caligari* and the Orientalist adventure fantasy *The Indian Tomb*), going through newspapers at breakfast (Figure 2.1). We see his face distorting in despair as he finds report after report about "unexplained" deaths of men. The causes of these deaths are described as "unknown" and "incomprehensible," yet it is clear from Körner's reaction that he reads the news in affective terms as the deaths of men who, like him, were attracted to other men. The opening anticipates Körner's own suicide toward the end of the film, when he kills himself to escape a blackmailer who destroyed his budding relationship with a young man. *Anders als die Andern* was inspired by the real cases of homosexual blackmail that Hirschfeld encountered in his clinic. Furthermore, deaths such as the high-profile suicide of the steel manufacturer Friedrich Krupp in 1902 received considerable public attention. Krupp, a married father of two who liked to holiday in Capri, where he entertained close relationships with young men, killed himself less than two weeks after the Social Democratic Party newspaper *Vorwärts* (Forward) published an article claiming that Krupp was homosexual.[64] *Anders als die Andern* examines the causes of such deaths and the silence that surrounds them. Produced as part of the educational outreach efforts of the Institute of Sexual Science, the film captures well the insidious ways in which the taboo subjects of homosexuality and suicide resided in early twentieth-century public discourse—not so much as a total absence but as a loaded silence that could contribute to a sense of collective despair and the feeling of an epidemic loss of queer life even as homosexual culture grew in affirmative terms.

Figure 2.1 Still from *Anders als die Andern* (1919), with Conrad Veidt as Paul Körner.

That verbal attacks, rather than necessarily physical violence, posed some of the most dangerous threats to queer existence is a recurring theme in Hirschfeld's writings. Discussing the consequences of persecution, for example, he deliberately offset German- and English-language expressions against each other to critique the transmission of antihomosexuality sentiments by the medical profession.[65] He recounts an encounter with an American patient who told him that when he had asked his doctor back home in Philadelphia for advice about his homosexuality, the physician responded that the only ways of dealing with it were masturbation, voluntary commitment to a psychiatric asylum, or suicide.[66] My translation here is a fairly literal rendering of Hirschfeld's German words. Hirschfeld himself records the incident in a way that makes clear that such a straightforward translation does not tell the full story.

The German passage includes the English-language expressions used by the American doctor, which are set apart in parentheses from Hirschfeld's own words. These English words give their own account of the doctor's negative stance toward homosexuality. They reveal that the doctor had advised his patient to "use his right hand," employing a slang term for masturbation, a practice which was at the time still largely a social taboo.[67] Next, the patient was offered the option "to place himself in a madhouse," a choice of words that reinforces the derogatory tone of the doctor's advice. While in the early twentieth century mental health issues were still understood in negative terms, the clinical terminology of the "psychiatric hospital" had by then replaced the older term "madhouse."[68] Most chillingly, the physician emphasized that the preferred action for his homosexual patient would be, "*better*, [to] commit suicide."[69] Hirschfeld does not translate "better," which I have emphasized. However, his decision to include the doctor's English words ensures that their devastating implications are not missed. From contextual evidence we know that Hirschfeld wrote for an educated audience, which would have been able to read both German and English. By recording in parallel the German and English words, the sexological text here draws attention to the deadly climax of the Philadelphian doctor's words. The professional objectivity of the Philadelphian doctor is undermined, alerting us to the complicity of certain medical discourses and certain doctors in perpetuating violence against homosexuals. This incitement to suicide is a powerful reminder that many, perhaps most, antihomosexual attacks are verbal and that the keepers of such verbal arsenals are frequently in positions of trust and power.

Dead Wilde

Of course not all queer people who died tragically or prematurely did so because they had taken their own lives. Hirschfeld's account of the reception of the death of arguably the most iconic modern homosexual, Oscar Wilde, indicates how the persecution of this famous figure affected both Hirschfeld and queer everyday life in the early twentieth century. Wilde's trial, and the wealth of public attention it received have been critically well documented. Considered a formative moment in modern homosexual culture when knowledge about sex between men was popularized, producing a stereotypical image of the (male) homosexual that would retain its cultural currency well into the twentieth century, scholars have examined in detail the events and their impact on homosexual culture.[70] The Wilde case is a reminder of the gendered history of same-sex sexuality—lesbianism entered English public discourse only in 1928 with the trial of Radclyffe Hall's novel *The Well of Loneliness*—and that modern same-sex history typically revolves around famous, often upper-class, figures. If Wilde himself does not fit the focus of this chapter on ordinary lives, Hirschfeld's writings about his death nevertheless reveal that Wilde's suffering affected everyday queer culture in the early twentieth century.

Wilde died in November 1900, at age forty-six, not long after he had been released from prison, where he had served a sentence of two years' hard labor following his conviction for homosexual conduct in 1895. The critical consensus is that Wilde's death was hastened by his deteriorating health, the result of the years in Reading Gaol. However, the exact details of what caused Wilde's death remain disputed.[71] In the late 1980s, the biographer Richard Ellmann popularized the controversial argument, first put forward by Arthur Ransome in 1912, that Wilde had contracted syphilis from female prostitutes during his time at Oxford in the 1870s.[72] Ellmann argued that the disease flared up more than twenty-five years later and caused the meningitis that he believes killed Wilde.[73] Subsequent studies have, however, convincingly discarded syphilis as the cause of Wilde's death.[74] In an article published in *The*

Lancet in 2000 to mark the centenary of Wilde's death, the pharmacological expert and psychiatrist Ashley Robins and the otolaryngologist Sean Sellars reexamined Wilde's death certificate and medical reports by his physician. They agree with other findings that suggest that Wilde died from meningoencephalitis, an infection of the brain. Robins and Sellars argue that the effects of this infection were compounded further by its treatment, an invasive surgical procedure that cost Wilde a lot of money, pain, and ultimately, his life.[75] They support their claims with a picture of Wilde on his deathbed (Figure 2.2), contending that the flower arrangement next to Wilde's ear was placed there deliberately to hide the extensive wounds the surgery had caused around his right ear. Unlike the visual representations of Wilde's trial, which circulated widely in the contemporary press, the death-bed photograph has not entered the popular archive of images by which Wilde is remembered, either in the early twentieth century or today. This does not mean that Wilde's death went unnoticed, however. While his plays were banned on the British stage, they became hugely popular in many countries, including Germany where Wilde's name also came to feature prominently in homosexual rights debates.[76]

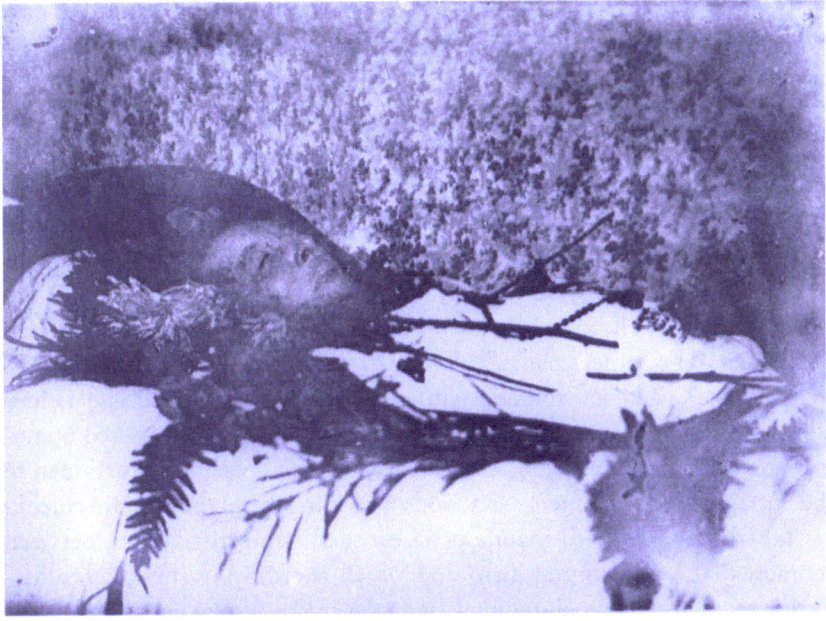

Figure 2.2 Photograph of Oscar Wilde taken the day after his death. Courtesy of Jeremy Mason.

Hirschfeld mentioned Wilde quite frequently to illustrate "the hell experienced by homosexuals" because of persecution.[77] Yvonne Ivory, in a painstaking reconstruction of Wilde's reception in the German homosexual rights movement, has examined in detail how "Hirschfeld's circle was inspired by Wilde and used his case and his name strategically to publicize the plight of homosexuals."[78] But references to Wilde's name ran deeper than political rhetoric might suggest. Hirschfeld's writings indicate the personal and collective upset caused by Wilde's persecution and premature death. Writing in the 1930s, Hirschfeld explained that his earliest sexological study, *Sappho und Sokrates*, was not only inspired by the suicide of his young patient but published in 1896 "synchronously" "with the trial of Oscar Wilde [when] Wilde's writings (especially his 'Picture of Dorian Gray') were widely read in Germany."[79] The temporal proximity in which this narrative places the suicide, Wilde's trial, and the beginnings of Hirschfeld's sexological work lays a powerful claim to the emotional connectedness of homosexual life at the turn of the nineteenth century. This argument is not about establishing a cause-and-effect relation between the Wilde trial and the young man's death—indeed there is no indication that the young man mentioned Wilde in the materials he left for Hirschfeld. Instead, Hirschfeld's work emphasizes that same-sex lives, however distinct, were governed by similar, hostile terms of reality.

Witnessing, directly or indirectly, the violent or premature deaths of men who loved other men caused emotional shockwaves that rippled far across the modern world. In Hirschfeld's case, this is made tangible in his account of a visit to Cambridge sometime between 1905 and 1907. We can date the visit because Hirschfeld mentions that it took place when Wilde's son, Vyvyan Holland, was a law student at Trinity College. Given that Hirschfeld was usually very keen to meet people on his travels—and that difficult personal encounters were a central component of his investigative method—it stands out that he deliberately avoided introduction to Holland when the opportunity presented itself, "as a courtesy," he explained, to a young man who felt "ashamed of his father's name."[80] Hirschfeld then goes on to claim that "the name Wilde" had come to evoke entirely negative and shameful associations since the trial, now sounding "like an indecent word, which caused homosexuals to blush with shame, women to avert their eyes and normal men to be outraged."[81] This sentence is at odds with the general tone of Hirschfeld's work, which seeks to dismantle precisely such crude distinctions between homosexuals and "normal men" and which is critical of stereotypical descriptions of female modesty in relation to sex. The turn to cliché signals the upset Hirschfeld felt because of Wilde's death. In times of stress, it seems, even an avid defender of homosexuality such as Hirschfeld resorted to drawing distinctions between (shamefully blushing) homosexuals and (outraged) heterosexual men. The account thus indicates the pernicious ways in which norms lodge themselves into the unconscious and thus continue to exercise their hold.

But Wilde's death also had a more positive legacy. Returning to his usual, more affirmative tone, Hirschfeld mentions an encounter with "a group of beautiful young male students" who had gathered to read aloud "The Ballad of Reading Gaol." What is remarkable is that the young men marked their allegiance to Wilde by attaching his prisoner number to their shirts.[82] The students thus symbolically aligned themselves with Wilde in an embodied form of memorialization that suggests that Wilde's tragic death—as much as his celebrated life—helped shape a sense of queer community around 1900. There is furthermore a physical aspect to Hirschfeld's own account of the meeting. He calls "The Ballad of Reading Goal" "markerschütternd," "the most earth-shattering outcry that has ever been voiced by a downtrodden soul about its own torture and that of humanity."[83] The German word *markerschütternd* literally means the shattering of bone marrow, a visceral choice of words that forges a physical connection between Hirschfeld and Wilde's suffering. Despite the imagery of somatic breakage, Hirschfeld ends the account on an upbeat note when he claims that his encounter with the young men reading Wilde's poem had filled him with a sense of "quiet joy and movement."[84] This affirmative, future-oriented turn to young men in the sad and upsetting narrative about Wilde's last years is typical of how Hirschfeld deals with the difficult realities of violent and premature death in homosexual life. While he does not shy away from pointing the finger at a hostile society that is responsible for the current suffering, he tends to counter despair with a forward-looking hope, here in the image of a queer community of young men that continues to flourish despite—and to some extent because of—death and persecution.

In some ways Hirschfeld's account of the impact of Wilde's death on homosexual subcultures anticipates some of the responses to the early AIDS crisis when political resolve and vitality was formed out of suffering. Yet unlike the many losses of queer life to illness in the 1980s, around 1900 it was the single death of a famous man who fell victim to antihomosexual legislation that caused wide-reaching upset. Hirschfeld's work offers insight into the impact of Wilde's death on homosexual men at that point in time when the trauma of Wilde's trial was still fresh and his public recuperation had not yet begun. His account of the aftermath of Wilde's trial supports the argument that death shaped modern queer culture, causing suffering but also forging a collective sense of belonging. Hirschfeld's writings show that Wilde's death had a culturally productive effect on homosexual men whose positive memorialization of Wilde in turn invigorated Hirschfeld's own work.

Affective Deaths

In the twenty-first century, an age of discursive explosions around difficult events and emotions—what Ann Kaplan and others have called "trauma culture"—it is easy to forget that extreme emotional experience and suffering have not always been publicly speakable.[85] Hirschfeld's writings on queer death and suicide tackle the difficulty of acknowledging emotional upset in relation to an identity—in this case homosexuality—that is discursively extremely restricted because of its lack of public legitimacy. Whereas the suicide of his patient grounds his professional work in personal trauma, his subsequent statistical work and account of Oscar Wilde's death indicate some of the emotional threads that held together queer lives collectively and across national borders at that point in time when sexology and related cultural, social, and political debates shaped modern sexuality. Attention to Hirschfeld's archive of death and suicide is not about recuperating his *scientia sexualis* as a model for twenty-first-century sexual activism or about denying the damage caused by sexological norms and the devastating practices of those doctors who tried to "cure" others of their unspeakable desires. Rather, I have examined the intersections between sexological practice, popular discourses about sexuality, and the lives of the women and men who inhabit the sexological texts with the aim of contributing to a better understanding of the terms that governed queer reality around the turn of the last century. According to Judith Butler such an understanding is needed for social transformation and the creation, in her words, of "a world in which those who understand their gender and their desire to be nonnormative can live and thrive not only without the threat of violence from the outside but without the pervasive sense of their own unreality, which can lead to suicide or a suicidal life."[86] An analysis of Hirschfeld's death narratives helps make visible the social norms that prompted many women and men to end their life because of the sense that their homosexual feelings and desires fundamentally denied their existence. These writings thus provide vital insights into the damaging terms that governed queer reality in the early twentieth century, revealing the powerful impact homosexual persecution and social rejection had on individual lives and collective existence at the time. They show that homosexual culture formed not just around political protest and affirmative cultural representations but also around injury, hurt, and death.

3

Normal Cruelty

Child Beatings and Sexual Violence

The previous chapters establish how colonialism framed the emergence of a rights-oriented sexual science and that both direct experiences of violence and the witnessing of violence against others shaped a collective sense of queer existence. This chapter shifts the focus to Hirschfeld's often overlooked writings on sexual crimes and what we would today call abuse.[1] This material constitutes a difficult archive, partly because it deals with the lives of subjects whose own voices cannot be heard independently from Hirschfeld's narrative and partly because the historically contingent categories of abuse and same-sex perversion remain closely tied in modern debates about sexual violence and its punishment. By tracking Hirschfeld's somewhat uneven engagement with protomodern debates about abuse, consent, and the treatment of sexual offenders and their victims, I aim to gain a better understanding of the overlaps and proximities between distinct histories of sexuality and sexual violence. The investigation is prompted by the realization that while the different kinds of abuse and violence discussed here all have their own distinct histories—historians of childhood have tracked the changing cultural attitudes and the social and legal transformations that gave birth to the notion of a "protected" childhood during the height of capitalist and colonial expansion in the West, feminist scholars have examined the long histories of violence against women, and historians of homosexuality have shown how movements against child prostitution were mobilized in the criminalization of sex between men—we still know relatively little about how sexual reform campaigners such as Magnus Hirschfeld engaged with these debates.[2]

The chapter begins with a historical overview that places the contemporaneous emergence of homosexual rights alongside child protection efforts before considering Hirschfeld's writings on sexual violence, which range from a critique of the castration of sexual offenders to comments on boy love, consent, sex education, systematic cruelty to children, and an oddly out of place discussion of intersex. This diverse and little-discussed body of work raises questions about what counted as violence around 1900, a time when individual behaviors (and the need to "correct" them) were typically considered in terms of their social implications. This is reflected in the language of the time, which deployed terms such as *decency* and *corruption* in place of the later category of *abuse*. Hirschfeld himself was among the first to embrace the emerging modern catalogue of "sexual offences," which included, in addition to older words such as *rape*, categories such as *coercion* and *violation*.[3] It was built around the understanding that individuals have "sexuelle[s] Selbstverfügungsrecht," or the right to determine whether they want to engage in sexual acts.[4] Yet if the emergence of this new vocabulary marks the beginning of a shift in understanding of different forms of interpersonal violence, the legal and medical debates around it indicate that older ideas about gender continued to influence what counted as abuse. Throughout the chapter I pay attention to Hirschfeld's own terminology, but I also use the anachronisms *abuse* and *sexual violence* as umbrella terms for acts of, in this case mostly physical, cruelty. The anachronistic choice of terminology is not to obscure historical specificity. Instead I follow Louise Jackson's observation that understanding of abusive behavior predated the modern coinage of the term,[5] using the category of "abuse" similarly to Shani D'Cruze in her work on the history of sexual violence to examine how different kinds of violence might be linked.[6] This broader approach emphasizes that homosexuality, and the violence against it, did not emerge in isolation but in a space of habitual, normal cruelty against bodies constructed as weak, perverse, or abhorrent. Hirschfeld's disparate writings on all kinds of injurious practices show that a degree of intimate violence was normalized in modern German society.

An Age of Sexual Exploitation

Considering the complex synchronicities between the histories of male same-sex sexuality and child sexual abuse debates is in many ways a problematic undertaking. It is problematic because of the persistence of pernicious stereotyping about predatory homosexuals and lesbians, a rhetoric that is still sometimes evoked in twenty-first-century discussions of pedophilia. It is problematic also because, as historians of homosexuality have pointed out, the emerging debates about the abuse and the protection of children—and childhood[7]—at times directly turned against men who had sex with other men. In England it was famously an investigation into female child prostitution in the mid-1880s that contributed to the introduction of repressive anti-same-sex legislation. In 1885 the journalist W. T. Stead published a series of articles titled "The Maiden Tribute of Modern Babylon" in the *Pall Mall Gazette*.[8] They contained the findings of an investigation Stead had conducted into child prostitution. His revelations of the ease of procuring sex with young girls—including details such as that some children were trafficked by their own mothers and that some doctors and midwives agreed to certify a girl's virginity—caused a public outcry. Stead's articles set in motion developments that would lead to Section 11 of the Criminal Amendment Act of 1885.[9] Also known as the Labouchère amendment, the new law not only raised the age of consent from thirteen to sixteen but, via inclusion of the category of "gross indecency," also effectively criminalized sex between men. Louise Jackson, in her study of child abuse in Victorian England, has pointed out that the focus of debate was almost entirely on the abuse of female children, "despite police knowledge of a market for adolescent boy prostitutes," because many of the social purity campaigners and philanthropists concentrated specifically on the rescue of fallen women and girls.[10] Furthermore, the diverse band of Victorian feminists who turned their attention to sexuality were predominantly concerned with women's rights over their bodies and the denial of women's access to sexual knowledge, topics that also preoccupied Hirschfeld's feminist colleagues at the institute.[11] The gendered focus of English sexual abuse debates and the introduction of laws against it—in addition to the increased age of consent, they also included criminalization of incest in 1908, although here too the focus was on girls—complicates the idea that legislation such as the Labouchère amendment was primarily driven by homophobia. Instead, as historians and critics such as Jackson and Jana Funke have in different ways made clear, such laws and "moral panics" were parts of broader attempts to protect children and women from male lust and sexual incontinence—even if in the process evidence of straight sexual abuse could turn into attacks specifically against men who had sex with other men.[12]

The age of classification when words such as *homosexuality* and *heterosexuality* were coined also produced the modern *pedophile*. While pedophilia debates fully gained momentum only in the later twentieth century, the term itself was coined in the 1880s when it circulated among medical professionals invested in diagnosing sexual transgressions as well as crimes. The Austrian psychiatrist Richard von Krafft-Ebing, famous for his authorship of one of sexology's first textbooks, *Psychopathia Sexualis*, introduced the expression "paedophilia erotica." Locating child sexual abuse in an emerging catalogue of sexual pathologies, which made little conceptual distinction between, say, shoe fetishism and abusive sexual behavior toward children, Krafft-Ebing defined "paedophilia erotica" as the phenomenon of "a sexually needy subject [being] drawn to children . . . by a morbid disposition."[13] He thus simultaneously pathologized and infantilized the abusive behavior. Krafft-Ebing's notion of the "needy subject" anticipates some of the psychoanalytic theories of Sigmund Freud. Freud, who was briefly mentored by Krafft-Ebing in the early stages of his career, wrote about the impact of child sexual abuse on his adult patients in the 1890s as part of his controversial *Verführungstheorie* (seduction theory), originally premised on his patients having experienced actual abuse. But Freud soon discarded the theory, claiming that patient accounts of sexual abuse should be understood as fantastic rather than real.[14] While neither Freud nor Krafft-Ebing explicitly linked child sexual abuse to sexual orientation, the two were often considered together—for instance, in the work of Wilhelm Stekel, one of Freud's early followers, who argued that pedophilia was a typical homosexual behavior, but also in the responses of some early homosexual activists whose attempts to distance the homosexual from the pedophile paradoxically reinforced the link.[15] This association between homosexuality and pedophilia was made in one of the earliest studies of child sexual abuse, conducted by the Frenchman Auguste Ambroise Tardieu in the mid-nineteenth century.[16] Largely ignored or dismissed by many of his scientific contemporaries, Tardieu gained infamy in histories of homosexuality for his measurements of male anuses and penises to determine whether a man had engaged in criminal sex with another man. However, his *Étude Médico-Légale sur les Attentats aux Mœurs* was also the first text to argue that child abuse was a widespread, rather than exceptional, occurrence.[17] The works of Tardieu and the later sexologists and psychoanalysts illustrate some of the complex proximities between historical debates about homosexuality and child abuse, in terms of both the false links drawn between the two and the difficulties of teasing apart their distinct discursive histories.

Contemporaneous with the scientific developments around child sexual abuse, discourses about boy love gained renewed cultural traction in the Hellenic revival that shaped educated, middle-class homophile subcultures in the nineteenth century.[18] Critics, who tend to treat these developments largely separately, have focused on the reception of Plato in homophile cultures where *pederasteia* was generally understood as the cross-generational friendship between an older, usually teacher-like, man and a boy.[19] The boys in question could range in age from child to young adult. For instance, in contrast to figures such as Oscar Wilde's Dorian Gray, the love object of Basil

Hayward, who was a young man stepping out into the world, some representations dealt with desire for younger boys.[20] The boys who were the object of attraction in the poems of William Johnson, a teacher at Eton, for example, were of school age, and Johnson himself was forced to resign because parents found a letter he had sent to one of his pupils. Martha Vicinus has pointed out that boy love is a difficult subject for twenty-first-century critics not least because the adolescent boy already was a complex figure in nineteenth-century female as well as male same-sex cultures—a "liminal creature [who] could absorb and reflect a variety of sexual desires and emotional needs."[21] According to Vicinus the "marginalization of the boy in analyses of literary history points to our own homophobia far more than to contemporary distaste for 'the love that dare not speak its name.'"[22] Yet if boy love could mean a number of things in the nineteenth century—and it is difficult to capture precisely the historical meanings of this multivalent concept that is today so overladen with abusive connotations—it is also clear that some of the nineteenth-century men who desired men were not only attracted to *pederasteia* but aware that relationships with, or even the public adoration of, youths might leave them open to charges of corruption. In a thought-provoking rereading of the work of the English literary critic and defender of "sexual inversion" John Addington Symonds, Jana Funke has noted that Symonds had made the distinction between his private acceptance, on occasion even celebration, of boy love and the need to represent homosexuality as a relationship between men.[23] Funke argues that Symonds, writing at a time when many members of the homophile movement were generally in favor of boy love, was uncomfortable with publicly supporting the practice, claiming that "we cannot be Greek now," by which he meant that members of his circle, who privately wrote quite extensively and positively about boy love, should not publicly discuss the issue if they were to avoid charges of corruption.[24]

There are numerous explanations as to why Symonds was so alert to possible public condemnation, including his controversial defense of "sexual inversion" and his having to step down from an Oxford fellowship after his amorous letters to a choirboy were discovered.[25] Furthermore, we might speculate that a public defender of homosexuality—albeit one with a fairly restricted readership such as Symonds—might have wanted to distance himself from the more overtly exploitative boy love narratives that circulated at the time. For example, in 1894 the Catholic convert John Francis Bloxham published under a pseudonym the short story "The Priest and the Acolyte," which describes the sexual relationship between a priest and a boy.[26] Lisa Hamilton, in her reading of the story, argues that "censure of their sexual relationship" is what drives them to commit double suicide.[27] However, the narrative leaves little doubt that it is the priest who not only initiates the sexual encounters between them but, once their relationship is discovered, coerces the boy into killing himself with the words "You can die for me; you can die with me."[28] "The Priest and the Acolyte" was published in the Oxford-based undergraduate journal *The Chameleon* alongside work by Oscar Wilde and Alfred Lord Douglas. During Wilde's trial in 1895 the prosecutor who cross-examined him read aloud the poem on shame that prefaced "The Priest and the Acolyte" in a bid to get Wilde to admit his knowledge of the author and the sexual practices alluded to in the story. The ensuing dialogue prompted Wilde, who called Bloxham's work "obscure," to utter the now famous defense of Douglas's poem "Two Loves," which mentions "the love that dare not speak its name."[29] The example illustrates how some antihomosexual efforts equated homosexuality per se with child abuse. The publication of Bloxham's story in the same journal with Wilde's work and Wilde's own antics with rent boys suggest that the boundaries between consenting same-sex subcultures and practices of sexual exploitation could be just as porous as the line between straight sex and abuse.[30]

The English debates provide a useful context for Hirschfeld's writings. While in contrast to England, age of consent played a comparatively small role in German homosexual rights legislation, questions about consent and abuse nevertheless implicitly underpinned many of the German discussions about sexuality. Hirschfeld frequently made reference to English contexts, claiming, for instance, that the English age-of-consent debates stand in "curious contradiction" to attempts to "'protect' youths from sexual education"[31] and citing Symonds's observations on Hellenic love in a discussion of "Jünglingsliebe" (love of male youths).[32] While Hirschfeld wrote relatively little on child sex or prostitution in Germany, he includes in *Die Homosexualität des Mannes und des Weibes*, in addition to the discussion of Hellenic boy love, a summary of the account of an American missionary to Peking who had visited various *Knabenbordelle*, or boy brothels.[33] The narrative explains in some detail the process of meeting boys as young as around twelve years old who could be bought "ready to do anything."[34] While Hirschfeld did not overtly condone the prostitution of these boys, unlike Stead in the 1880s he passed no moral judgment and paid little attention to the well-being of the boys. Instead he claimed to observe a specifically Chinese tolerance toward sex: "How little the [Chinese] people are offended by homosexual sex," he writes, "is indicated by parents themselves leaving daughters as well as sons, often at a young age, with public houses [brothels] in the belief that this will secure them a better future."[35] At this stage in his life, Hirschfeld had not yet traveled to China and relied on the words of a Christian missionary to make his assertions. While his knowledge of China was secondhand, his choice of words indicates that he tempered his observations for a German audience. Describing the fate of the young boys as a "profession" (*Beruf*), Hirschfeld explained that their age was *jugendlich*. In the above, I translate the word as "young age," but it can also mean "youthful." More precisely, however, *jugendlich* would have been understood as "adolescent" in the early twentieth century.[36] Hirschfeld thus subtly implied that the Chinese boy prostitutes were of pubertal age, a rhetorical move that dissociates them and their clients from child sexual corruption and exploitation even if, or because, it was offset against the knowledge that some of the "adolescent" boys looked a mere twelve years old.

Critics have demonstrated that ideas about sexual maturity change across time and according to different cultural contexts and that the modern concept of age of consent was established in many countries only around the turn of the nineteenth century. While age of consent is not one of the main hallmarks of German homosexual rights developments, the age of sexual activity was nevertheless debated by defenders of homosexuality in the country. Some looked back to classical Greece for affirmation of cross-generational same-sex relationships. Adolf Brand, one of the founders of *Der Eigene* (The Autonomous), an early homophile journal, for instance, argued in favor of "intimate relationships between youths and men."[37] Others, however, sought to distance themselves from association with "child sexual abuse and molestation."[38] Hirschfeld's reference to the age of the Chinese boy prostitutes suggests that he too was aware of changing attitudes about childhood and adolescent sexuality. Yet his retelling of a story of child prostitution in China paid little attention to questions of abuse, as he used the account instead to demonstrate an apparently particularly Chinese acceptance of homosexuality.[39]

Child Protection and Homosexual Rights

Whereas age of consent was less a feature in German debates about sexuality than in English debates, the widespread introduction of anti-same-sex legislation coincided with emerging debates about the protection of children in both nations. Unlike the English debates about corruption, the German focus was on protection and predominantly concerned with issues relating to the social welfare and the legal situation of children. For example, the first *Kinderschutz-Verein*, or society for the protection of children, was founded in 1869 and initially at least focused on the welfare of *Haltekinder*, children who were looked after by people other than members of their own family.[40] Historians of childhood have analyzed this development primarily in relation to shifting ideas about the family, society, and the state. However, the beginnings of the notion that children need special kinds of legal protection and social welfare also coincided with the emergence of the first affirmative same-sex activism. Around the same time as debates about the legal guardianship of children began to gain momentum—including in relation to the development of a foster care system and processes that would allow the state to remove children from parents deemed unsuitable—the Hanoverian lawyer Karl Heinrich Ulrichs first started to publish pamphlets in support of what he called "mannmänliche Liebe" (man-manly love).[41] Ulrichs first spoke out publicly against the criminalization of sex between men during a legal congress in Munich in 1867, which had gathered to discuss the development of a common penal code for the independent German states. In his speech he argued that man-manly love was a naturally occurring phenomenon and should therefore not be criminalized. While Ulrichs, who derived his ideas from Plato's *Symposium*, elsewhere in his work referred to men who love boys, his terminology of man-manly love—which emphasized the adult nature of this love—suggests that he publicly sought to distance modern male same-sex love from classical *pederasteia*.[42] The conceptual nuances of Ulrichs's terminology were, however, lost on his Munich audience, which rejected the demand for the decriminalization of sex between men. According to Ulrichs's account of the events, which was published in the book *Gladius furens* (Raging sword), his speech was met with outrage, even prompting some of the audience members to shout out an emphatic demand to "crucify, crucify" Ulrichs.[43]

The contrast between Ulrichs's emergent philosophical-legalistic homosexual rights discourse and the demand that he be crucified symbolizes the struggle between religious and secular authority that marks Western modernity. Ulrichs's reception in Catholic Munich not only reveals the prevalence of religiously grounded social prejudice even in professional, secular contexts but also anticipates the so-called *Kulturkampf* (culture war), a power struggle between church and state that marked the first decade or so of the new Wilhelmine Empire. The term *Kulturkampf* was coined by the influential physician Rudolf Virchow, one of Hirschfeld's doctoral examiners, who is famous today for his work on pathology and public health.[44] It refers to the clash between the Catholic Church and the (Protestant and Prussian dominated) German Empire, which sought to separate religion from the state. More broadly, the term also describes a time of heightened tensions within the German Empire when antisemitism was on the rise and social and political conflicts—especially in relation to the rise of socialism—marked the divide between conservatives, liberals, and political radicals.[45]

By the time Hirschfeld started his sexual activism in the 1890s the main battle between the Catholic Church and the German Empire was over. The

Church had somewhat softened its stance, and agreements had been reached over previously contested issues such as civil marriage, a prospect causing widespread discomfort among Protestants as well as Catholics. However, concerns about the regulation of bodies continued to shape social and legal debates in the new German Empire, and these debates were frequently couched in the language of a struggle between cultures—language that also indicates the different political allegiances of sexual rights activists and framed their discussions of sexual violence and abuse. Most famously, perhaps, the radical Austrian psychoanalyst Wilhelm Reich returned to the terminology of the *Kulturkampf* in 1936 in his book *Die Sexualität im Kulturkampf* (Sexuality in the culture war), in which he argued that the attempts of reformers such as Hirschfeld had failed because they left unchallenged the capitalist framework that fed bourgeois sexual taboos, supported repressive institutions such as marriage, and enacted laws against a wide range of bodily practices including abortion and sex between men.[46] If Reich was right in pointing out that Hirschfeld and his colleagues did not manage to effect comprehensive sexual reforms, it is also worth noting that the framework within which Hirschfeld placed his efforts was inspired by socialism and communism even if his realization of new modes of living remained limited.

In the 1920s Hirschfeld became increasingly interested in the politics of the new Soviet Union. He looked to the country for alternative ways of changing social attitudes to sex. In 1929 he wrote an article titled "New Morals for Old in Soviet Russia," based on his travels though the country. It was published in the *Illustrated London News* in 1929—with the disclaimer that "the opinions expressed are [Hirschfeld's] and not necessarily editorial"—to coincide with the meeting of the World League of Sexual Reform in London.[47] At this meeting Hirschfeld presented talks on the history and current state of sexology, as well as a paper on indecency. The paper ostensibly dealt with incest and rape but also critiqued the uses of the word *indecency* in the antisemitic rhetoric that was gaining prominence in Germany. Hirschfeld held that *indecency* was no longer just a word for rape and incest but also used to describe an alleged "pollution" of "Aryan blood" caused by sex with Jews.[48] Hirschfeld, deeply concerned about political developments in the country he still considered home, looked favorably on the Russian Revolution. Despite opening his article with the cautious statement that it was "too early to say whether [Lenin's new civilization] is a success or a failure," Hirschfeld clearly approved of the "fundamental . . . change in human relationships . . . adopted by the Soviets with respect to the family and the relations of men and women" and the "complete emancipation [of] women."[49]

The article includes a brief discussion on "protecting the child." Noting with approval that "the protection of the child is the chief consideration of the

[Soviet] courts"—whereby "protection" in this context means legal guardianship—Hirschfeld argues that Soviet courts had a better understanding of family with their focus on the needs of the child.[50] He cites the example of a couple who had abandoned their newborn but seven years later demanded that the foster parents return the child to them. Hirschfeld explains that the demand was "in accordance with the letter of the law" but that the court "decided to leave the child where it was happiest," giving the fosterers the official status of parents.[51] In other words, then, Hirschfeld approved of the idea that family is not based on biological relationships. Yet while his focus on the legal guardianship of children in Soviet Russia mirrors the debates of the German child protection movements and while he admired the innovations of Soviet Russia, especially in relation to the redefinition of family and sexual legislation—a second article he wrote in 1929 dealt specifically with modern Russian sexual law—Hirschfeld did not apply his newfound knowledge to critique fully the restrictions and inequalities of German family life.[52]

Violent Guardianship

In German, the vocabulary used to describe the legal relationship of one person to another suggests that a degree of violence is conceptually inherent to life in the family and state. The German word for violence, *Gewalt*, describes a multitude of power relations ranging from the state to the parental. The word goes back to the Old High German *walden*, which similar to its Old English counterpart *weldan* (also *wieldan* or *wealdan*) means "to wield, have power over, subdue." In an English-speaking context, the introduction of the word *violence* in the thirteenth century—from Norman *violence* and Latin *violentia*, both associated with vehemence, impetuosity—effected a separation between *violence*, primarily associated with physical force and injury, and the political strength associated with the word *power*. While a similar distinction exists in German, in which *Macht* does some of the work of *power*, *Gewalt* nevertheless retains its associations with both physical violence and the exercise of power in all its forms. As *Staatsgewalt* it describes sovereignty and the institutions by which the state exercises power over its citizens. In the expression *Gewalt ausüben* it describes both the exercise of power and structural and interpersonal violence. Most revealingly, perhaps, in the phrase *in seiner [ihrer] Gewalt sein*—which literally translates as "being subjected to his [her] violence"—*violence* is a synonym for legal guardianship, usually that of an adult over a child. The bracketing of the feminine version of the phrase signals that this power remained unequally gendered for much of modern German history. For while in the nineteenth century the emerging feminist movement successfully campaigned for reformed divorce laws and the introduction of protection for mothers (*Mutterschutz*, which today is the term for paid maternity leave), the mother's legal position toward her child remained unequal compared to that of the father until well into the twentieth century.

Around the time when Hirschfeld published his first book, the father's legal and physical power over his children de facto increased. In addition to having sole legal power over the child—which went back to the 1794 Prussian Legal Code and would remain law until 1958, when the mother, as well as the father, gained the legal right to exercise "violent care" over her child[53]—the father's right to use "appropriate physical force"[54] on his children was introduced in 1896 as Paragraph 1631 of the civil code of the German Empire and subsequently adopted into the revised penal code of 1900.[55] The father's right to beat his child coincided with the violence of German colonialism—1896 was the year the Great Industrial Exhibition of Berlin made a show of the victims of Germany's colonial conquests—and the rising success of the feminist movement, which, while still struggling to change the legal position of German women, nevertheless increasingly let women's bodies slip out of male control.[56] The strengthening of the father's legal power at this time is a forceful reminder that the loosening of certain forms of gendered and classed oppression did not bring equality. For instance, while women's rights to property improved, and as Lynn Abrams has noted, the new German divorce laws were "comparatively liberal and tolerant" when viewed against the laws of many other European countries, these laws nevertheless denied women full financial and legal independence, and a divorce furthermore carried the risk that the woman would lose her "property and guardianship of any children."[57] In other words, despite the introduction of laws that aimed to provide greater autonomy for women and improve the rights of children, a married woman and her children remained legal subjects of the husband-cum-father.

Given that Hirschfeld was in favor of gender equality and supported child reform, it stands out that he paid so little attention to the abuse that might take place in a family context. Instead here too his focus was on presenting what we might today call sex-positive arguments for social reform. In 1930, for example, partly inspired by his visit to the Soviet Union, he published a book on *Sexualerziehung* (sex education), which was cowritten with the twenty-seven-year-old Ewald Bohm, a Swiss-Danish psychiatrist who would gain fame in the 1950s for his textbook on the Rorschach test.[58] By the time Hirschfeld and Bohm turned their attention to the topic of sex education, the phenomenon of child sexuality had already received considerable attention, ranging from Krafft-Ebing's early accounts of the very existence of the sexual child to Freud's model of formative child sexuality and to Hirschfeld's own "Das urnische Kind" (The urning child), which he presented in a talk in 1903.[59] Here he made the case that the "Uranian's particularity" is already evident early on, typically manifesting itself in boys through their femininity, while both Uranian girls and boys tend to be introverted but good at school.[60] Rather than addressing questions of child sexuality, however, the talk focused on the manifestations of homosexuality, a topic that continued to occupy Hirschfeld at the time. In contrast, his rival Albert Moll published an influential study, *Das Sexualleben des Kindes*, translated into English in 1912 by Eden Paul, one of Hirschfeld's translators, as *The Sexual Life of the Child*, which dealt more specifically with the debates about child sexuality. Moll, who was against the political application of sexual science, insisted that child sexuality was different from adult sexual desires and emotions and hence could not be understood by merely extrapolating adult accounts of their desire.[61]

Hirschfeld and Bohm's later work on sex education shifted the focus from questions about an innate child sexual consciousness to the social contexts in which it was formed. Deeply critical of what they considered the potentially deadly contemporary sexual morality—the high death rate from illegal abortions and the belief that "most suicides . . . are caused by sexual concerns"—Hirschfeld and Bohm set out a long list of instructions on how to ensure that a child could develop free from social taboos and constraints.[62] If this work might seem to echo Jean-Jacques Rousseau's Romantic ideal of natural childhood as developed in *Émile* (1762), Hirschfeld and Bohm's claims about childhood and education were derived from a critique of social problems such as abortion, prostitution, and the "thirst for [sex with] children."[63] In contrast to Rousseau's philosophical ponderings, Hirschfeld and Bohm explicitly distanced their views on sex education from contemporary protopedophilia debates. Many of the points they made were radical for the time, such as that children should be told the truth about sex and reproduction, that the emphasis on gender distinctions through clothing should be delayed, and that all forms of corporal punishment should be abolished.[64] Given the outspoken, comprehensive discussion of all kinds of sexual topics, and in light of their claim that "love ennobles every kind of sexual act," it is striking that Hirschfeld and Bohm mention only in passing the importance of learning to distinguish right from wrong, or rather, in their words "truth and falsehood."[65] This is a small but significant point, for it suggests that understanding issues of consent was not yet on the agenda even in a project that challenged the silences around sex.

From Straight Castration to Intersex

Hirschfeld wrote about sexual abuse in more detail elsewhere, but with a focus specifically on the men who committed the abuse. In 1924, not long after founding the Institute of Sexual Science, Hirschfeld published a book on sexuality and criminality, *Sexualität und Kriminalität*,[66] which covered many topics, including the treatment and punishment of *Kinderschänder* (male child abusers).[67] While Hirschfeld acknowledged certain debts to Krafft-Ebing, he nevertheless avoided the term *pedophilia*, suggesting that he understood the men who sexually abused children not merely as "types." Instead Hirschfeld was particularly concerned with what he considered the coercive use of castration—or the "forced removal of the gonads"—in the treatment of men imprisoned because they had been convicted of sexual offenses against children.[68] These men were often presented with the option of having their gonads removed, usually in exchange for a reduced prison term. Hirschfeld called the practice a "violent mutilation" and an example of an injurious state punishment in which the bodies of certain kinds of offenders—namely, men who have sexually abused children—are deliberately mutilated.[69] In many ways, the argument anticipates current twenty-first-century debates about "voluntary surgical castration" in Germany, where a castration law first passed August 15, 1969, is still in place. It allows imprisoned sexual offenders to apply for surgical castration. While observers are divided over the ethics and efficacy of such a drastic step, according to one study more than one application by prisoners who volunteer to undergo the procedure is approved each year.[70] The legally supported treatment of sexual offenders with surgical castration contrasts markedly with another German initiative, the project Kein Täter Werden, or Don't Offend. Inaugurated in 2005, Don't Offend focuses on the prevention of sexual abuse. It provides confidential support for people—mostly men—who have already abused children or fear they may do so in future.[71] Under German law, patient confidentiality is absolute, and doctors are not permitted to report offenders to the police. The Don't Offend initiative matches potential and current offenders anonymously with a therapist, who then works with them to prevent abuse or stop it. Writing in the 1920s Hirschfeld anticipated some of the current debates about treatment and prevention. His views on the topic were, however, oddly contradictory at times, especially when questions of gender and sexuality entered the frame.

Hirschfeld's discussion of intersex in this context is especially troubling, indicating the problematic historical situatedness of intersex bodies in the regulatory spaces between law and medicine. Despite his apparently unequivocal opposition to the "violent mutilation"[72] of state-supported castration, Hirschfeld emphasized that in certain cases those accused should be able to decide "whether they would prefer to lose their gonads or their liberty"[73]—namely, in cases when castration might cure what he calls a "dangerous disturbance of the sexual drive."[74] According to Hirschfeld, who claimed that only very few "Anomalien" (anomalies) fall into this category, it was specifically intersex men and women who might chose to have their reproductive organs removed to ensure that they "do not come into conflict with the law."[75] Hirschfeld noted that he observed in intersexual people who selected castration "a complete cessation of the sexual drive," making no further comment on the violent policing of gender norms that informs such decisions.[76] It is difficult today to recover the voices of the intersex people who came to Hirschfeld's clinic, not least because some of his discussions of the patients who "want[ed] to align their physical appearance with their inner feelings" obscure the boundaries between intersex and transgender.[77] Yet the above quotation clearly refers to intersex rather than access to medical technologies for transgender people seeking to change their bodies to fit their gender. By describing intersex bodies as "dangerous," Hirschfeld troublingly fails to distinguish between intersex people and sexual offenders. Elsewhere in the text he claims to have met personally "tens of thousands" intersex people, arguing that their bodies are of no real "criminal importance" except that their "hermaphrodite" status can force them into situations that cause them end up in court.[78] However, his insight that it is the law rather than intersex people that is dangerous is undermined by the argument that surgery can be an appropriate "protective" measure for people whose bodies and genitals do not conform to social norms and expectations.[79] Hirschfeld's favoring of surgery on intersex bodies, despite his claims that gender often remains undetermined or undiagnosed, appears at odds with his arguments that "sexual difference is quantitative"[80] and that "everything in the universe flows into each other; nature knows no jumps, no crass opposition."[81] It anticipates the normalization of surgical mutilation of intersex bodies, bringing Hirschfeld in line with those medical practitioners who continue to perform irreversible operations on the bodies of people—often infants—whose genitals do not conform to the binary standard.

What might have motivated Hirschfeld's writings here? Sufficient evidence supports the argument that his work on sexuality and criminality was influenced by a wish to ensure that homosexuality would be clearly taken out of the criminal equation and that this focus at times obscured his full apprehension of gender-based violence. His discussion of child sexual abuse, for instance, focused on the case of a married man who abused young girls. Hirschfeld observed that when the man first came to his clinic, he was stuck in a cycle of sexually abusing girls, being imprisoned for it, and then on release immediately turning to abuse again. According to Hirschfeld his patient—whom he describes as "hardworking [and] quiet" and who arrived at the clinic accompanied by his wife—suffered from a "typically underdeveloped body" and a "playful sexual drive" that was satisfied when he touched little girls.[82] Hirschfeld diagnosed the man with what he calls "psychosexual infantilism," arguing that people who suffer from this condition would positively benefit from what he now simply called "Eingriff" (procedure), meaning castration.[83] According to Freud's "Totem and Taboo," published in 1913, this kind of infantilism is characteristic of the neurotic who has failed to develop into an appropriate adult heterosexuality, instead failing "to get free from the psychosocial conditions that prevailed in his childhood or [returning] to them."[84] Whereas Freud is typically heteronormative, Hirschfeld's analysis of "psychosexual infantilism" troublingly aligns mental and physical disability with child sexual abuse. "In honor of humanity it must be said," he writes, "that upon careful examination most abusers of children turn out to be not arbitrary, malicious criminals, but people who are mentally, physically, and genitally underdeveloped."[85] The argument that child sexual abusers are "underdeveloped" is problematic on a number of levels, including the attitudes it reveals to disability and its perpetuation of the racist and imperialist assumption that "neurotics" are akin to underdeveloped "savages." Furthermore, Hirschfeld's emphatic separation of what he calls the "male psychopaths who lay their hands on children" from an implicitly normal majority of the population lends these crimes an exceptional status, which does not reflect reality.[86]

In her study *The Subject of Murder*, Lisa Downing has persuasively argued that society awards murderers an exceptional status in a bid to put a safe psychic distance between their crimes and the lives of "normal" people.[87] Hirschfeld's distinction between an implicitly normal social majority and the underdeveloped sexual abusers of children similarly obfuscates the everydayness of such abuse, and his recommendations for treating sexual offenders problematize his claims for the transformative potential of "rational sex education."[88] In the course of the narrative it becomes clear that the man had come to seek Hirschfeld's advice because as a repeat sexual offender he was facing either further imprisonment or commitment to a psychiatric hospital. Linguistic slippages in this paragraph make it difficult to gauge whether Hirschfeld goes on to describe his own actions or that of his colleagues. But we know that he was involved in the man's court case, recommending that the man be presented with the option of castration instead of a jail sentence. This was granted, and the man selected to undergo castration. While it is not clear whether Hirschfeld was involved in the procedure itself, he apparently closely monitored his patient's progress, and three years after the castration he considered the man cured.

Hirschfeld's advocacy of the castration of an offender he had diagnosed with "psychosexual infantilism" raises questions about his own involvement in "corrective" surgeries on the bodies of people who were deemed to suffer from a psychological disorder.[89] It further problematizes his views on intersex surgery, showing that despite his arguments for a more dispassionate scientific, rather than moralistic or emotional, response to sexual acts and bodies as well as sexual offenses, he considered surgery a solution to certain kinds of sexual "problems"; both sexual offending and intersex fell into this category. Hirschfeld presented surgery as something that would be in the interest of intersex people without citing the view of those affected. Similarly, his comments on the sexual abuse of children ignore the voices of the victims. Instead the analysis focuses on Hirschfeld's broader interests in the criminalization of sex and a related concern with the treatment of what he called "Geschlechtsnot," meaning both gender and sexual need. He thought that *Geschlechtsnot* affected women, men, and youths at the time because of a lack of sex education that caused all kinds of issues ranging from shame and suicidal feelings to an increase in abortion and prostitution.[90] While he suggested that sexual science could provide a solution to these problems by *educating* lay people and legislators on matters of sex, both his passing comments on intersex and his analysis of the married man who abused young girls reveal that Hirschfeld's sexological practice was implicated in coerced surgical procedures.[91]

Beating Pedagogues

While Hirschfeld's sexological practice was open to people whose sexually abusive acts were seen to render them beyond empathy and cure, his focus on the treatment of offenders tended to sideline the victims of abuse. This is illustrated by a little-known article Hirschfeld wrote in 1929 on corporal punishment, "Prügelpädagogen," which manages simultaneously to critique the socially condoned abuse of children and ignore the experiences of victims.[92] The word *Prügelpädagogen*, which has no single English equivalent, describes educators who use beatings and other forms of physical violence against children as part of their methods of discipline. By his own account, Hirschfeld was prompted to write the critique after revelations about the "unglaublichen Misshandlungen" (unbelievable mistreatment) of children in the state-funded Bavarian children's home Mariaquell.[93] The abuse was brought to public attention in spring 1929 by the Social Democrat councilor Therese Ammon, who would later be arrested by the Nazis and die in the

Theresienstadt concentration camp in 1944.[94] According to an article in the radical left-wing feminist paper *Die Unzufriedene* (The discontent woman), Ammon reported that around seventy children who lived in Mariaquell suffered sustained physical abuse and cruelty under the governance of a medical doctor, Dr. Klippen, and a Jesuit pastor named Blumen.[95] Three- and four-year-old children were regularly beaten with sticks and other implements; they were tied up and sometimes stuffed into sacks and left imprisoned in dark, airless cupboards for prolonged periods. Furthermore, even the smallest misdemeanors in the classroom—such as mere inattentiveness—were punished by withholding the small financial allowance that paid for the children's food. As a result the youngsters were generally starving and weakened by the physical and mental effects of their cruel mistreatment.[96]

Perhaps one of the most shocking aspects of this sad case is that despite Ammon's exposé and the subsequent investigation it prompted, the people responsible for the abuse—Hirschfeld ironically calls them the "pious friends of children"—were never charged or tried for these acts.[97] In other words the cruel and violent treatment of the children was not considered criminal. There is a dearth of contextual information on this case. However, according to the law of the time—the 1912 amendment to the German Criminal Code that made child abuse an "aggravated bodily injury"—the perpetrators should have been prosecuted.[98] The introduction of this law did not mean that social attitudes to child-rearing changed fundamentally. Not until 2000, for instance, was a clause inserted in the German Civil Code that asserted a child's right to be raised without violence (*gewaltfreie Erziehung*). However, while the 1990 UN Convention on the Rights of the Child (UNCRC) pledged to ensure that children's upbringing be without "physical or mental violence [or] injury or abuse," hitting children nevertheless remains part of everyday life across the world, including in countries such as the United States—which is famously only one of three nations with UN membership (the others being Somalia and the Sudan) not to have ratified the UNCRC—and the United Kingdom, which has signed the UNCRC but with the condition that parents may smack their child as long as the smack does not leave a mark on the child's body.[99] In 1920 the Mariaquell abuse in Germany, while extreme, nevertheless was on the spectrum of normal, everyday violence, especially against poor, orphaned, and abandoned children whose very existence was often seen as a marker of shame, transgression, and disorder.

Critics of corporal punishment and other injurious practices aimed at children have tended to conceptualize this violence as a form of interaction that seeks to undo children, reshaping them according to the perpetrator's expectation. In contrast a thought-provoking reassessment of the issues at stake by Karen Wells and Heather Montgomery makes the case that "the intention of violence against children is not to 'unmake the world' but to make it by incorporating the child into it in specific ways."[100] Rather than considering violence as a form of control that seeks to isolate the abused subject from the social, Wells and Montgomery argue that "the violence of everyday life . . . [enters] children into the social order" in particular ways.[101] The events in Mariaquell and their reception support this point. They indicate not only that violence was used to shape the children into an, admittedly particularly cruel, institutional routine. But they also suggest that a degree of physical violence was considered a normal, and to some extent an unremarkable, part of child-rearing in the early twentieth century.

Victims Denied

Hirschfeld similarly critiques the permissibility of certain forms of everyday abuse. The article quickly shifts from the abuse at Mariaquell to a broader discussion of what kind of violence is socially condoned. Hirschfeld cites the example of the treatment of a physical education teacher who was tried for touching his female pupils. The man, "P.Z.," lost his job and was sent to prison for acting "tenderly toward a thirteen-year-old child."[102] Noting that he himself had been an expert witness in P.Z.'s court case, Hirschfeld emphasized that in his opinion the teacher was not guilty of a crime because he had lacked "unzüchtige Absicht" (indecent intent) when touching three girls, known as A, B, and C. Asking why the physical mistreatment of children in schools and care homes is so widely accepted while the "affectionate" touch of a male teacher is inevitably considered criminal, Hirschfeld writes:

> We certainly support the extensive protection of the young, but we are brave enough to say openly that the unequal measurement of a physical blow compared to a kiss on the cheek is one of the many inconsistencies that will be incomprehensible in a more enlightened society.[103]

The "we" in this sentence refers to the team behind the *Die Aufklärung*, which was one of two journals published by the Institute of Sexual Science. While the other journal, titled *Die Ehe* (Marriage) and edited by the physician Ludwig Levy-Lenz, a pioneer of gender reassignment surgery, focused specifically on marriage, *Die Aufklärung* had more wide-reaching sex reform aims, publishing commentaries on all kinds of topical debates about sex alongside book reviews, anthropological studies, and German translations of extracts from Radclyffe Hall's famous novel about female sexual inversion, *The Well of Loneliness*.

Die Aufklärung literally translates into English as "the enlightenment," but in German it could also mean sex education more specifically. The journal was cofounded by Hirschfeld and the anthropologist Maria Krische at the Institute of Sexual Science in 1929. The German historian of sexuality Volkmar Sigusch has argued that Krische's work can barely be distinguished from that of her husband, Paul Krische.[104] However, Krische was an active member of various sexual reform initiatives, and her single-authored articles in *Die Aufklärung*, which dealt mainly with sexual anthropology and, as so many other studies of the time, had a tendency to racial stereotyping, indicate that she worked independently on sex reform questions. Her contributions were perhaps further obscured by Hirschfeld's coeditorship of the journal, not least because he had established an international reputation and dominated work at the institute by the time the journal was launched. Hirschfeld's "we" in the above quotation implicitly linked his own analysis of P.Z.'s case to the homosexual reform demands that were at the heart of his political efforts. This contextual information helps explain what influenced Hirschfeld's position toward P.Z. In defense of the teacher who "tenderly" touched three young girls, Hirschfeld appropriated arguments that were first developed in affirmative (male) homosexuality discourses, which favored classical models of *pederasteia*—or the relationship between older male teachers and their students—as a homosexual ideal. What is problematic about the narrative shift in focus from the victims of abuse in Mariaquell to the criminalization of a teacher who had touched his pupils is that Hirschfeld here first abandons the children who had been tortured in the care home and then fails to take account of the schoolgirls who had been subjected to the teacher's touch.

Hirschfeld does not stop to ponder how the girls might have felt at the receiving end of what he calls the "fleeting, impulsive, nonpremeditated" touch of their teacher.[105] Instead he notes that the teacher's "touching" (*das Anfassen*, which can also be translated as "groping") had "not extended to the girls' private parts," thus implicitly suggesting that P.Z. had not acted abusively because he had not touched the girls' genitals.[106] Antu Soreinen, in an analysis of how in the 1950s a series of cross-generational relationships between women and girls in a Finnish care home were misconstrued as abusive because they challenged heteronormative ideas about intimacy, has shown that careful attention to the multiple voices of all involved in such relationships is necessary to establish consent and the conditions of possibility that deny or enable it.[107] Hirschfeld's account of P.Z.'s case fails precisely because it relies entirely on one narrative: that of the teacher whose gender and professional position lent him the kind of authority that has historically been complicit in perpetuating, denying, and ignoring sexual abuse and violence against women, children, and young people.

While Hirschfeld is right to challenge the criminalization of the adult touch per se because it fosters damaging ideas about physical contact, it is equally problematic to fail to acknowledge unwanted forms of touch. The absence of a consideration of the girls, let alone whether they might have felt molested by the teacher suggests that Hirschfeld's understanding of what counts as abusive behavior had gendered limits. The disjuncture between his criticism of the beating of children, which he considered a fundamental social problem, and the gendered blind spots that marked his take on a teacher touching his female pupils may come from a place of defense of homosexual relationships and the discursive need for establishing the tender, caring aspects of this socially ostracized form of intimacy. Yet Hirschfeld's critique of the criminalization of the teacher who touched his pupils nevertheless perpetuates a long tradition of marginalizing female experience, here treating the bodies of women and girls as objects that are available to the male touch.

Impeded Empathy

In the twenty-first century, gender politics are once more at the forefront of critical debate and activism. As many homosexual rights are won, including entry into conservative institutions such as marriage, itself part of a long history of structural violence against women, political battlegrounds are shifting toward transgender and intersex rights, slowly beginning to loosen the crushing grip of binary gender norms. Yet while visibility and recognition are no doubt greater today, ongoing gender inequalities—such as the recent spate of trials against people accused of "gender fraud," the "bathroom debates," and the continued surgical mutilations of intersex infants—serve as powerful reminders that binarism has a deep structural and social reach. Hirschfeld's work challenged many of these assumptions, but it too was not always free of them. At times it was the parochialism of his own homosexual politics that obscured or denied his apprehension of other forms of suffering. For while Hirschfeld challenged many abusive practices and behaviors and argued for a new understanding of gender, his focus on straight abuse produced what we might call an *impeded empathy*: in this case an overt concern with dissociating (male) homosexuality from pervasive and pernicious stereotypes.[108] Hirschfeld's writings on, and reaction to, different kinds of abuse show that certain physical interventions, both medical and social, were normalized in the early twentieth century. If his accounts of child abuse suggest that there was an everydayness to adult-child violence, they also indicate that gendered assumptions about age and authority governed whether the touching of certain bodies was permissible. In many ways this history has been difficult to excavate because even today antihomosexual stereotyping is sometimes superimposed on discussions of child sexual abuse. Furthermore, an element of violence as discipline has historically been a part of everyday child-rearing, if not necessarily in practice then certainly in assumption. Yet Hirschfeld's work reveals more than the problematic historical convergences between antihomosexuality and child abuse discourses. His writings on sexuality and criminality, and especially his discussion of intersex in this context, show that the broader unspeakability of sexual matters created defensive blind spots in affirmative homosexual activism, which struggled at times to apprehend and challenge gender-based violence.

4

From Fragile Solidarities to Burnt Sexual Subjects

At the Institute of Sexual Science

The previous chapters show that colonial violence formed the hidden framework of emerging homosexual rights discourse, that both direct experiences of persecution and witnessing of attacks against others wrought a collective sense of queer existence, and that certain kinds of physical violence were normalized in modern society. This chapter examines how violence shaped the relationship between sexological archives and the people who inhabit them. It focuses on Hirschfeld's Institute of Sexual Science in Berlin, which housed the first full archive of modern sexology, including some of the first modern lesbian, homosexual, bisexual, transgender, and intersex collections. Exploring life at the institute, a space in which sexual research and subcultural life intersected, the chapter's opening parts consider the institute's relationship to other intellectual and political contexts of Weimar Berlin, its gender politics, and broader questions about the possibilities and limits of queer and transgender (self) archiving. The remaining parts then examine the impact of the "deviant" collection, first, on the people who in some way saw their own desires and sense of self reflected in the objects gathered at the institute and, second, on the Nazi men who attacked the institute in May 1933. By reassessing life and work at the Institute of Sexual Science and its destruction, then, I here address broader questions about what Hirschfeld's archives can tell us both about the imbrication of sexology in modern queer and transgender self-fashioning and about the violence issued against bodies that did not fit binary sex/gender norms and the spaces that archived their existence.

An Institute of Men?

While the history of the institute has been documented in some detail, existing studies tend to pay relatively little attention to the feminist connections that shaped its work.[1] The institute was founded by Hirschfeld in 1919 as a space for "research, teaching, healing, and refuge" that could "free the individual from physical ailments, psychological afflictions, and social deprivation."[2] At the institute Hirschfeld and his colleagues hoped to realize a new kind of sexology that would be open to all members of the public and use science, including eugenics, to bring about greater social and sexual justice.

The institute was housed in the former home of the German ambassador to France. Hirschfeld had bought the building during the reshuffling of property and political power in the immediate aftermath of World War I. Around the same time, he also set up the Magnus Hirschfeld Foundation, a charitable organization that would—using donations from anonymous private supporters and Hirschfeld himself—provide the necessary funding for the institute's many activities. The American birth control reformer Margaret Sanger, who visited what she called "The Institute of Sex Psychiatry" in 1920, described it as "a most extraordinary mansion," "sumptuously" furnished and full of "pictures of homosexuals."[3] Sanger noted that the institute "was not a place [she] particularly liked" but that she was nevertheless "interested to see how a problem which had cropped up everywhere in the post-War confusion was attacked."[4] The description of a "problem" to be "attacked" is typical of Sanger's eugenicist take on birth control, which for her was a means of regulating what she considered social problems such as the spread of "feeble-mindedness," "degeneracy, crime and pauperism."[5] While Sanger was part of the antidisabilist and antipoor strand of the emerging birth control movement her observations on the institute refer not to birth control but homosexuality. In the early 1920s, the institute's fame rested primarily on its work on sexual and gender deviancies despite the fact that its activities covered a broad range of clinical research and practice, including development of medical, anthropological, and psychological research on all aspects of gender and sexuality and marriage counseling, eugenics research, and provision of sexual health clinics.

The institute was a male space, not least because all the medical practitioners employed were men. Yet its work was nevertheless also shaped by a sometimes uneasy dialogue between homosexual rights activists and contemporary feminists.[6] Hirschfeld was close to several influential feminists, one of whom was his sister, the writer Franziska Mann, with whom he felt connected[7] and who in a private note affectionately described her "joy" at realizing that "nature had given her a brother who was also a friend."[8] In 1918, in the lead up to the foundation of the institute, the siblings published a pamphlet together, *Was jede Frau vom Wahlrecht wissen muß!* (What every woman needs to know about the right to vote!), which tried to impart a sense of urgency to the feminist cause by claiming that the end of World War I offered a unique opportunity for action as "the eyes of the world are now resting on German women."[9] Hirschfeld also had close links with Helene Stöcker, the radical feminist activist who in 1905 cofounded the Bund für Mutterschutz und Sexualreform (League for the Protection of Motherhood and Sexual Reform) and a related journal, *Mutterschutz* (later renamed *Die Neue Generation* [The new generation]).[10] Stöcker, like Hirschfeld, was critical of the institution of marriage not least because it restricted women's financial autonomy. Also like Hirschfeld and many other sex reformers, she actively promoted eugenics as a way of protecting "the health of the race" at a time when prostitution and the spread of venereal disease were thought to threaten national well-being.[11] The journal she edited promoted Hirschfeld's work by, for instance, reviewing positively his *Jahrbuch für sexuelle Zwischenstufen* (Yearbook for sexual intermediaries).[12] It published articles by other sexologists such as Iwan Bloch, whose contribution on "love and culture" reiterated some of the ideas of his *Das Sexualleben unserer Zeit*,[13] and Havelock Ellis, who published articles on pregnancy[14] and prostitution.[15] Stöcker and Hirschfeld shared the belief that feminist reform and homosexual reform were connected and that science—via the discriminatory practice of eugenics—would provide the way to a better future. In 1909 they joined forces when a proposed legal reform threatened to extend the remit of Paragraph 175 to criminalize female as well as male same-sex sexuality.[16] Stöcker subsequently joined Hirschfeld's Wissenschaftlich-humanitäres Kommitee (WhK; Scientific Humanitarian Committee) as the first woman on the board of directors, and in the 1920s she helped set up the World League of Sexual Reform, an international organization that brought together feminist, sexual, and social reformers and that had office space at the Institute of Sexual Science.[17]

The links between Stöcker and Hirschfeld were further strengthened by Hirschfeld's support of the campaigns for the reform of the antiabortion Paragraph 218 of the German Penal Code.[18] In 1928 he published with the communist Richard Linsert, who was also a member of the WhK, a study of birth control, which became recommended reading for women seeking advice on family planning matters.[19] Stöcker in turn shared Hirschfeld's pacifist views, which by the 1920s had taken firm root, and published a critique of violence in 1928.[20] While it is thus fair to say that women were not formally employed by the institute, Stöcker's role in some of the key organizations associated with it shows that women were involved in its work, helping shape, as Kirsten Leng has argued, "the elaboration of a field of knowledge" around sexual matters.[21]

At Home at the Institute of Sexual Science

The institute was more than a place of work, however. It was also a home. Hirschfeld himself occupied rooms on the second floor with his long-term partner Karl Giese; other rooms were rented out to permanent and temporary staff, visitors from around the world, and Hirschfeld's widowed eldest sister, Recha Tobias. Recha, who would be murdered by the Nazis in Theresienstadt in 1942, rented rooms to Walter Benjamin, who stayed for around three months.[22] Benjamin mentioned the view from his window of Berlin's Tiergarten park, but made no reference to the institute's work in his writings.[23] Dianne Chisholm, who has pointed out the absence of sexological references in Benjamin's work, notes that "despite his expressed fascination with transvestism and transsexuality . . . Benjamin shows no familiarity with [Hirschfeld's] groundbreaking research on 'sexual intermediaries.'"[24] This silence indexes a curious footnote in Berlin's radical and reform history: the parallel existence of the city's various intellectuals even when they were brought into physical proximity. After Benjamin left, Recha rented out his rooms to the recently widowed philosopher Ernst Bloch.[25] Bloch too did not write about his time in Hirschfeld's institute or sexology more generally. If these silences indicate a disjuncture in the 1920s between sexual reform and other kinds of philosophical and political efforts, the biography of another famous institute occupant, the communist Willi Münzenberg, the press officer of the German communist party and a member of parliament, nevertheless suggests that the institute deliberately made space for radical left-wing activities. Münzenberg, together with his partner, the political activist and publicist Babette Gross, organized many meetings of the Comintern, the Communist International, from his rooms at the institute. In her biography of Münzenberg, Gross referred to Hirschfeld as the socialist "with a heart for communists,"[26] a moniker that alluded to Hirschfeld not only offering Münzenberg accommodation at the institute but also being known for his fascination with Soviet Russia and publication in 1919 of a pamphlet in support of nationalizing health care.[27] While the Comintern did not directly engage with the institute's sexological work, Gross nevertheless noted that she and her comrades had greatly valued the institute because the busy space was well suited for meetings with "illegal visitors from abroad."[28]

While the institute was a hive for radical political as well as sexual reform activities, it was also characterized by the blurring of boundaries between professional and private space. On the occasion of the tenth anniversary of its founding, for instance, one of the librarians wrote a curious celebratory note in the voice of the institute, thanking the "beloved papa," Hirschfeld, for setting up a "life and work community."[29] Despite the avowedly communal aspect to the institute, everyday life was in many ways similar to other middle-class households at the time. For instance, the recollections of Hirschfeld's own housekeeper, Adelheid Rennack, which were recorded under her married name Adelheid Schulz in an interview with her granddaughter, suggest that the workload of domestic servants remained fairly heavy, in keeping with the conventions of the time. According to the Hirschfeld Society, Adelheid Schulz's working hours were from 7 A.M. to 6 P.M. Schulz herself, however, who remembered her time at the institute fondly, explained that she worked "as much as necessary," which could include long workdays.[30] In Münzenberg's revolutionary rooms a certain Frau Kröger, who had previously worked as a cook on a country estate, managed domestic affairs. Little is known about her other than that she was employed on Hirschfeld's recommendation. According to Gross's biography of Münzenberg, Frau Kröger would withstand a Nazi interrogation that took place after the Reichstag burning of 1933, during which she did not reveal the identities of the communist visitors to Münzenberg's flat.[31] Gross dismissed the significance of this brave act of resistance, trivializing it by suggesting that Frau Kröger was not politically motivated but simply "charmed" by Münzenberg.[32]

Such glib and sometimes contemptuous attitudes to women working in domestic service have a long history. A recent study by the geographer Rosie Cox, *The Servant Problem*, shows that even in the twenty-first century the professional commitments of middle-class households remain propped up by cleaners and private child minders whose pay and working conditions tend to be poor and who are often immigrants, legal and illegal, whose disenfranchised status is reinforced through the precarious nature of their employment.[33] A growing body of scholarship on the history of domestic service in turn has further problematized the contingencies of servitude including in relation to the interactions between radicals, writers, and artists and their servants. Alison Light's *Mrs. Woolf and the Servants*, for example, has turned attention to the difficult, sometimes abusive, relationship of the modernist feminist icon with the women she employed as servants.[34] A similar point about the limits of middle-class feminism was already put forward in 1909 by the feminist Edith Lees Ellis in a roman à clef titled *Attainment*. Based on the London-based socialist Fellowship of the New Life, whose members included founder Thomas Davidson, as well as Edith herself and her husband, the sexologist Havelock Ellis, *Attainment* lampooned the failures of the radical community to involve their domestic help in their reform efforts.[35] The critiques of servitude highlight the classed and gendered blind spots of middle-class householders, showing that domestic labor remained one of the areas in which the perpetuation of gender inequality was most deeply entrenched—including in homes that otherwise challenged the status quo.

The domestic arrangements at the Institute of Sexual Science both affirm and complicate this history. While domestic labor at the institute was mostly conventionally gendered, there were some notable exceptions to this rule, which give a queerer—if not a more feminist—framework to the institute's domestic life. For example, the English archaeologist Francis Turville-Petre—another of the institute's renowned inhabitants, who was famous for his excavations in the Galilee region of Palestine and involved in the work of the WhK[36]—employed a certain Erwin Hansen as his servant on the recommendation of Hirschfeld's partner Giese. Hansen in turn hired a boy named Heinz, and the two of them ran Turville-Petre's household affairs.[37] Unlike the institute's female housekeepers, whose lives remained separate from those of their employers, the lives of Erwin Hansen and Heinz became intimately entwined with those of Turville-Petre and his friend, the American writer Christopher Isherwood, who also resided at the institute. Isherwood gave an account of his time there in the autobiographical *Christopher and His Kind*, which was written in the third person and not published until 1976, the time when gay liberation had gained momentum in the wake of the Stonewall Riots.[38] According to Isherwood, Francis and Erwin socialized together, "bringing with them one or more boys from Berlin's bars" when they returned to their home at the institute. We are also told that Isherwood started a relationship with Heinz and that "as soon as Francis realized that Christopher and Heinz were going to bed together, he announced that Christopher must pay half of Heinz's wages."[39] In the early 1930s the four men traveled together to Greece. Isherwood and Turville-Petre would not return with Erwin and Heinz to Germany, which by then was already in the grip of Nazism. It is not known what happened to Heinz, the boy without a surname, but Erwin is believed to have been murdered in a Nazi concentration camp.[40] The queer connections between the four men, then, started out as a financial contract but went far beyond the conventional terms of a relationship between male servants and their employers, and they were enabled by life in the environment of the Institute of Sexual Science.[41]

A Space for Transgender

The institute was not only a place where homosexual relationships could flourish. It also provided a safe space for people whose assigned gender did not match their sense of self. In 1910 Hirschfeld coined the term *transvestite*, today associated with cross-dressing but then describing a much wider range of transsexual and transgender phenomena and identities.[42] K. J. Rawson, in the introduction to the special issue "Archives and Archiving" of *Transgender Studies Quarterly*, comments on the complex history of transgender terminology as well as the lives indexed by certain words in certain spaces and at particular moments in time. Paying attention to the fairly recent emergence of the term *transgender*, Rawson acknowledges that by using the word in historical research "we must always be mindful of how we are imposing an identity category onto pasts in which that identity is anachronistic and onto places where that identity is foreign."[43] Rawson also notes, however, that "problematic as it may be, *transgender* appears to be the most efficient and effective mechanism available for us to cohere . . . transhistorical and transcultural practices under the same banner."[44] Or to say this differently, the reason for using words such as *transgender* is not to obscure historical detail or reduce the range of experiences under discussion but to indicate that there is a shared realm of experience—and transition, whatever form it may take—for people who do not maintain the gender that they were assigned at birth. With this in mind, I refer to Hirschfeld's coinage of "*transvestism*" and related historical words where they appear, but I too use *transgender* as an umbrella term when trying to capture something of the historical realities of people at the Institute of Sexual Science who, in the words of Susan Stryker, "move[d] away from the gender they were assigned at birth, people who cross[ed] over (*trans-*) the boundaries constructed by their culture to define and contain that gender."[45]

Hirschfeld first set out his ideas on the subject in a study, *Die Tranvestiten* (1910), which examined the etiological, critical, and historico-ethnographic contexts for different kinds of transgender phenomena.[46] While *Die Transvestiten* was in many ways radical—Stryker calls Hirschfeld "a pioneering advocate for transgender people" because of it and his related work—the study also indicates some of the gendered limits that, somewhat paradoxically, circumscribed Hirschfeld's ideas.[47] As Geertje Mak has pointed out, the introduction of the "transvestite" focused mostly, albeit not exclusively, on male-to-female *transitioning*, relegating female-to-male transitioning to the realm of *passing* for economic privileges or sexual fulfillment.[48] While Mak's attention to assigned gender in some ways runs counter to the recovery work of transgender history, it nevertheless usefully documents that assigned gender shaped the conditions of, and possibilities for, transitioning. For Hirschfeld, male-to-female transvestites were defined by their gender identity and, as Mak and Darryl B. Hill have shown, heterosexual identifying.[49] In contrast, he understood female-to-male "passing" mostly either in economic terms, as a way for women to gain male privileges, or in relation to their perceived sexual inversion. The difficulties of thinking masculinity without men have been aptly demonstrated by Jack Halberstam in the groundbreaking study *Female Masculinity*.[50] There is little question that Hirschfeld's transvestite categorization helped inaugurate a new way of speaking transgender collectively and publicly and that his work could offer, as Ina Linge has argued, a "prosthetic support" for the way people articulated their sense of self.[51] However, his work also is an example of the persistence of binary gender norms even in projects that overtly challenge them.

The Institute of Sexual Science prided itself in supporting transvestites in a number of ways.[52] Perhaps most famous today are the medical interventions it offered, but it also supported, more widely, transgender people whose lives were threatened by gender-related laws and social norms. One of the institute's surgeons, Ludwig Levy-Lenz, for example, a gynecologist who took part in many of the early *Genitalumwandlung* operations (the term literally translates as "transformation of the genitals"), wrote in his memoirs that because it was difficult for "transvestites to find a job . . . we did everything we could to give such people a job at our institute."[53] He points out that the institute employed five "male transvestites" as maids, claiming that they were "the best, most hardworking and conscientious domestic workers we ever had."[54] Levy-Lenz emphasized that no visitor to the institute "notice[d] anything" when encountering these maids. Christopher Isherwood, in his third-person account of his time at the institute, describes how the disclosure that an "apparently female guest was a man" challenged his perception of himself: "Christopher had been telling himself that he had rejected respectability," he writes, but "the Hirschfeld kind of respectability disturbed his latent puritanism."[55] Isherwood's words, which suggest that initially at least he was uncomfortable with encountering transgender people, reveal some of the fault lines between homosexual and transgender cultures at the time. They reinforce why doctors such as Levy-Lenz and Hirschfeld wanted the institute to be an oasis for people whose bodies did not match their assigned gender and who were, as Rainer Herrn has shown, sometimes in conflict with the law because of it.[56]

The domestic labor of the transgender maids shows that a certain kind of class expectation shaped the expression of transvestite femininity at the institute, where it was located in the domestic sphere.[57] Katie Sutton, in a meticulous analysis of the emergence of a transgender subculture and its public reception, has shown that a particular kind of "middle-class transvestite identity" dominated debates in Weimar Germany. She reveals that a "politics of respectability" underpinned both affirmative subcultural and scientific discourses about transvestism, which sidelined those people deemed unrespectable, including prostitutes, criminals, "female-to-male and homosexual transvestites [and] individuals who voiced what would now be termed 'transsexual' desires."[58] In 1930 the institute offered rooms to one of the newly founded protransvestite organizations, the Vereinigung D'Eon (D'Eon Union, named after an eighteenth-century nobleman who lived the later part of his life as a woman).[59] While it thus supported on a number of levels people who wanted to transform their assigned gender, the institute also was part of a larger movement of making transvestism respectable.

Arguably the most famous of the institute's maids was Dora, more commonly known as Dorchen, the diminutive form of her name. Born Rudolph Richter, Dorchen was referred to the institute by a judge after having been arrested for cross-dressing. The institute became the place where Dorchen's body was transformed. In 1922 she underwent a castration procedure, followed by hormone treatment, which was overseen by Hirschfeld. In 1931 she received a penectomy and a vaginoplasty. The success of these operations was widely publicized, publicity that, according to Joanne Meyerowitz, formed part of the institute's attempt to establish itself as *the* place of expertise for *Genitalumwandlung*.[60] It soon became famous not only for its sex change work but also for its hormone-related research, including early experiments with hormone treatments relating to "rejuvenation" and impotence.[61] These activities, which show that apparently specialized transgender-related medical innovations have close links with treatments considered more mainstream, considerably raised the institute's national and international profile. An article in the English-language *Malayan Saturday Post*, for instance, noted that the experiments by Hirschfeld and Bernard Shapiro, one of the institute's leading experts on andrology, had led to cutting-edge insights into the treatment of impotence via hormonal treatments.[62] Thus, technologies developed to transform physical sex and those aimed at people adapting to heteronormative expectations were interdependent, as the hormone research, for instance, was also used in the budding erectile dysfunction and popular beauty industries.

Dorchen's operations were performed by one of the institute's own doctors, Levy-Lenz, and the surgeon Erwin Gohrbandt, who worked at some of Berlin's most renowned hospitals and who had invented the vaginoplasty technique.[63] Only a few years later, Levy-Lenz, who was Jewish, had to flee Nazi Germany, while Gohrbandt added the role of chief medical advisor to the Luftwaffe (the Nazi air force) to his portfolio. In this role he would contribute to discussions about experiments conducted in the Dachau concentration camp, thus giving them "an appearance of legitimacy" that would further contribute to normalizing the dehumanizing cruelty of Nazi medicine.[64] While it would be both reductive and misleading to read Gohrbandt's Nazi work back into his involvement in the institute's sex change surgeries, it nevertheless reminds us of the ethical issues raised by advances in medical technology, advances that at times rested on the treatment of patients as subjects of experimentation rather than medical care. In Dorchen's case her status as a patient was complicated by her role in the household. She was given a home at the institute, working as a maid there until the Nazi raid of 1933. Dorchen's fate is yet to be discovered—there are speculations that she was killed around the time of the raid—but her life story survives as a case study by Felix Abraham, the institute's specialist in transvestism.[65] Abraham described her surgery as a "radical treatment for extreme transvestism," a diagnosis conflating his understanding of cross-gender and cross-dresser identifications. Abraham was a sympathetic doctor who emphasized Dorchen's medical needs. He countered claims that genital operations were "a kind of luxury surgery with a playful character"[66] with the argument that it was better to operate if the patient asked for the procedure because otherwise they would in all likelihood mutilate their bodies.[67] Indeed Dorchen herself, as Rainer Herrn has shown, had already tried to castrate herself before seeking help at the institute.[68] In the absence of Dorchen's own words, it is difficult to gauge the extent to which she had a say in her medical treatment. Yet while ultimately her feelings and desires, and the external pressures she might have experienced, are lost to us, the surviving evidence from Dorchen's time at the Institute of Sexual Science suggests that here she found a space, literally and metaphorically, to live.[69] Attention to the domestic life of the institute thus helps close some of the critical divide between the discursive and social histories of sexology and the gaps in experiential evidence, even as it shows how transgender identity was put into a certain kind of place in Weimar Germany.

Sexual Bodies in the Frame

How, then, did Hirschfeld and his colleagues treat the people who came to the institute's clinics? Arguably the most famous aspect of the work was Hirschfeld's so-called sexual intermediaries work. *Sexual intermediaries* describes the existence of infinite variations in gender and sexual desire.[70] Hirschfeld understood sexual desire and the manifestation of gender to be encoded in the body, arguing that infinite variations exist in desires, bodies, gender expressions, and the intersections between them.[71] To some extent the overlaps and confusions between the terms Hirschfeld used to describe same-sex and transgender phenomena reflect the impossibility of producing neat sex-gender distinctions. Hirschfeld swung, for instance, between a focus on gonads and ovaries as "primary sex markers"[72] and discussions that destabilized the fundamental categories of man and woman with the argument that "infinitely variable mixtures" of "femaleness" and "maleness" could exist in a human.[73] For some critics these inconsistencies mark Hirschfeld's essentialist failings.[74] However, given that Hirschfeld worked at a time when binary gender essentialism was the norm and that he overtly tried to challenge this norm, framing his work entirely in terms of the constructionism versus essentialism debates that concerned gender theorists in the 1980s and early 1990s forecloses understanding of the issues that preoccupied Hirschfeld and the people whose self did not match their assigned gender. While essentialist debates about biology and nature clearly played a role in the conceptualization, self-understanding, and medical views of transgender, the in many ways more urgent questions dealt with issues relating to the silences around transvestism and the livability of lives that did not conform to binary norms and expectations.[75]

If as Judith Butler has argued, the discursive framing of lives in the public sphere is directly linked to the apprehension of lives as such, it is perhaps not surprising that one of the key aims of gender "deviants" and their allies was to insert their existence into the public frame.[76] Trying to document the existence of sexual intermediaries formed a key part of Hirschfeld's work at the institute. Figure 4.1 indicates how he went about this process with the help of photography. It shows photographs of sexual intermediaries produced as part of the work at the institute. The upper part and side of the wall are taken up with nonstandardized images of varying sizes, which are mounted behind glass and framed in thin dark wood. They depict, as we can just about make out, individual images and occasionally a set of pictures of the same person in differently gendered outfits and poses. The main, lower part of the wall is taken up with large, dark panels, each of which includes a set of four pictures. The subjects of these images, which sometimes depict a single person and sometimes a couple, are, as a large text panel announces in English, French, and German, "Sexuelle Zwischenstufen": individuals whose bodies, desires, and gender *presentations* challenged the conventional binaries about femaleness and maleness, femininity and masculinity.[77] Unlike the photographic traditions of criminology and anthropology, which tended to put certain humans on display to act as specimens that would reveal truths about larger groups of people, the photography here focused on individuals, displaying them together to prove the larger point that an infinite number of gender variations existed in nature.[78]

The sexual intermediaries panels had a practical function. Used both as research data and to illustrate Hirschfeld's ideas, they played an important

Figure 4.1 Hirschfeld's archive, including display panels depicting "sexual intermediaries," 1925. Bildarchiv Preussischer Kulturbesitz, 10002255.

role in transmitting long and complex written texts to a wider audience by depicting at a glance phenomena that in their written exposition covered hundreds of pages of scientific writing. In contrast to the often forbidding size of the printed books—and as part of some of his publications—the photographs offered a visual shorthand to the ideas of sexual intermediaries, providing more instantaneous access to Hirschfeld's ideas. Furthermore, the display panels were portable, which increased the audiences Hirschfeld was able to reach with them, because he and his colleagues used the panels in public talks. The sexual intermediaries panels thus opened up the institute's archives, making them accessible to the wider public who were introduced via the photographs to people who were "anders als die andern": different from the others.[79]

Critics have rightly questioned the ethics of turning humans into objects of scientific study in this way, which exposed them to the gaze of expert and lay viewers. This criticism seems particularly apt in relation to the institute's collection of close-up photographs of the genitals of intersex people, which employ the visual language of medicine and criminology to turn people into case studies by training the lens on certain parts of their bodies—such as the breasts or genitals—to highlight somatic deviations from a standard male or female norm.[80] In recent years the medical interventions aiming to "correct" intersex bodies have come under sustained criticism, led by people who were subjected to invasive surgeries as children and including scholarship on the links and overlaps between intersex history and other histories of sex, gender, and the body.[81] Hirschfeld's role in this context was complex. For he too considered intersex in relation to questions of "treatment," as discussed in Chapter 3, but his main interest in intersex related to the support it lent to his sexual intermediaries idea. David James Prickett has argued that while there was a "normative message" to Hirschfeld's use of photographs, the message was nevertheless "intended to guarantee those of 'abnormal' gender performance, sex, and/or sexual orientation the same legal rights as those in 'normal' society enjoyed."[82] With this in mind, the photographic display of people and their bodies at the institute cannot be understood merely within a framework of pathologization. According to Katie Sutton the institute's photographs "illustrate how cultural representations of 'third sex' individuals . . . do not simply posit sexual science as a pathologizing, hierarchical force, nor are they uncritical of the theories and practices of sexologists."[83] Instead, she suggests, these photographs are "cultural translations of sexological knowledge [that] employ science as a resource in actively redefining categories of sexual citizenship."[84] In other words, the institute's photographic collection cannot be understood merely as an archive of medical practice. It also constitutes an early auto-ethnographic document of modern queer and transgender lives.

Hirschfeld's own role in Berlin supports this point. He was a well-known figure in the city's sexual subcultures, which he frequented with his lover, and where he was also known, as his American colleague Harry Benjamin later noted, as "Tante Magnesia."[85] An early book, *Berlins Drittes Geschlecht* (1904; Berlin's third sex) can be described as an anthropological study about, but also to some extent *for*, the city's sexual subcultures. Hirschfeld gathered stories and pictures about Berlin's "third sex," an endeavor clearly indebted to the personal links he had forged. For instance, the book includes a photograph of a twenty-five-year-old "female invert" and a handwritten note explaining that the woman was "delighted to present [Hirschfeld] with [her] experiences of, and views on, female homosexuality."[86] The combination of photo and explanatory note reinforce that the sexual intermediaries collection was not merely an archive of clinical images but also a document of Berlin's sexual subcultures.

Many of Berlin's cross-dressers and other "sexual deviants" visited the institute and had their picture taken. These portraits were then displayed alongside images of the institute's transgender and intersex visitors and patients.[87] Margaret Sanger, in the account of her visit to the institute, described how "on the walls of the stairway there were pictures of homosexual men decked out as women in hats, earrings and feminine make-up; also women in men's clothing and toppers."[88] This description is an example of the use of *homosexual* as a catch-all term for all kinds of sexual "deviancies" in the 1920s. "Further up the steps," Sanger continued, "were photographs of the same individuals who had been brought back to normality, some of them through adaptation of the Voronoff experiments[89] in the transplantation of sex glands."[90] If Sanger's encounter with the sexual intermediaries photographs challenged her perception of gender, it did not prompt her to become more accepting of gender variation. Instead she interpreted the visual display, according to her own set of expectations, as a journey from abnormality to normality, thus figuring the institute as a place dedicated to fixing or curing gender.

Sanger's reading of the photographs as a straight(forward) journey into normality contrasts with accounts of queer visitors for whom the photographs and other objects collected by Hirschfeld and his colleagues had an affective appeal. According to Christopher Isherwood, for instance, it was precisely the encounter with the objects, rather than the people, gathered at the Institute of Sexual Science that proved to be transformative. In *Christopher and his Kind* he writes that

> Christopher giggled nervously when Karl Giese and Francis [Turville-Petre] took him through the Institute's museum. . . . Christopher giggled because he was embarrassed . . . because, at last, he was being brought face to face with his tribe. Up to now, he had behaved as though the tribe didn't exist and homosexuality were a private way of life.[91]

Here, then, the institute's collection of objects, rather than its people, is given center stage. Isherwood suggests that the encounter with the "sex museum"— the fetishes, fantasy pictures, and photographs—forced him to "admit kinship with these freakish fellow tribesmen and their distasteful customs."[92] This is in many ways a curious passage, as it displaces sexual identification from people to the objects that are used to document their existence. But this displacement also provides for an intimate archival encounter: a flash of recognition that makes real for Isherwood the existence of homosexuality, which he now no longer understands in terms of private acts but, for better or worse, as a public display. In other words, the publicly framed material archive of Hirschfeld's sexology, the objects of fantasy and desire gathered at the institute rather than the humans who pass through it, prompt Isherwood's affective admission of queer kinship.

The End of the Institute

The objects and materials gathered at the Institute of Sexual Science became one of the earliest points of attack after the Nazis rose to power. On Saturday, May 6, 1933, Nazi men raided the institute, an event that not only destroyed Hirschfeld's life work but also marked the end of the first phase of European sexology. The attack, which took place after months of observation and threats against the institute, inaugurated a new phase in the intensification of Nazi terror. It happened in three stages: in the morning, Nazi students entered the institute and began to destroy its interior. In the afternoon, members of the Sturmabteilung—the paramilitary wing of the Nazi Party known as the SA—joined the fray to conduct a more systematic search. Together they removed large parts of the institute's library, which were then loaded onto trucks, ready for stage three of the attack, the destruction of the materials four days later in what would be the first in the series of infamous Nazi book burnings.[93]

The raid on the Institute of Sexual Science has received considerable critical attention, not least because it inaugurated a most violent time in the history of attacks against queer women and men.[94] Between 1937 and 1939 alone, persecutions under Paragraph 175 increased nearly tenfold and the number of forced castrations on men who were, or were considered to be, homosexual, multiplied.[95] On April 4, 1938, a Gestapo directive ordered that men convicted of homosexuality be incarcerated in concentration camps. According to the historian Rüdiger Lautmann, an estimated ten thousand inmates held in various concentrations camps were classified as homosexual; the number who died remains uncertain.[96] The raid on the institute foreshadowed this escalation of organized violence against homosexuals and anticipated the antisemitic pogroms that preceded the death camps. Since the Jewish contribution to sexology was considerable, including at the institute, where many prominent members—such as Hirschfeld, Abraham, and Levy-Lenz—were Jews, it should come as no surprise that antisemitism as well as homophobia fueled the attacks.

While Levy-Lenz claims that what he calls "the purely scientific institute" became "the first victim which fell to the new regime" because its members "knew too much" about the taboo subject of sexuality generally and the sexual behavior and proclivities of German women and men more specifically,[97] the critical consensus today is that it was precisely the institute's associations with both homosexuality and Jewishness that made it the focus of Nazi attack.[98] The details of the attack remain, however, somewhat contested. This is partly because of differing views on what the actual target under attack was. According to a Nazi rallying call, "Brenne Hirschfeld" (Burn

Hirschfeld), which was picked up by the contemporary press, Hirschfeld himself was the symbolic target of the raid—symbolic because it was known that he was no longer resident at the institute.[99] If this suggests that all his work was under attack, according to an eyewitness there was a degree of selection in the raid on the institute. The unnamed observer who was present during the attack claims that after the morning's indiscriminate vandalism by the students, the SA seemed to approach their destructive task in a more methodical fashion: after having removed "basket after basket of valuable books and manuscripts," including "bound volumes of periodicals," "the material belonging to the World League for Sexual Reform," and "the whole edition of the journal *Sexus*," the SA then "wanted to take away several thousand questionnaires . . . but desisted when they were assured that these were simply medical histories."[100] The questionnaires were one of the most famous and controversial aspects of Hirschfeld's work. He first developed what he called the Psychobiologischen Fragebogen (psychobiological questionnaire) in 1900 for use as a diagnostic tool in his clinic.[101] According to Walter Benjamin, "Some of the prominent [Nazis] had been patients of Hirschfeld [which] is why his records and books and his Institute were destroyed so promptly."[102] While others too have argued that what they call "the *apparent* destruction of the Institute" was in fact "a cover operation to retrieve . . . incriminating evidence against both prominent Nazi leaders and their opponents,"[103] the Hirschfeld biographer Charlotte Wolff has claimed that "confessional" materials such as the questionnaires were deliberately spared so that they could later be used by the Gestapo to root out homosexuals.[104] None of these arguments seems entirely convincing, however, if we remember that it was a group of students, rather than Nazi soldiers, who were first let loose on the institute and that a careful selection of materials would have been difficult in such an attack.

However, attention to material circumstances, rather than questions of intent, can deepen understanding of how the events played out. The questionnaires, for example, were distinguished from other medical books and manuscripts held in the institute's library less by their content than by their physical form: they consisted of a large volume of loose paper. Each questionnaire contained more than a hundred questions ranging from inquiries about language development in childhood to reflections on sexual preferences in adulthood.[105] By the time of the Nazi raid, Hirschfeld had collected more than ten thousand questionnaires, the longest of which was 360 handwritten pages and had taken almost six months to complete.[106] If these numbers are correct, it seems possible that the practical difficulties involved in removing such a large amount of loose paper aided the serendipitous survival of this archive. The end of the institute, which marks the escalating Nazi violence against certain groups of people, also indicates, then, that the life and death of archives is subject to a degree of random circumstance and that attention to such circumstances can provide insights into why certain collections of paper and objects come under attack.

Handling Homosexual Texts

That the library earmarked for destruction contained "deviant" writing posed a particular problem for those managing the destruction of this material: how to handle it without being tainted by sexual perversion and degeneracy. Judith Butler, in her observations of what she calls the "risk of sociality" in torture, has emphasized the complex role played by the body in negotiating the relationship between the subject and the social. She writes:

> As bodies we are exposed to others, and while this may be the condition of our desire, it also raises the possibility of subjugation and cruelty. This follows from the fact that bodies are bound up with others through material needs, through touch, through language, through a set of relations without which we cannot survive. To have one's survival bound up in such a way is a constant risk of sociality—its promise and its threat.[107]

If we accept that our relationship to others is partly mediated through the body, then homophobia and transphobia can be understood as forms of aggressive risk management by those who feel threatened by the proximity of bodies and desires that challenge their sense of self. The idea that the body exposes us to a "constant risk of sociality" is particularly useful for understanding how homophobia, transphobia, and antisemitism shaped the messy interplay between visceral and psychic forces in the attacks on Hirschfeld's institute. Whereas materiality played a role in the serendipitous survival of certain texts, their content influenced how these materials were handled. Seen as a threat as much as objects of desire, the queer content of the institute's library could not be touched by the Nazi men without raising questions about the relationship established in the encounter.

Photographs taken during the raid on the institute suggest that the Nazi thugs, consciously or unconsciously, attempted to manage the "risk of sociality," which emerged for the Nazi men in the encounter with queer objects under attack. Figure 4.2 indicates that the dissociation of Nazi men and homosexuality was taken seriously. The photograph shows a student and an SA man standing atop a mountain of books and photos. Both men appear to be intently focused on the materials in front of them. The student is looking

Figure 4.2 Members of the Hitler Youth select material for the book burning, 1933. Magnus-Hirschfeld-Gesellschaft.

at pictures, while the soldier is reading a page in a book. Closer inspection suggests that the photograph was staged in a way that sought to dissociate the Nazi men from the content of the materials in which they are so immersed. The picture is well lit and carefully composed. Strategically placed at the front of the mountain of books and papers are a number of photographs of topless women, apparently taken from the journal *Die Ehe*, the institute's publication on marriage. The conspicuous inclusion of these images heterosexualizes the materials handled by the Nazi men. Nazi propaganda and policy tended to decry and persecute both pornography and homosexuality.[108] However, here the prominent placing of photographs of topless women suggests that homophobic anxieties shaped the raid on the Institute of Sexual Science. The representation of Nazi hands on naked women manages to maintain the institute's association with sexual immorality even as these images also ensure that the Nazi men sent to cleanse the institute of its holdings are dissociated from homosexuality. Sharon Patricia Holland has argued that "if touch can be interpreted as the action that bars one from entry *and* also connects one to the sensual life of the other, then . . . *racism has its own erotic life*."[109] Holland's observation on "the erotic life of racism," by which she means the paradoxical intimacy of racist acts and gestures, complicates understanding of the issues at stake in the Nazi raid on the Institute of Sexual Science. It helps us see these acts not merely as part of the general group psychology of Nazi totalitarianism but more specifically as evidence of how antisemitism and homophobia together dictated the actions during the attack on the institute. The photographs are evidence of the influence of deeply entrenched cultural fantasies about Jews and homosexuals and "tradition[s] of homophobia" as well as the antisemitism that guided the simultaneously quotidian and spectacular destruction of the institute.[110]

Other evidence exists that Nazi men were forbidden from engaging with Hirschfeld's work. In 1934, the *Palestine Post*, the leftist predecessor of today's *Jerusalem Post*, when reporting on the escalation of Nazi violence mentioned the case of a German student who "ha[d] been excluded from the Nazi party . . . his offense being that he was found reading the book on the Great War morals by the Jewish author Dr Magnus Hirschfeld."[111] There is no indication whether the article refers to Hirschfeld's jingoistic commentary on World War I, published in 1915, or his later, more critical, reassessment of events. What is clear, however, is that the *Palestine Post* picks up on the importance the Nazi regime placed on dissociating itself from the influence of the Jewish and homosexual Institute of Sexual Science.

Hirschfeld's Head at Stake

The role of the institute in the Nazi book burnings is often forgotten in mainstream histories of the events and their aftermath even as their images have gained a degree of iconic status in twentieth-century historiography, where they have become synonymous with the Nazi attack on culture. In Anglo-American popular discourse, the book burnings are seen as the moment when Nazi barbarism revealed itself, inaugurating the escalation of the regime's reign of terror and anticipating the mass killings in the camps. However, in a recent reassessment of contemporary reactions to the book burnings, the historian Matthew Fishburn has shown that they did not immediately influence debates in the United States and United Kingdom. He points out that famous responses, such as the letter of President Theodore Roosevelt to the American Bookseller's Association meeting in 1942, which includes the much-quoted line that "people die, but books never die," were only gradually assembled into the neat narrative of condemnation by which the book burnings are memorialized in Anglo-American culture today.[112] According to Fishburn, an article in a 1940 issue of *Life* magazine brought together many of the words and images of disapproval that are today associated with Anglo-American responses to these events, including the focus on the destruction of "literature."[113] While Fishburn thus rightly points out that a significant number of the texts destroyed were nonliterary, it is noteworthy that he does not mention that the first book burning was largely fueled by materials removed from Hirschfeld's institute.

Few contemporary observers in 1933 would have failed to notice that Hirschfeld and the institute played a key role in the Nazi book burnings. In the lead up to the raid Hirschfeld had frequently come under attack by right-wing hatemongers. While most of the violence directed against him was verbal or visual—the Nazi tabloid *Der Stürmer* published several Hirschfeld caricatures—he also suffered physical attacks,[114] most famously surviving the 1920 beating by right-wing thugs that left him so severely injured that he was mistakenly declared dead.[115] Just over a decade later, in 1932, a portrait of Hirschfeld featured in a Nazi election poster as an example of Jewish and homosexual un-Germanness.[116] The poster, which was directed against Hitler's opponent Paul von Hindenburg, describes Hirschfeld as a "famous expert witness in the courtroom and fighter against Paragraph 175," a statement that indicates that homosexuality itself retained a degree of unspeakability in Nazi propaganda even as it was acknowledged as a political concern. The historian Dagmar Herzog, who has undertaken a detailed examination of how "Nazis eager to advance a sexually conservative agenda drew on the ambivalent association of Jews with both sexual evil and sexual rights," makes a persuasive case for why Hirschfeld was a particular target: his "contention that sexual orientation was biologically determined."[117] His image on the Nazi campaign poster further indicates how attacks on Hirschfeld came to focus on his head as a symbol of un-Aryanism. The poster depicts Hirschfeld alongside portraits of nine other Hitler opponents, ranging from members of the Social Democrats to MPs from the staunchly conservative Center Party. They are brought together under the heading "We vote for Hindenburg!," which is rendered in pseudo-Hebraized font. The images of these ten men are contrasted in the lower half of the poster with portraits of leading Nazis, including Herrmann Göring, "Hauptmann Röhm," and "Dr Goebbels," whose allegiance is pronounced in bold neo-Gothic lettering that declares, "We vote for Hitler!" At the bottom of the poster, even larger neo-Gothic writing exclaims, "If you look at these heads, you will know where you belong!" The poster's divisive visual language insists on a distinction between Aryan and non-Aryan physiognomies, a distinction typical of Nazi polemic against Jews. Yet it is noteworthy that many of the Nazi opponents included here were, in fact, not Jewish. However, by likening them to the well-known Jews Magnus Hirschfeld and Bernhard Weiss—the vice president of Berlin's police force—the poster made a claim for the visibly un-German facial features of these men.

A few months after the poster's circulation, Hirschfeld's head would again play a key role in the violent symbolism of the Nazi book burnings when the physically absent Hirschfeld would be figuratively burnt at the stake. A single, blurry photograph survives that shows a bronze sculpture of Hirschfeld's head being paraded through the streets of Berlin on May 10, 1933 (Figure 4.3). The bust, made by the Jewish sculptor Kurt Harald Isenstein (1898–1980) and presented to Hirschfeld on his sixtieth birthday in 1928, had been removed during the raid on the institute on May 6.[118] Four days later it was carried through the city to be thrown onto the bonfire in Berlin's Opernplatz. The famous left-wing author Erich Kästner, who witnessed these events and the burning of his own work that night, later described the sense of disturbance he felt at seeing how "the head of a smashed up bust of Magnus Hirschfeld, staked high above the crowd, swayed to and fro" amid the crowd that had congregated to watch the events.[119] Hirschfeld himself, who witnessed the events from the precarious safety of his French exile, where he saw in a Paris cinema a newsreel of the attack, wrote in his diary about his deep distress, removing himself from the symbolism of the action by referring to his bust simply as a work by the sculptor Isenstein.[120] The display of Hirschfeld's head in this way clearly heightens the threatening symbolism of the book burnings by reminding the audience of the link between the human body and the textual corpus committed to the flames. But the carrying of the bust on a stake also tells us something about the psychic structures of hate and antihomosexuality behind these attacks. While the stake clearly serves as a means of display, ensuring that the Hirschfeld bust could be seen by as many spectators as possible, it also created distance between the bust and its bearers, who avoided direct touch to safeguard the Nazi men from Jewish homosexuality.

Nazi film footage of the events on May 10 makes clear that some planning had gone into constructing the bonfire. It shows that, to enable the burning of more than ten thousand books and other materials, the Nazis had stacked up numerous wooden palettes and filled them partly with books, constructing a solid framework for a bonfire that would need to be slow burning yet well ventilated. The footage also shows men and women, some in Nazi uniform, others in civilian clothes, move around the lit fire, throwing whole books at it as well as what looks like the occasional individual sheet of paper or piece of cardboard, items that appear only just heavy enough to make the short flight into the flames. The labor involved in this task creates visceral links among the perpetrators and between them and the objects they pass through their hands. In one scene, twenty-eight seconds into the footage, we see a human chain passing books from an unseen place somewhere in the dark toward the fire, while in another scene we see a civilian in a shirt

Figure 4.3 The bust of Magnus Hirschfeld, taken from the Institute of Sexual Science, is carried through the streets of Berlin. Magnus-Hirschfeld-Gesellschaft.

and tie gathering piles of books from the ground and hurling them toward the flames. The voiceover explains that German students had "eingesammelt" (collected) the books for burning. The camera then moves to Hitler's propaganda minister, Joseph Goebbels, who addresses the masses, trying to impress on them what he calls the "strong, great and symbolic undertaking" of "entrust[ing] to the flames the intellectual garbage of the past."[121] According to the historians George Mosse and James Jones, "The tossing of the bust of Hirschfeld into the flames is the sole instance where an image was burnt with the books."[122] It is not clear, however, whether the bust actually reached the flames—some historians have argued that it would simply have been too heavy to be tossed into the fire. It is likely not only that the bust was present on that night but that it somehow withstood the Nazi attack.

A story goes that the Hirschfeld bust was found the day after the bonfire by a street cleaner who took it home and kept it safe until after the end of World War II, when he donated it to the Berlin Academy of Arts, where it is on display today. Whatever the truth of this account, it is fair to say that circumstances aided the bust's survival as much as the street cleaner's initiative. The sculpture of Hirschfeld's head was made from bronze, an alloy containing copper and tin. The melting point of bronze, which varies according to the ratio of its constituents, tends to be significantly higher—between 1,900 and 2,100 degrees Fahrenheit—than the temperature reached by burning paper, which combusts at around 1,500 degrees Fahrenheit. Wood also burns at about 1,100–1,500 degrees Fahrenheit, so the book bonfire simply would not have been able to reach a temperature high enough to melt the bust. The Hirschfeld bronze, symbolically rendered untouchable when it was staked up high above the hands of Nazi men, thus literally remained untouched by the brutal events of May 1933.

An (Im)Material End

Maryanne Dever, in a thought-provoking reassessment of the archive, has argued "for the necessity and value of moving away from our ingrained habit of ignoring the material instantiation of the archival artifacts with which we work."[123] Dever, who is specifically concerned with "the potential of the thing that is the paper," demonstrates beautifully that attention to the materiality of archival documents can aid the process of recovery and deepen understanding of how the material relates to the cultural.[124] My own analysis of the Institute of Sexual Science in this chapter differs in significant ways from Dever's project, not least because I have not lingered on my own encounter with the materiality of the objects under discussion. I am well aware that it might, therefore, seem somewhat disingenuous to close with a reference to Dever's work. But I mention it here because her insistence that understanding the material is central to our relationship to the archive and what we might recover from it helps bring into relief my own concern with the Institute of Sexual Science as a place in queer history. The Institute of Sexual Science was in many ways the first LGBTIQ archive, a place where certain kinds of information were formally collected, stored, and analyzed. But this archival work, which anticipates the development of later, formal library collections, was undertaken not in institutional isolation but amid the activities, private and political, of people who called the institute home and went about their everyday lives within its walls. It was precisely the institute's very real presence in interwar Berlin and in the international sexual reform circles of the day that made it an easy point of attack for Nazi thugs. Attention to the Nazi violence that brought to an end both the institute and the activist sexology that had gained prominence via Hirschfeld's work reveals how the materiality of the objects got caught up in the psychic realms of hate and a fear of contamination that shaped how the attack was conducted.

The blurring of boundaries between antisemitism and homophobia during these attacks indicates that it can be difficult to untangle the histories of homophobia from other forms of hatred. Similarly, as the earlier part of the chapter shows, it can be difficult to distinguish queer histories from feminist or transgender histories because the lives and discourses that inhabit such histories often overlap, even as different vocabularies or groups of people come to compete with each other. The aim of this chapter is not to untangle the messiness of this past but to reveal the knots and fine threads that held together sexual lives and labors at the Institute of Sexual Science and that would eventually unravel, collectively but also in many cases on an individual basis, in the violence of the Nazi onslaught. By focusing on the Institute of Sexual Science in this way, I have shown how attention to the materiality of sexology encourages broader thinking about the sexological archive and the violence issued against the place and the people who inhabited it.

5

Lives That Are Spoken For

Queer in Exile

That queerness and exile often go hand in hand is a well-rehearsed argument in studies concerned with diaspora and the queer subjects of (trans)national communities. While some scholars have focused on the transformative aspects of queerness in global context,[1] others have challenged liberatory readings of mobility and what Sara Ahmed has called "the conflation of migration with the transgression of boundaries."[2] Furthermore, inward-looking analyses of queer people whose aesthetics and emotional allegiances rendered them out of sync with their contemporaries have taken up the tropes of exile to extend understanding of the manifestations of queer precarity. In a reassessment of what she calls Walter Pater's "forced exile," for example, Heather Love has argued that Pater's "shrinking politics"—his refusal "to approximate the norms of modernist political subjectivity"—must be understood as a form of double displacement, because Pater inhabited "a threatened position as someone with secrets to keep and as someone whose particular form of secrecy was fast becoming superannuated."[3] In this chapter I take the debates about the shapes and effects of queer exile as my prompt for reconsidering Hirschfeld's final years, specifically his account of a journey through America, Asia, and the Middle East, which he undertook to escape Nazi persecution in Germany. Critics have read his published travelogue, *Die Weltreise eines Sexualforschers*[4] (The world journey of a sexologist; published in English as *Men and Women: Impressions of a Sexologist*), as an example of Hirschfeld's overall progressive, if historically contingent, sexual and racial politics.[5] I want to complicate these readings by paying attention to not only the existence of global sexual reform networks that enabled Hirschfeld's exile—networks that challenge the Eurocentric focus of many histories of sexuality—but also his citational practices, or what Sara Ahmed calls the textual *"screening techniques"* that index "how certain bodies take up spaces by screening out the existence of others."[6] In some ways, this line of investigation is similar to the questions I ask in Chapters 1 and 3 about racial and gender violence and whose voice is admitted into writing. But here I use the concept of Hirschfeld's queer exile to tease out his movable, sometimes moving, allegiances and disavowals during a time of political upheaval and personal uncertainty. Organized roughly chronologically, the chapter examines Hirschfeld's visit to the United States; turns to his writings on Japan, India, Egypt, and Palestine; moves from his "straight turn" in America to the feminist allegiances he claimed in Asia despite rarely allowing women's voices into the narrative, and concludes with a consideration of Hirschfeld's complex political stance as an anticolonial supporter of Zionism. The travelogue reveals the connectedness of modern sexual debates across different parts of the world even as it shows that Hirschfeld's anecdotal and epistemological efforts, while not actively screening out the existence of others, nevertheless tended to speak over their voices.

Straight in America

Die Weltreise marks an exile that was for Hirschfeld both traumatic and a respite from rising Nazism. Over the course of the 1920s he had increasingly expressed concerns about his future. In January 1929 he wrote about the financial struggle to maintain the institute.[7] Seven months later, he claimed that he had mended his financial issues.[8] However, by that stage it is clear that he had begun to worry about the loyalty of some of his colleagues. In his "Testament," a diary that also functioned as a will, he noted his fallout with his former collaborator Max Hodann over the running of the institute, claiming that Hodann was not suited to combining idealism with the practical sense needed to run the facility.[9] In contrast, Hirschfeld praised the continued support of Karl Giese, his long-term partner whose role it was to oversee the institute archive, and Friedrich Haupstein, the institute's administrative lead.[10] Concerned with the future of the institute, he furthermore announced the wish that his longtime colleagues Bernhard Shapiro, an endocrinologist, and Felix Abraham, who led the institute's "transvestite work," together with the gynecologist Ludwig Levy-Lenz take over the institute's running after his death. As it happens all three men were Jewish. That Hirschfeld was well aware of the dangers they faced is indicated by his proviso that they work "as long as possible."[11] The expression foreshadows the impossible conditions for Jews after the Nazis officially took power in 1933. While Hirschfeld's three medical colleagues escaped Germany, only two of them, Shapiro and Abraham, would survive the war. Abraham took his own life in Florence in 1937. Karl Giese, who after Hirschfeld's death and the closure of the institute ended up living impoverished and isolated in Brno (now in the Czech Republic), also committed suicide, in 1938.

Hirschfeld could not have known precisely how events would unfold in Germany. However, in 1930, on the eve of what would become his world journey, it was clear that he perceived a precarious future. In light of this it is not surprising that he readily agreed to an invitation by his old friend Harry Benjamin to lecture in America. Benjamin, a German-born endocrinologist, had visited the United States in 1913 and decided to remain in the country after the outbreak of World War I.[12] Benjamin freely acknowledged that it was during "the many times in the 1920s [when he] visited Hirschfeld and his Institute" that his interest in the people whose gender did not conform to binary norms and social expectations first developed.[13] Hirschfeld's trip to New York provided him not only with an opportunity to escape from the deteriorating situation in Germany but also an emotional respite as it allowed him to renew old friendships at a time when some of his institute colleagues turned their backs on him.

Hirschfeld arrived in New York in November 1930. At Benjamin's invitation, he first presented a lecture to a group of German-American physicians.[14] Delivered in German, the talk dealt with current debates about sexual pathology, a topic that was close to Hirschfeld's main interests.[15] Other speaking engagements followed and Hirschfeld was soon busy presenting talks to a wide range of audiences.[16] A pattern developed during his early days in America according to which his talks were inflected differently if they were presented to German-speaking or English-speaking audiences. While he gave his usual lectures on all kinds of sexual matters, including homosexuality, to German-speakers, his English-speaking talks were tailored more specifically to issues relating to "scientific partner selection and eugenic marriage counselling."[17] Shortly after arriving in New York, for example, the *New York Times*, which at the time had a daily circulation in the region of 450,000–500,000, reported that "Dr Magnus Hirschfeld ha[d] come here . . . to study the marriage question."[18] This contrasted with Hirschfeld's reception in the German-language *New Yorker Volkszeitung*, a socialist daily, which at the height of its success had a circulation of 20,000 but closed in 1932 during the Depression and was replaced by a weekly paper, the *Neue Volks-Zeitung*.[19] It announced Hirschfeld's intention to "discuss 'love's natural laws,'" a turn of phrase that Hirschfeld frequently used when making the case for the naturalness of homosexuality.[20] While his German audiences in New York thus heard talks that were similar to the kind of lectures he gave at home in Berlin, it soon became clear that Hirschfeld sought to appeal to English-speaking American audiences by representing himself in straight terms, courting publicity as a specialist on marital love instead of advocating on behalf of the people whose desires or genders ran against the normative grain of the time.

What was behind this change? It would be reductive to claim that Hirschfeld's "straight turn" in the United States is simply evidence of internalized homophobia, often seen as the underpinning of queer silences on same-sex matters. Instead, as Heather Love has pointed out, it is important to acknowledge that while "the historical experience of shame and secrecy has left its imprint on queer subjectivity," a more "'homeopathic' approach to political subjectivity" is needed if we want to "incorporate rather than disavow the causes of social inequality."[21] Or to phrase this differently, attention to shame alone can obscure the violent historical contingencies that prompted queer people into silence in certain contexts and at certain points in time. In her analysis of Walter Pater's work, Love argues that Pater suffered "exclusion" from classic male same-sex culture and the emergent modern homosexual cultures of his own time.[22] Hirschfeld, like Pater a privileged white man, similarly experienced the exclusion—and sense of a loss of support network—that comes with enforced exile. While he had chosen to leave Germany, the decision had arguably been taken out of his hands given the rise of Nazism and the dangers it brought to his life. With this in mind, Hirschfeld's decision to present himself in the United States, initially at least, as an expert on marriage and related issues, seems to have been a direct response to the perilousness of his political exile.

At the end of November 1930, not long after arriving in the United States, Hirschfeld gave an interview to the *Milwaukee Sentinel* that would set the tone for how he presented what we might call his American public persona. The interview was conducted by George Sylvester Viereck, the son of one of Hirschfeld's Berlin acquaintances, the Social Democrat Louis Viereck. Unlike his father, George Viereck was politically on the far right. While it is not clear what continued to bind Hirschfeld and George Viereck even after Viereck had become outspoken in his support of Nazism, in late 1930 and early 1931 they were united in their efforts to promote Hirschfeld's work to the American public.

In his first interview with Viereck, Hirschfeld laid out his views on marriage in the United States. The topic was controversial. Margaret Sanger's birth control campaign, which focused, initially at least, on women and was concerned with the reproductive effects of heterosexual sex, was the subject of considerable public debate. Hirschfeld's marriage talk in contrast deliberately appealed to heterosexual American men in search of sexual pleasure. He set himself up as a "European" expert on "romantic love" who could help American men to capitalize on what he claimed was the country's "sexual awakening" after World War I.[23] In a shrewd appeal to the American capitalist imagination, Hirschfeld claimed to have observed a change in American attitudes to love. He argued that while "the American man [used to] divert into his business the libido—the desire or urge—. . . [that led] Europeans to seek romantic adventures," after World War I American men had started to develop their "romantic" side even as they maintained their astute business sense.[24] In other words, Hirschfeld appealed to American audiences by claiming to have identified a trend according to which American men were now developing together business and erotic capital. When Viereck interrupted Hirschfeld with a reminder that America was in fact in the middle of an economic depression, Hirschfeld was quick to retort that the Depression would pass soon, thus flattering his intended audience of romantic yet economically go-getting heterosexual American men. If the links drawn between romance and business and the emphasis Hirschfeld placed on the economic astuteness of American men appear out of tune with the general tone of his work, they show a new sense of dependency on his audience, borne from the increasing precariousness of Hirschfeld's professional situation.

The interview, a curious mixture of confident expert talk and anxious appeal for the sympathy of an implicit straight-male American reader, hides the traumatic reality of Hirschfeld's flight from Germany. At the time when he left the country he not only feared the rise of Nazism. He also was "shocked and disappointed" by many of his sexological colleagues, notably Richard Linsert, who together with others had opposed Hirschfeld as leader of the Wissenschaftlich-humanitäres Kommitee (WhK; Scientific Humanitarian Committee). Hirschfeld had stepped down as the WhK's leader after a tenure of thirty-two and a half years, claiming that the majority of members still supported him but that he no longer wanted to expose himself to what he called the *Kesseltreiben*, or the systematic defamation campaign conducted against him by some of his former close colleagues.[25] The professional struggles were accompanied by, or perhaps the cause of, a bout of ill health. Early in 1930 Hirschfeld's long fight with diabetes was compounded by a painful infection of his left arm, diagnosed as polyneuritis, which also caused pain in his thighs, face, and teeth and by his own account made him feel "very disabled."[26] On arrival in America some of these concerns lifted, and he "subjectively [felt] very well on this trip, certainly better than [he had] felt the past few years in Europe."[27] The interview with George Viereck marks the moment of transition when Hirschfeld, while anxious about the uncertainties of exile, started to look forward again to the future.

A main concern that would mark Hirschfeld's final years was financial: how to make a living as a sexologist in exile? In addition to fees for his sexological work he had income from investments in a major Dutch department store, De Bijenkorf, and the production and sale of the so-called Titus Pearls, a medical remedy Hirschfeld had developed at the Institute of Sexual Science in the 1920s.[28] In the German context, the pills were claimed to heal the "shattered nerves" of men who had survived World War I and related forms of depression that were seen to be the cause of "sexual weakness."[29] American advertising in the 1930s, in contrast, widened the target market for the Titus Pearls. One advertisement claimed, for instance, that the pills treated "high blood pressure, hardening of the arteries, physical exhaustion after work or exercise, dizziness, depression, neurasthenia."[30] Another promised that the Titus Pearls would restore "youthful strength" to women as well as men.[31] These advertisements, which announced that the pills were created by "Dr. Magnus Hirschfeld, the world-known authority on Sexology," were placed in newspapers across the United States, ranging from the small Texas weekly the *Bowie Booster* to the famous anti–Ku Klux Klan *Muncie Post-Democrat*, which was based in Indiana. Hirschfeld's self-representation as an expert on marital love during his early days in America was directly tied to financial concerns. By affirming his status as an expert on (hetero)sexual matters he appealed to as broad an audience as possible.

The manufacturer of the Titus Pearls would formally sever the link with Hirschfeld when the Nazis came to power in 1933. However, the sale of the pills was a source of income during Hirschfeld's world journey.[32] His reputation in America was boosted—and indelibly shaped—by a second interview with George Viereck in February 1931, published simultaneously in the *Milwaukee Sentinel* and other newspapers across the United States, from the *Washington Herald* to the *Los Angeles Examiner*. In the second interview, Viereck, who had links to the conservative Hearst press empire and hence managed to get his work widely noticed, described Hirschfeld as the "Dr. Einstein of Sex."[33] The moniker, which sought to capitalize on the publicity surrounding Albert Einstein's recent arrival at the California Institute of Technology in Pasadena, would henceforth shape Hirschfeld's reception in North America and beyond.

While Hirschfeld's early appearances in the American media no doubt shaped an image of him as a (heterosexual) "sex expert," it would be wrong to claim that Hirschfeld did not discuss homosexuality during his four months in the United States. At the famous bohemian Dill Pickle Club in Chicago, for instance, he was announced as "Europe's Greatest Sex Authority" who would present a talk on "Homosexuality" with "beautiful revealing pictures."[34] The talk, which initially had to be postponed for unknown reasons, was thought to have attracted an audience of over three hundred people.[35] In San Francisco, his last destination on the U.S. mainland, Hirschfeld presented talks on homosexuality both to a specialist medical council and to the wider public at the Plaza hotel.[36] During his time in California he also strengthened his existing cultural and political allegiances. Visiting Hollywood, he met, for example, the Hungarian director Paul Fejos at MGM Studios. Fejos had become famous for his film *The Last Performance* (1927), about a menacing magician. It starred Conrad Veidt, the lead actor in the Hirschfeld-supported anti-homosexual-blackmail movie *Anders als die Andern* (Different from the others; 1919). At the time of Hirschfeld's visit, Fejos was working on the silent movie *Menschen Hinter Gittern* (*Men behind Bars*),[37] which would be released in 1931. The film, which follows the story of an otherwise upright man who drunkenly kills another man, critiques the treatment of criminals in prison. Both alcoholism and prison reform were topics close to Hirschfeld's heart. Early in his career, for instance, he wrote a critique of the effects of alcohol on family life, and he repeatedly addressed the failings of the criminal system, especially when it came to sexual questions.[38] In San Francisco, Hirschfeld visited the famous San Quentin prison to meet Thomas Mooney, the left-wing political activist widely thought to have been framed for a deadly bomb attack on the Preparedness Day Parade in San Francisco in 1916.[39] The visit clearly had an impact on Hirschfeld. He returned to it in a letter written in Haifa, Palestine, in 1932, in which he argued that Mooney and his coaccused Warren Billings were victims of a national "fear neurosis" that had started to take hold during World War I.[40]

Hirschfeld thus maintained his connections to left-wing reformers and artistic subcultures during his stay in America. However, it was his image as the "Einstein of Sex" that captured the American public imagination. If the moniker indicates that Hirschfeld became known in the United States primarily as a sex expert rather than a defender of homosexuality, the role that had made him (in)famous in Europe, it also testifies to the psychic and financial pressures that shaped Hirschfeld's exile.[41]

The Travelogue

While in America, Hirschfeld realized that it would be impossible for him to return to Germany. Having anticipated the possibility of a more permanent exile, he hatched a loosely formed plan to continue his travels by moving eastward. In due course, the journey would take him across Asia and the

Middle East before returning him to Europe, where he eventually settled in French exile. Hirschfeld's written account of his travels, *Die Weltreise eines Sexualforscher*, has been examined primarily for what it can tell us about Hirschfeld's resistance to and complicity in the perpetuation of colonial power dynamics.[42] Liat Kozma, for instance, has argued that "the uniqueness of Hirschfeld's narrative [in *The World Journey*] lies in his awareness of power relations that dictate social norms and practices: colonialism, gender inequality and heteronormativity."[43] But while the narrative is often astute in its comments and offers many unique insights into an international network of sexual reformers willing to host Hirschfeld during his time in exile, it also raises questions about what Anjali Arondekar and Geeta Patel, in a different context, have called the "citational underpinnings" that shaped Hirschfeld's apprehension of the people he met on his travels.[44] Arondekar and Patel use the expression *citational underpinnings* in their reappraisal of the relationship between queer studies and area studies. They critique the elevated role played by the United States (and some European contexts) in studies of sexualities in global perspective in which, as they point out, "geopolitics provides the exemplars, but rarely the epistemologies."[45] Arondekar and Patel are not mainly concerned with the forgotten or obscured histories that are at the heart of my project. Instead they explore "why certain vocabularies of the geopolitical achieve prominence while others get relegated to the ash heap of (queer) history."[46] Yet their observations on the (Euro-)American[47] centrism of twenty-first-century queer scholarship also lend themselves to tracing the apprehensive boundaries of Hirschfeld's *Die Weltreise*. Attention to the book's "citational underpinnings," by which I mean Hirschfeld's points of reference in the text, not only reveals the global travel of ideas and people before World War II. It also shows that despite Hirschfeld's developing critical understanding of racism and colonialism, there are gendered limits to whose voices he admits into the narrative: he aligns himself with local male elites, some of whom he had first met back in Berlin, and relegates women's voices to the exemplary rather than the epistemological.

Primarily a travelogue—the *Canadian Jewish Chronicle* called it "rambling, un-literary [but] an interesting conversation with an elderly man who has seen much and is moved by nothing"—*Die Weltreise* is a personal account of Hirschfeld's exiled journey through Hawaii, Japan, Taiwan, China, Indonesia, the Philippines, India, Egypt, and Palestine.[48] The narrative, which is often somewhat disjointed and mostly impressionistic, was first published in German in Switzerland in 1933 and then translated into English by Oliver P. Green in 1935. It was published in America under the title *Men and Women: The World Journey of a Sexologist*. The change of words grammatically links men *and* women, thus adding a heterosexual gloss to the original title that might appeal to Hirschfeld's straight American audience. The British edition of the book, in contrast, which was substantively the same translation by Oliver P. Green, was glossed in colonial terms as *Women East and West: Impressions of a Sex Expert*.[49] The English edition of what I henceforth refer to as *The World Journey*, furthermore deliberately linked the book to works such as Hermann Heinrich Ploss, Max Bartels, and Paul Bartels' colonial anthropology *Woman*, a three-volume compendium that in translation from German was also published by Heinemann in 1935 and is advertised on the dust jacket of *Women East and West*.[50] If, according to Homi Bhabha, the narration of nation is achieved via "complex strategies of cultural identification and discursive address that function in the name of 'the people' or 'the nation' and make them the immanent subjects of a range of social and literary narratives," the translations of *The World Journey* suggest that the representation of the nation's other(s) were similarly inflected according to circumstance.[51] It is surely no coincidence that a work by the "Einstein of Sex," unpublishable in his own home country, was figured in implicitly heterosexual terms for the depression-hit British and American markets, with the British edition further adding a nostalgic allusion to the heyday of the country's colonial power.

The English titles obscure the book's actual content. *The World Journey* no longer engaged in the kind of heterosexually focused self-marketing that had characterized Hirschfeld's arrival in the United States. Instead it signals a return to Hirschfeld's queer concerns. While he claimed that it was a worldwide interest in sexology that helped him cover the "not insubstantial cost of the world journey," it was in fact the personal and professional friendships Hirschfeld had forged over the course of his career that enabled his journey, by offering paid lecture engagements and, not infrequently, a place to stay.[52] As director of the Institute of Sexual Science in Berlin and copresident of the World League of Sexual Reform, which in a series of meetings in the 1920s brought together sexual reformers and scientists from different parts of Europe, America, China, Japan, and elsewhere, Hirschfeld had forged alliances that would enable him to tour the world as an expert on a wide range of sexual topics.[53]

During these travels, while in Shanghai, Hirschfeld met a twenty-three-year-old man, Tao Li,[54] who would become his companion henceforth.[55] Throughout *The World Journey* he represented their liaison as an idealized "teacher-pupil relationship," emphasizing their professional connection, for instance, by noting that Tao Li was already well versed in European sexology when they first met.[56] Tao Li's father threw a farewell party for the two men, expressing his hope that "his son would become the Dr. Hirschfeld of China," figuring their relationship in teacher-pupil terms that would later be picked up in public discussions of their relationship, such as a short commentary in a Viennese paper that announced Hirschfeld's completion of a world journey in the company of Tao Li, who was planning to complete his medical studies in Europe.[57] *The World Journey* does not linger on their relationship. Instead it shifts attention from the personal to the sexological as Hirschfeld holds up Tao Li as an example to support his argument that personal circumstance but most of all "congenital characteristics and inclinations" shape humans across the world. "The 400 to 500 million Chinese people are individually just as distinct," he writes, "as the 100 million Germans or 50 million English people."[58] While Hirschfeld did not publicly represent his relationship with Tao Li in intimate terms, he frequently wrote about their companionship, and plenty of other evidence survives of the life they forged together until Hirschfeld's death.[59]

Citational Limits in Japan

It was an invitation by a Japanese colleague, Keizō Dohi, that prompted Hirschfeld to embark on his travels from America to the East. Dohi, whose first name Hirschfeld spells as "Keijo," was a dermatologist with a special interest in venereal diseases. Born in 1866, he trained in Germany and Vienna before returning to Japan, where he became an influential medical figure. Dohi maintained close links with the German-speaking world, including via the German translation of his *Beiträge zur Geschichte der Syphilis in Ostasien* (Contributions to the history of syphilis in East Asia) (1923), which claimed that syphilis was introduced to Japan by Spanish and Portuguese traders in the sixteenth century.[60] Dohi died only a few months after Hirschfeld's visit. His friendship and instrumental role in kick-starting Hirschfeld's world lecture tour was evidence that by the 1930s there existed a global network of researchers with a shared interest in sexual matters, even if Dohi's professional training suggests that sexological research remained oriented toward Europe.[61] Jana Funke, who examines the intersections in *The World Journey* between sexology and anthropology, has argued that Hirschfeld "was positioned both at the centre and on the margins of Western discourses," that while his role as a Western sexologist implicated him in the colonial transfer of power, his "creative dialogue" with the people and objects he encountered on his travels also broadened what she calls "the scope of the Western sexual imagination."[62] Yet the Japanese narrative suggests that Hirschfeld kept control of whose voice was heard in this dialogue.

Hirschfeld often sought out, at least initially, the Western colleagues who had settled in the countries he visited. On his first stop in Hawaii, for instance, he met with two resident German doctors who had set up practice in

Honolulu.⁶³ In Indonesia he spent time in the company of the South African ethnologist and lawyer F. D. Holleman, who had trained in the Netherlands and became an influential legal anthropologist in the Netherlands and South Africa.⁶⁴ During Hirschfeld's final days in Tokyo, the German director of the Japanese-German Cultural Institute, Wilhelm Grundert, acted as Hirschfeld's translator. In *The World Journey* Hirschfeld argued that the "distinguished" scholar Grundert should be given a chair at a German university, a hope that would come true not long afterward, when Grundert joined the Nazi Party in 1934 and two years later was appointed as the head of Japan Studies at the University of Hamburg, followed by a rapid promotion to the role of the university's chancellor in 1938.⁶⁵

In the main, however, Hirschfeld's time in Japan was characterized by his meetings with Japanese colleagues, new acquaintances and people he had previously met in Berlin. He reconnected, for instance, with his old friend "S. Iwaya," who had been a Japanese tutor at Friedrich-Wilhelms-Universität (today's Humboldt University) between 1900 and 1902.⁶⁶ During his time in Berlin, Iwaya was introduced by a friend to the WhK and wrote an article on pederasty in Japan for the *Jahrbuch für sexuelle Zwischenstufen* (Yearbook for sexual intermediaries).⁶⁷ Iwaya's work is an example of the complex travel of sexual ideas between Japan and Germany in the twentieth century. He took Hirschfeld to Tokyo's Meiji Theater to meet his son, who worked there as the technical director. Iwaya junior introduced Hirschfeld to female impersonators of the Kabuki, a traditional dance form. The meeting marks a return of Hirschfeld's long-standing interest in sexual and gender questions. While there is no surviving record of the conversation between Hirschfeld and the two men from the Iwaya family, he claims that one of the Iwayas acted as his translator, allowing him to have a conversation with a young actor who sought affirmation that he really looked like a woman.⁶⁸ At this point the narrative turns its back on Hirschfeld's hosts. Embarking on a discussion of the Kabuki tradition, Hirschfeld does not cite his local guides, even though one of them is a theater professional. Instead he mentions a work by the Western observer Maria Piper as the source of his knowledge of Japanese theater.⁶⁹ On the basis of Piper's analysis, Hirschfeld then applied his sexological schema to the "female impersonators" of the Japanese stage, classifying them as "normal," "transvestite," or "homosexual."⁷⁰

The citational evidence gleaned from Hirschfeld's account of Japanese theater suggests that he privileged his existing, European (and at times North American) frame of reference, thus screening out the knowledge he might have gained from his Japanese hosts. Instead he recast Japanese people and traditions in a Western frame of reference. The Japanese narrative problematizes Hirschfeld's famous argument that the "individual sexual type is stronger and more important than a racial type," by which he meant that sexuality in all its manifestations exists across all parts of the world.[71] It problematizes the claim because it raises questions about how he came to formulate his arguments. This critique is not about disputing that all kinds of sexual acts may exist in all kinds of places but to question the naming practices of Western observers such as Hirschfeld who seemed convinced that sexological classification could be applied across the world.

Speaking for *Women in India*

The question of whose voice is heard in sexological discourse has preoccupied scholars concerned with the relationship between scientific and "lay" cultures in the articulation of modern sexuality. It is specifically the voices of women that have been marginalized, or rather, spoken for and over, both in sexology and the related scholarship. In *The World Journey* the denial of women's voices is somewhat obscured by the fact that Hirschfeld frequently lavished enthusiastic praise on members of the women's movement. He claimed, for instance, that his "most remarkable encounter" in Japan had been with the leaders of the Japanese feminist movement—"Shidzue Ishimoto; Fusaye Ishikawa; Hannayo Ikuta."[72] In the account of his time in Egypt he further argued that the local feminists occupied a "high intellectual level," citing as his example an encounter with the famous Egyptian feminist and publisher Hoda Charaoni,[73] who, he claimed, was the same "type of woman"[74] as other strong women leaders he had met, including in China a certain "Mrs. Ma,"[75] which most likely refers to the Hong Kong–based YMCA member and advocate for Christian women Ma Huo Quintang, and in India "Lady Bose," the wife of the scientist Jagadish Bose and aunt of Hirschfeld's colleague and host in India, Girindrashekhar Bose, and the scientist Debendra Bose, who would later coedit *A Concise History of Sexual Science in India*.[76] Despite his praise for these feminists and global feminism more broadly, Hirschfeld rarely admitted the voices of women into the narrative of *The World Journey*, however.

Hirschfeld's account of his time in India most clearly illustrates his habit of speaking for women. While he commented favorably on many of the women he met, he largely excluded their words from his text. He arrived in India in late September 1931 and stayed there until mid-November, when, sick with malaria, he boarded a Middle East–bound ship in Bombay. The account of his relatively short time in the country, which forms the central part of *The World Journey*, has received considerable critical attention, partly because of Hirschfeld's engagement with Indian sexology, from which developed his long-standing interest in what he called "the Indian art of love."[77] Veronika Fuechtner, for example, has argued that the Indian narrative can be understood as "a complicated reaction against the rise of fascism," a reaction that both enacts "power relations" and "unfolds a counter-hegemonic potential."[78] While Hirschfeld's account of his time in India is where he articulated most clearly his anticolonial stance, this was not the first time that he spoke out against colonialism. During his time in Indonesia he criticized the Dutch colonization of the archipelago. Despite his critical stance—he compared colonialism to slavery—the Indonesian account remained curiously indebted to the language of nineteenth-century scientific racism.[79] This is most apparent in Hirschfeld's focus on the perceived difficulties of white women and men to adapt to Indonesia's tropical climate. He claimed, for instance, that white women found it harder than white men to adapt to tropical heat, evoking an old stereotype about the climatic contingencies of gender.[80] According to Hirschfeld this apparent physical difference forced many European women to return to Europe—or indeed never to leave home in the first place—while white men were able to settle in Indonesia, where they often ended up marrying indigenous women.[81] Hirschfeld's account here uncritically repeats the sexist and racist assumptions about gender and climate that had been a mainstay of nineteenth-century scientific—including sexological—discourse. By the time of his visit a European middle class had emerged in Indonesia, which was made up of both women and men.[82] Hirschfeld argues elsewhere that professional European women, mainly doctors, seem to adapt well to life in a tropical climate, yet in the Indonesian chapters his reduction of women to their bodies—and throwaway remarks about the "romantic conflict" caused by attempts to "import" European women to the tropics—draws gendered boundaries around Hirschfeld's apprehension of colonial agency.

Hirschfeld arrived in India when the independence movement was gathering momentum. He was well received as "the foremost sexologist of Berlin."[83] His work appealed to a wide range of outward-looking Indian political activists, who were, in Sanjam Ahluwalia's words, "especially keen to project a 'modern' image of India" and who imagined *swaraj* (freedom and independence) "as an inauguration of modernity."[84] Hirschfeld in turn aligned himself with members of "the Indian elite," arguing that they were "in character and knowledge entirely able to lead their nation."[85] By "elite" he meant the influential men who hosted Hirschfeld in India. He stayed, for instance, with Jawaharlal Nehru in Allahabad, having first met the man who would become India's first prime minister in Berlin.[86] Hirschfeld's main host was Girindrashekhar Bose, the first president of the Indian Psychoanalytic Society and a member of an influential family of scientists, who looked after Hirschfeld directly or via recommendations to friends for most of his stay in India.[87] Perhaps it was partly these friendships that prompted Hirschfeld to claim that he had "supported Indian freedom for fifty years" because "it is one of the biggest injustices in the world that one of the oldest civilized nations . . . cannot rule independently."[88] Birgit Lang has argued that Hirschfeld's identification with Indian anticolonial activists constitutes a form of "anticolonial mimicry," an allegiance that expressed itself affectively and as an intellectual affinity rather than an actual involvement in political action.[89] Indeed his support of Indian independence appears to have been largely a private expression, as Hirschfeld's public talks in India, as elsewhere, continued to focus on topics such as "love, sex and marriage," "sex pathology," and the question "Is homosexuality in man and woman inborn or acquired?"[90]

The one major intervention made by *The World Journey* is in the controversy surrounding the publication of Katherine Mayo's *Mother India*. Published in 1927, not long before Hirschfeld's arrival in India, Mayo, an American historian, articulated a sustained attack on Indian society, which was built around a critique of sexual politics and practices in the country. *Mother India* was attacked by Indian audiences because, as Mrinalini Sinha has argued, it "painted a highly sensationalized picture of rampant sexuality and its consequences in India: masturbation, rape, homosexuality, prostitution, venereal diseases, and, most important of all, early sexual intercourse and premature maternity."[91] Indian activists, including Mahatma Gandhi, who also critiqued child marriage, attacked Mayo's work, arguing that it deliberately fueled the British imperialist agenda by suggesting that Indian sexual customs were cruel and out of hand unless checked by British rule.[92] Hirschfeld aligned himself with Mayo's critics, dedicating a whole chapter of *The World Journey* to what he called the "sexual caricature" Mayo presented of India.[93] Arguing that *Mother India* "falsified" evidence to provide "England-friendly propaganda," Hirschfeld stressed that sexual exploitation and oppression were not exclusive to India.[94] He argued that every country has its own "sexual scandals," noting that in his youth a sexual scandal had rocked England itself, alluding presumably to the child prostitution controversy prompted by W. T. Stead's investigative journalism in the 1880s.[95] Veronika Fuechtner has pointed out that Hirschfeld "reject[ed] the category of the [Indian] exotic altogether," arguing that, according to Hirschfeld, "what is moral, *sittlich*, always stands in relationship to local custom, *Sitte*."[96] However, while Fuechtner is right to point out that Hirschfeld challenged colonial views of India such as those expressed by Mayo, it is also important to note that the cultural relativist terms in which Hirschfeld formulated his response remained embedded in a Western frame of reference. Or to say this differently, while Hirschfeld clearly distanced himself from the outright racism that propelled colonial discourses, he too spoke *for*, rather than *with*, the girls and women whose lives had become a discursive battleground in the debates about English rule over India.

Hirschfeld's arguments in some ways echo the work of contemporary anthropologists such as Bronislaw Malinowski, who shifted the critical framework from a moralistic to a relativistic understanding of cultural difference. Yet while Malinowski, in the words of Havelock Ellis, no longer considered the "peoples [who are] not completely under the influence of our own civilisation" merely as scientific objects but as "witnesses to unfamiliar aspects of our common human nature," this kind of anthropological endeavor remained subject to an unequal transfer of power, which often remained unacknowledged.[97] The titles alone of many of Malinowski works—*Sex and Repression in Savage Society* (1927) or *The Sexual Life of Savages in North-Western Melanesia* (1929), for example—indicate that cultural relativists retained much of the conceptual baggage of scientific racism as well as a Eurocentric frame of reference.[98] A similar charge can be levied against Hirschfeld in relation to his writings on the role of women in India. While his narrative at times overtly sought to resist racial hierarchies, it nevertheless retained a fairly uncritical belief in the accuracy of Hirschfeld's own observations on the people and cultures he encountered.

The World Journey shows that despite Hirschfeld's sympathies with anticolonialism and a loosely defined global feminism, his narrative only rarely let women speak. Instead his encounters with Indian girls and women are typically represented as fairly superficial anecdotal curiosa. For instance, his critique of practices such "contempt of widows" or the sexual exploitation of young girls who were forced to become "temple women,"[99] a position that made them vulnerable to sexual abuse including by the temple's priests, was indebted to the narratives of others, including Western observers such as Mayo and an English doctor named N. J. Balfour,[100] as well as Indian men of privileged social standing such as Nehru.[101] While Hirschfeld might not have heard the voices of disenfranchised Indian women because of linguistic difficulties and the structural inequalities that would have made it difficult for him to gain unmediated access to the poorest, most exploited women, there is little evidence that he attempted to speak with the women he wrote about. Gayatri Spivak, in her influential critique of poststructuralist conceptions of the subject, "Can the Subaltern Speak?," has criticized "the unrecognised contradiction within a [Western] position that valorises the concrete experience of the oppressed while being so uncritical about the historical role of the intellectual."[102] *The World Journey* shows little awareness of its own limits and exclusions. Instead Hirschfeld's account, for all its anticolonial claims, continued to speak for—and over—Indian women.

That Hirschfeld's way of speaking over women was not restricted to the loss of the voices of the poor and uneducated is illustrated by the account of a talk he presented at the women-only Lady Hardinge Medical College in

Delhi.[103] Here he commented not on the intellectual insights of the students but on the "lovely view" he encountered when faced with a large lecture theater full of "good-looking female students in their Indian dress." The objectification of Indian women in *The World Journey* is underscored by the inclusion of a photograph that shows Hirschfeld "talking to a thirteen-year-old mother."[104] It depicts him side on, wearing a light-colored tropical suit, literally talking down to the young girl, whose eyes are directed away from him and toward the sleeping child in her arms. The composition of the bodies and the way they are hierarchically linked via the direction of Hirschfeld's gaze reinforces the unequal transfer of power between the European sexologist's gaze and the young Indian mother who is turned into the object of his study.[105]

While Hirschfeld refers to quite a number of encounters with women in India—he laments, for example, a cancelled meeting with Annie Besant and mentions that his talk "Love in the Light of Science" at the "Bombay Ladies-Branch National Indian Association" had attracted an audience of three hundred women—the only example of his citing a woman occurs in a description of his time in Darjeeling, when he asked a European woman if she was afraid of the "natives" while walking alone, and the woman responded that her only worry was "English soldiers."[106] The references to "highly educated" Indian women such as Kamala and Krishna Nehru, in contrast, are not substantiated by similar quotations. Sara Ahmed, writing in the context of twenty-first-century debates about sexism and institutional racism, has argued that citation practices are a "successful reproductive technology, a way of reproducing the world around certain bodies."[107] Hirschfeld's *The World Journey* illustrates how Western, male-centric knowledge is (re)produced. Despite the evidence it presents that Hirschfeld met with both female and male sexual reformers, women, and Indian women specifically, tend not to figure through their own words in *The World Journey*. These silences appear doubly problematic given the text's anticolonial framework and emphasis on the existence of localized yet internationally connected feminist and sexual reform movements. *The World Journey* is a reminder that prejudice can lurk in unacknowledged ways even in projects that overtly proclaim their own progressiveness and solidarity with oppressed people.

Retrospection and Zionism

The geographical arc of Hirschfeld's journey back to Europe was accompanied by an increasingly reflective, paradoxically retrospective and forward-looking mood. He had already started to think about what might await him on return to Europe during his time in India. In a diary entry from October

1931, for instance, written while in the Indian city of Patna, he reflected on his relationship with Tao Li, describing it as one of the biggest "Gewinne" of his travels, a word that carries connotations of both "gain" and "victory."[108] While he still portrayed the "loyal" and "affectionate" Tao Li as a "pupil," he added a note in English to the German text that expands on their close relationship and anticipates a precarious future.[109] Formally written, signed and dated in the manner of a will, it pronounces Tao Li to be Hirschfeld's beneficiary and asks that, in the event of Hirschfeld's death during his travels, Tao Li take his ashes to Berlin to hand them over to Karl Giese and Fritz Haupstein at the institute. Hirschfeld further stipulates that Tao Li "shall keep everything I have with me, especially also my manuscripts and money," concluding with the plea that Tao Li be "considered in every way as a quite confidential friend."[110] If the informal will expresses fears about what would happen to Tao Li, and to Hirschfeld's body, after his death, the diary also increasingly reveals a sense of nostalgia. The entry for Christmas Eve 1931, for instance, written in Alexandria, records Hirschfeld's plans to take Tao Li to a "Bavarian beer hall" in the city because he missed his Institute of Sexual Science. Nishant Shahani has argued that queer experience is defined by "a certain kind of retrospection" that may take any number of forms—"returning to a primal scene" and "belated cognition" are just two of the examples provided.[111] In *The World Journey*, which is primarily an account of historic transformation rather than psychic life, Hirschfeld's backward glances to the time before exile are noticeably rare. This lends extra force to the fleeting moments of retrospection, which indicate not only some of the emotional pressures on Hirschfeld but that he tried to keep them in check by issuing forward-looking pleas to "keep going: work, hope, don't give up."[112]

Besides the Middle East's geographical proximity to Europe, Hirschfeld's encounters with old acquaintances from Berlin might have prompted his thoughts to turn toward the Institute of Sexual Science. On arrival in Cairo he found that medically informed sexual debates were thriving, sustained both by the renewed interest in Egyptian, Arab, and Ottoman histories that developed in response to the British occupation and, as Liat Kozma, has shown, by the work of people such as the medical doctor and self-styled sexologist Faraj Fakhri who "presented [himself] as liberating [his] readers from the hold of custom and organized religion and thus situated [himself] as the vanguard of a modern and enlightened East."[113] Fakhri had spent time at Hirschfeld's institute during the first half of the 1920s, and while Hirschfeld does not mention him in *The World Journey*, he lists numerous encounters with Egyptian medical colleagues, representing Egypt as a place in which sexual science was thriving. Hirschfeld's claims are supported by historical developments in the country that, from around the 1880s, turned attention to matters relating to gender and sexuality, including broader debates about feminism and masculinity, as well as more specific concerns with marriage, prostitution, and masturbation.[114] Hanan Kholoussy has shown that the "monitoring and medicalising of sexuality"[115] at the time affected the lives of both men and women as the emergence of a sexual science in Egypt was imbricated, in Kozma's words, in the "construction of productive citizens whose bodies, habits, inclinations and practices were increasingly regulated by the state and tied to the construction of new middle-class mores and values."[116] Hirschfeld, like many of his colleagues, considered sexology a harbinger of progressive social change, noting, for instance, that his university lectures were attended by European as well as Egyptian women—some of them veiled—whose presence he considered the marker of new times.[117] His talk "Love in the Light of Science" covered topics as diverse as the "natural laws of love," "marriage," and "sex pathology," but his reception in the popular press—which also carried advertisements for the Titus Pearls—supports the argument that the primary audience for sexology was Egypt's emerging middle class.[118]

While Hirschfeld emphasized the scientific foundations of sexual modernity, he also claimed in his private notes that "to the Arabs . . . homoerotic love practice is something natural [and that] Mohammed could not change [this attitude]," picking up on a prevalent trope about Arab sexuality.[119] Writing in *The World Journey*, in contrast, Hirschfeld mentioned a meeting with the Egyptian minister for health, Mohamed Shahin Pasha, who according to Hirschfeld considered homosexuality an "illness" but whom he nevertheless represented as a progressive figure.[120] Hirschfeld, praising what he considers Pasha's willingness to engage in dialogue, made space for Pasha's voice, reproducing a quotation according to which the Egyptian politician expressed his joy at having met Hirschfeld. Here Pasha argued that the "illness" he calls "aberration of the sexual drive" needs the "careful attention of doctors and the implantation of preventive measures" that would allow a new generation to thrive.[121] Hirschfeld's alignment with a man who explicitly argues for the treatment—and hence future eradication—of homosexuality seems out of keeping with his views. It suggests that in the early 1930s his allegiances were not only to same-sex cultures but also the thriving international scientific community. Homosexuality is noticeably marginal to Hirschfeld's extensive account of his time in Egypt, which instead picks up on national debates about gender and colonial rule. He commented favorably, for instance, on Egypt's thriving feminist movement and made the case for Egyptian independence from British rule, cementing his argument with the observation that "the average ethical and intellectual level [of Egyptians] was equal to that of European nations."[122] While *The World Journey*'s Egyptian narrative thus focuses on Hirschfeld's involvement in debates about the social dimensions of scientific progress, his diary entries from his time in Egypt reveal a nostalgic retrospection, as anxieties about the future were compounded by ill health, diabetes, and malaria, which Hirschfeld traced to his stay in an "Indian-run hotel" in Agra.[123]

The tone of Hirschfeld's writing changes when he arrives in Palestine, where a new, albeit contingent, optimism begins to mark his words. He initially takes on the tone of a tour guide, mocking the tourists who pass through the Holy Land on three-day itineraries in pursuit of "illusions" supported by "belief" and "fantasy."[124] Contrasting their travels with his own five-week stay, he lays bare his attachment to Palestine, claiming that he had "never found it so hard to tear [himself] away from a place than it was to leave Jerusalem, that [he] had never found it harder to leave a country than it was saying farewell to Palestine."[125] The affective introduction to Jerusalem as the *Glanzpunkt*, or highlight, of Hirschfeld's travels stands out in a narrative that generally reveals little about Hirschfeld's own feelings. Here we find another example of retrospection, this time, however, harking back to Hirschfeld's seldom-mentioned Jewish background. He claims to experience *Jugenderinnerungen*, or memories from a young age, which lent familiarity to the figures, stories, and places associated with Palestine, a familiarity that is derived from his knowledge of the Old and New Testaments.[126] The passage reveals Hirschfeld's biblical knowledge, as he mentions, for instance, the stories of Sodom and Gomorrah, Abraham and Isaac, the Cave of Machpelah, Jesus and Pilate, and Jericho.[127] However, he is quick to reject religion, claiming that "Gottesfurcht," a German synonym for religious belief that literally translates as "fear of God," "is nothing but a real kind of physical fear similar to the fear of death."[128]

While Hirschfeld's connection to Palestine is not presented as a religious expression, he openly admired the "adoringly moving and heartwarmingly natural" young Jewish "pioneers" who were forging new lives in Palestine.[129] Praising Tel Aviv for having established itself as "the only uniformly Jewish city in the contemporary world,"[130] he speaks out in favor of Zionism, influenced by his own experiences of the "success" of Zionism in Palestine.[131] Hirschfeld, like many supporters, was critical of certain aspects of Zionism, predominantly in relation to internal debates. He disagreed, for instance, with racial definitions of Jewishness on the grounds that "'pure' races" cannot exist "among white people if one acknowledges that every individual has a genealogy of fathers and mothers [that] might encompass thousands, or possibly even hundreds of thousands of generations."[132] He also disagreed with the introduction of Hebrew as the lingua franca, going as far as to claim that if it was not for the linguistic barrier, he might have considered retiring to Palestine.

It is not difficult to see why in the 1930s Jewish life in Palestine seemed so appealing to Hirschfeld. In addition to the escape it offered from antisemitism, especially in its violent escalation in Nazi Germany, Jewish settlers—also known as the *yishuv*—had begun to experiment with radical new forms of living that were far removed from the restrictions of bourgeois European society.[133] Sexual reform was part of this process and both psychoanalytic and sexological work circulated readily.[134] By the time of Hirschfeld's visit, his former student at the Institute of Sexual Science the medical doctor Chaim Berlin had established a sexological practice in Tel Aviv, and shortly after Hirschfeld left Palestine another doctor who had trained at the Berlin institute, Avraham Matmon, would open the Tel Aviv Institute of Sexual Science.[135] By his own account Hirschfeld gave around a dozen well-attended talks during his time in Palestine—in Tel Aviv, Jerusalem, Haifa, kibbutz Beit Alfa, kibbutz Ain Charod, and elsewhere.[136] Given the popularity of sexual science in the *yishuv* it stands out that *The World Journey* paid little attention to the "sexual intermediaries" that preoccupied Hirschfeld elsewhere, focusing instead on *Lebenslust*, *Lebenskraft*, and *Lebensbejahung*—roughly "lust for life," "vitality," and "affirmation of life"—among Jewish settlers.[137] While Hirschfeld mentioned that he had observed all kinds of sexual concerns[138] in Palestine except for transvestism, the main part of his discussion deals with collective ways of living, including the fostering of what we might today call body-positive attitudes and the benefits of communal child-rearing.

Hirschfeld expressed admiration for the *Kolonialisten*—the colonizers—who according to him were able to shed old taboos and inhibitions and start a freer life.[139] Today the cost paid by the Arab and Muslim inhabitants of Palestine has been well documented in critiques of the unequal conditions of livability in the region.[140] At the time of Hirschfeld's visit the full-scale military occupation of Gaza and the West Bank undertaken after the founding of Israel in 1948 was yet to come. There was, however, already violence between Jews and Arabs that anticipated later events. When Hirschfeld visited Jerusalem, for instance, the city was recovering from the bloody aftermath of the 1929 fighting over access to the Western Wall. Hirschfeld was aware of the disputes, making space in his account of Palestine for a section on what he called the "Arab claim." He recalled the arguments for Arab independence put to him during a meeting in Cairo with a man he called "Anni Abdul Hadis," who according to Hirschfeld was a member of "Istik Cal."[141] "Anni Abdul Hadis" presumably refers to Awni Abd al-Hadi, founder of 'hizb al-istiqlal al-'arabi, the Arab Independence Party, which was opposed to the Zionist effort.[142] Abd al-Hadi was a founding member of the Paris-based *al-fatat* group, which supported Arab independence and unity. According to Hirschfeld Abd al-Hadi, an influential and well-connected figure, spoke "fluent German" during their meeting, setting out his case for why Palestine should not be called a "Jewish land."[143] Given Hirschfeld's tendency to ignore other voices, it is significant that he made room for Abd al-Hadi's account of the history of Palestine, including his critique of English rule and the arrival of "100,000 Zionists."[144] Yet rather than engaging with Abd al-Hadi's claims, Hirschfeld shifted the focus to the "extraordinarily difficult situation in which Zionism has placed Judaism in Palestine," extolling the virtues of the "brave, joyful, and optimistic" outlook of the Jewish "pioneers" in the face of adversity.[145]

The encounter between Hirschfeld and Abd al-Hadi illustrates the deep opposition that already marked lives and politics in Palestine. Elsewhere in the text Hirschfeld recounted the fate of a Jewish settler from Poland who had set up home with his family near Haifa and was shot dead in his own living room one night, killed by an unseen assassin who hid in the darkness outside.[146] It is likely that this murder was a real event rather than merely anti-Arab rhetoric. Yet Hirschfeld's inclusion of it in *The World Journey* nevertheless draws attention to what he does not discuss: the impact of Zionism on the Arab and Muslim inhabitants of Palestine. While he mentioned elsewhere positive encounters with Arab Christians in Palestine, acknowledged that both Jews and Arabs have suffered and caused suffering, and emphasized the need for reconciliation, framed in terms of "panhumanism," "cosmopolitanism," and *Menschenliebe*, or the love for other humans,[147] *The World Journey* is weighted toward "the achievements of the Zionists in Palestine" in the face of Arab resistance.[148]

From our vantage point today Zionism in 1930s Palestine points to the future formation of the state of Israel and what Palestinians call *al-nakba*, or the catastrophe of the forced expulsion from their home.[149] At the time when Hirschfeld was visiting Palestine, however, his attention was primarily on the deteriorating situation in Germany, which made the prospect of a "state-like" form where Jews could escape from persecution clearly appealing. The devastation of the Holocaust would later play an important role in the case for the state of Israel.

Hirschfeld closed the written part of *The World Journey* with a couple of lines from Ferdinand Freiligrath's poem "Trotz alledem" (Despite everything; 1843), which was inspired by the Scottish poet Robert Burns's 1795 celebration of socialism "Is There for Honest Poverty" (also known as "A Man's a Man for A' That") and published by Karl Marx. The poem gained popularity in early twentieth-century socialist and communist circles for its emphasis on egalitarianism. Yet Hirschfeld's plea for equality is somewhat undermined by *The World Journey*'s visual denouement. The final page of the book is given over in its entirety to a photograph of two men. Titled "Arab merchant with (boy)friend,"[150] it replaces the political focus of the previous discussion with a visual reminder of Hirschfeld's concern with same-sex sexuality. The picture alludes to Hirschfeld's discussion of his time in Egypt when he had praised what he called the "sexual tolerance" of Islam. According to Hirschfeld this "tolerance" does not express itself as an overt prohomosexuality stance but as the ability to discuss the topic and disagree over it.[151] Dialogue, however, is precisely what is avoided by the use of a photograph that reverts to a representation of Arab men as objects of the gaze of a Western observer, an observer who here apprehends their existence primarily in sexual terms. If the image can perhaps be read as a utopian expression of Hirschfeld's hope that same-sex affinities will transgress political and racial divides, it nevertheless also shows how easily his focus on homosexuality *screened out* the lives of the people he met on his travels.

(After)Life

Hirschfeld died unexpectedly on May 14, 1935, his birthday, in exile in Nice. The last years of his life had been precarious. He had already received news of the deteriorating political situation in Germany while still on his travels in India and the Middle East. On arrival in Europe, where his first stopover was in Athens, Hirschfeld noted that the same kind of "hounding" he previously experienced had already caught up with him and that he considered "the situation at home more atrocious than ever."[152] In the 1920s Hirschfeld had experienced hate in a way that occasionally left physical damage, as discussed in the Introduction. However, it was only when he returned from his travels in the spring of 1932 that he actually feared for his life. "I can hardly believe it," he writes in his diary, anticipating a future that would bring death in exile.[153]

Hirschfeld's last major appearance among the international sexological community was during the congress of the World League for Sexual Reform in Brno (Brünn).[154] His account of it is brief, focused on describing his ill health and the support of Tao Li.[155] Hirschfeld's colleague Edward Elkan later remembered that "Hirschfeld was already a very sick man" when he met him in Brno, noting that Hirschfeld "was always accompanied by his close friend Dr Giese" but claiming not to know "the Chinese doctor" (Tao Li), whom he photographed together with Hirschfeld.[156] Elkan, a Jewish socialist and birth control advocate who had a medical practice in Hamburg, would soon experience himself Nazi violence at firsthand. At the beginning of 1933, he "was almost beaten to death . . . by a gang of Nazi thugs who attacked him. . . . He was dragged from prison to prison and finally, his arm still in a sling, allowed to emigrate to London."[157] The year would be decisive for Hirschfeld too, starting with an attempt by Bernard Shapiro to remove him from the directorship of the Institute of Sexual Science and culminating in the Nazi destruction of the institute, which prompted Hirschfeld to leave Ascona "secretly" because he feared that his former colleagues would betray him and provoke events that could lead to his arrest or even death by Nazi hands.[158] To escape this threat he fled to France, where he initially lived in Paris with both Karl Giese and Tao Li. He retired to Nice after Giese was arrested, imprisoned, and eventually deported from France after "unhappy circumstances"—Hirschfeld also described them as a "trifle"—led to this chain of events.[159] Hirschfeld does not give further details, but according to a contemporary observer the events started with an "occurrence" in the swimming baths.[160] After the traumatic time in Ascona and Paris—in a letter to his old friend the sexologist Norman Haire, Hirschfeld writes about his "depression" about the events in Berlin—Nice seemed to offer a glimpse of hope for Hirschfeld.[161] He notes an improvement in health, starts to make plans for a new institute, and is emotionally buoyed by meetings with old acquaintances, including Eden Paul, who together with his wife, Cedar, would translate and posthumously publish Hirschfeld's *Racism*, and Ernst Maass, Hirschfeld's great-nephew, who would be with Hirschfeld on the day of his death and oversee the funeral arrangements.[162]

Despite Hirschfeld's own life and death being subjected to violence because of his sexual reform work and Jewishness, his account of his travels shows that contrary to his political claims he did not always fully apprehend everyone on equal terms. By examining Hirschfeld's queer exile, then, this chapter troubles the European and North American focus of many histories of sexuality by teasing out some of the coeval developments of modern sexuality across the modern world. But most of all it turns attention to the lingering influence of long histories of oppression even on those who overtly claim to reject racism and sexism. *The World Journey*, despite its accounts of friendship and hospitality, is a text that largely speaks for, rather than with, its subjects, and as such is symptomatic of the limits of Hirschfeld's global homosexual rights activism, which often brushed over localized contingencies and individual experience. *The World Journey* reveals how a degree of detachment[163] allowed Hirschfeld to screen out the voices of the people he encountered on his travels, limiting, to adapt Arondekar and Patel's words, their lives to the exemplary and not the epistemological.[164] Given Hirschfeld's avowed support for anticolonialism, feminism, and social justice, *The World Journey* is perhaps most accurately understood as an example of insidiously transmitted, rather than necessarily overt, sexism and racism, which exposes how affirmative global homosexual politics could retain and perpetuate practices that support discrimination and exclusion even when speaking out for justice.

Coda

How was Hirschfeld's work received after World War II? I examine in the Introduction the complex fate of Hirschfeld's own archive and the serendipitous circumstances that brought some of it back to light, first in 1994 and then in the early 2000s. Here I conclude with a consideration of Hirschfeld's discursive afterlife in the postwar years, using the example of his reception by Alfred Kinsey and his contemporaries as a way into discussing how death and violence animate contemporary debates about queer culture and politics. To some extent the Coda is a reorientation of the forward-looking understanding of sexual debates in the 1950s, debates that are often conceptualized not in the present but as phenomena *in anticipation* of the sexual revolution and the gay liberation movements. Instead I give centrality to the backward glances of Kinsey and his contemporaries to Hirschfeld's earlier sexological efforts, not out of a genealogical impulse—there is no denying the deliberate rupturing with the past of much postwar sexual rhetoric—but to examine what Sara Ahmed has called the "lines that accumulate privilege and are 'returned' by recognition and reward."[1] If Ahmed's concern is with a specific "way of inhabiting the world by giving 'support' to those whose lives and loves make them appear oblique, strange, and out of place," I explore how antiqueer sentiments are transmitted across time before concluding with a consideration of the shifts in alignment between power and queer politics in the twenty-first century.[2]

Hirschfeld and Kinsey in the Nuclear Age

World War II and its immediate aftermath led to the end of what we might call the first phase of sexology in Europe. After the war the center of sexological research shifted from Europe to America as the rights-oriented sexology of Hirschfeld and his colleagues at the Institute of Sexual Science was replaced by the large-scale studies of "American" sexual behavior conducted by Alfred Kinsey and his colleagues at Indiana University.[3] Unlike Hirschfeld, whose reception in gay history has been generally positive and sometimes reverent, Kinsey's contribution to American sexual politics has been more controversial. While some critics have described Kinsey as a "sex crusader"[4] whose "research and the public debates it stirred in the United States helped to legitimate discussion of homosexuality and spur the growth of a gay political movement,"[5] others have argued that the popularization of the distinction between "heterosexual" and "homosexual" supported the persecutory politics of the McCarthy era,[6] not least because, as Janice Irvine has pointed out, Kinsey's "refusal to take stands on political or social issues of the day" fashioned a particular "white, middle-class, heterosexual" sexology.[7]

The diverse responses to Hirschfeld and Kinsey share that they tend to examine prewar German and postwar American sexologies separately.[8] Yet points of connection existed between the geopolitically distinct strands of sex research. Perhaps the most obvious link is Kinsey's impact on West German discourses about sex in the 1950s, where his work received considerable public attention, not least because the newly set-up American cultural institutions in the country—the Amerikahäuser and Deutsch-Amerikanischen Institute—promoted Kinsey's work as part of their efforts to "reeducate" and "reorient" a German population that had been complicit in the Nazi regime.[9] Whereas in Germany, as Sybille Steinbacher's research suggests, Kinsey's work was deployed as part of a sociocultural, American-centric denazification process, in the United States Kinsey figured as a scientist whose rational objectivity encapsulated the values and scientific optimism of the beginning nuclear age. Arguing from the outset that his work represented "scientific fact completely divorced from questions of moral value and social custom,"[10] Kinsey insisted in a later work, *Sexual Behavior in the Human Female* (1953), that he rejected the common assumption that "sexual behavior is either normal or abnormal, socially acceptable or unacceptable, heterosexual or homosexual; and [that] many persons do not want to believe that there are gradations in these matters from one to the other extreme."[11] In place of the established binaries, he presented a model of sexual behavior that favored the metaphor of the continuum over the fixed categories of sexual types that had preoccupied many, but not all, earlier sexologists. One might argue that Hirschfeld's "sexual intermediaries" in their infinite variations anticipated some of Kinsey's thinking, although it is worth noting that Hirschfeld's emphasis on gender as well as sexual desire was considerably more complicated than Kinsey's Heterosexual–Homosexual Rating Scale. Kinsey mentioned Hirschfeld's work in his first major sexual study, *Sexual Behavior in the Human Male* (1948). These fleeting references constitute unique sites of "deconstructive contestation"—points of access to the norms of the postwar past—revealing the (homosexual) limits of Kinsey's avowedly value-free science of sex.[12]

Not long after Hirschfeld's visit to the United States in the 1930s, Kinsey shifted his research focus from zoology to human sexuality. Acknowledging his debts, Kinsey notes that "Hirschfeld deserves considerable credit for having tried on a larger scale than anyone had before to ascertain the facts on a matter that has always been difficult to survey."[13] By "matter that has always been difficult," Kinsey means homosexuality, a turn of phrase that indicates his take on the issue. Kinsey emphasizes his methodological connection with Hirschfeld, figuring the German sexologist as a scientific predecessor when he argues that "down to the beginning of the present study, no more serious attempt [than Hirschfeld's study of homosexuality] has been made."[14] Yet the tone of writing changes quickly. Kinsey takes issue with the fact that Hirschfeld's psychobiological questionnaire was aimed at examining the occurrence of homosexuality in German society, as I discuss in Chapter 2. Kinsey claims that "the uncritical acceptance of these inadequate calculations has delayed recognition of the magnitude of the medical, psychiatric, social, and legal problems involved in homosexuality, and delayed scientific interpretations of the bases of such behavior."[15] Here we find a subtle shift in emphasis from the discussion of method to that of readership, as Kinsey suggests that Hirschfeld's work *delayed* sex research by encouraging an "uncritical" audience response that perpetuated his "inadequate calculations" within a nonscientific sphere. This dismissal problematizes Kinsey's claim in the opening pages of *Sexual Behavior in the Human Male* that his aim is to provide an account of "the man of the street" by "the accumulation of a body of scientific fact that may provide the basis for sounder generalizations about the sexual behavior of certain groups and, some day, even our American population as a whole."[16] The rejection of an audience response in relation to Hirschfeld's work suggests that it was important for Kinsey that the "man on the street" did not set the research agenda. This point is reinforced further by Kinsey's reference to Hirschfeld's "Sex Institute" in Berlin. Kinsey claims that Hirschfeld's data is "uninterpretable," because the patients and visitors who filled out the questionnaire, in Kinsey's view, did not constitute a representative part of society.[17] Ironically, Kinsey's later study, *Sexual Behavior in the Human Female*, would be subject to similar criticism of "methodological inadequacies," because, as one commentator argued, "almost all [women interviewed] came from urban white collar or professional families."[18]

Kinsey's suggestion that Hirschfeld's work was too bound up in the milieu in which it was produced was a direct jibe against the queer orientation of Hirschfeld's work at the institute. If Kinsey clothed his critique of Hirschfeld in terms of methodological differences, his collaborator and coauthor of *Sexual Behavior in the Human Male* Wardell Pomeroy in a later account of their work suggests that methodology was not the main divisive factor between Kinsey and Hirschfeld. Pomeroy points out that Kinsey's findings and Hirschfeld's findings were in fact remarkably similar. For instance, while Kinsey's provided more varied data on homosexuality in relation to age, class, and religion,[19] overall, according to Pomeroy, his findings chimed with Hirschfeld's, whose "famous questionnaire on homosexuality had produced . . . an estimate of 27 percent of such behavior in the population, not far from Kinsey's own figure."[20] Pomeroy goes on to explain that Kinsey objected specifically to the-homosexual-as-scientist, claiming that Kinsey was "offended by Magnus Hirschfeld's open proclamation of his own homosexuality—not because of the behavior, but because he thought Hirschfeld was a special pleader in his work and not an objective scientist."[21] This helps explain the paradoxical position Hirschfeld occupied in Kinsey's work, acknowledged both as the American's most important predecessor in the study of homosexuality and as someone who "delayed" science because of a flawed methodology that drew its conclusions from what Kinsey believed to be a biased database: for Kinsey, Hirschfeld's homosexuality disqualified him as a scientist.

Kinsey's complex relationship with Hirschfeld reveals that he considered heterosexuality both the norm and an implicit condition of scientific objectivity. This reading concurs with observations by some of Kinsey's own homosexual subjects of study in a later reflection of their role in his survey of homosexuality. In an oral history project by the Gay, Lesbian, Bisexual, Transgender Historical Society of Northern California conducted in 1983, historian Len Evans interviewed one of Kinsey's unofficial informants, Samuel Steward, whose account of his working relationship with Kinsey is revealing. On the one hand, Steward emphasizes Kinsey's positive attitude toward homosexuality, recalling with great fondness Kinsey's "liberating influence" and explaining that "we [homosexuals in the 1940s and 1950s] looked upon [Kinsey] as a savior. He was the liberator. He was our Stonewall."[22] On the other hand, however, Steward suggests that Kinsey was keen to dissociate himself from the homosexual participants in his work. Pointing out that Kinsey engaged "a lot of unofficial collaborators whom he depended upon to a very large extent," Steward notes that these collaborators remained "unofficial" in the sense of not being publicly acknowledged.[23] Although this could be explained by the persecution of homosexuals at the time, Steward claims that there were other reasons too: Kinsey "felt he couldn't have any homosexuals on his staff or officially connected with him, because he thought it would taint the study."[24] According to Steward's experience, then, Kinsey's rejection of any official collaboration with homosexuals was not simply a response to the repressive political climate of his time but indicative of Kinsey's assumption that homosexuality tarnished scientific authority.

The Discursive Half Life of Homophobia

Kinsey's disqualification of homosexual authority through the figure of Hirschfeld shows how the process by which, as Heather Love puts it, "the history of queer damage retains its capacity to do harm in the present" is played out in the past.[25] Kinsey recycled a particular homophobic discourse of the prewar years when he discredited Hirschfeld's authority by emphasizing the sexologist's homosexuality. Overtly, Kinsey set out to challenge norms, arguing, for example, in his later work on female sexuality that "somehow, in an age which calls itself scientific and Christian, we should be able to discover more intelligent ways of protecting social interests without doing such irreparable damage to so many individuals and to the total social organization to which they belong."[26] However, the encounter with Hirschfeld, even more than Kinsey's nod toward Christian America, shows up his own need to protect science, making clear that while Kinsey might have been supportive toward his homosexual subjects of study, he was deeply invested in not granting scientific authority to the homosexual to speak for himself.

This kind of policing of authority causes its own damage, as it reshapes expressions of homophobia in a way that allows them to return within new discourse formations. The reception of *Sexual Behavior in the Human Male* illustrates this point through the ease by which postwar commentators similarly reverted to older assumptions about sexuality when formulating their response to Kinsey's work. Most contemporary American responses to the Kinsey reports tended to focus on the extent to which Kinsey's findings reflected accurately on the state of the American population, as well as analyzing the implications of his findings.[27] In West Germany, in turn, Kinsey was a feted figure, seen to be part of the inauguration of a progressive new nation ready to sever its links with the recent Nazi past.[28] That such change operated, however, largely on the level of remodeling rather than rupturing the locations of power and privilege in German society is indicated, for instance, by the fact that one of the main people promoting Kinsey's work in the country was the journalist Walther von Hollander, who had worked as a scriptwriter at Universal Film AG during the Nazi regime. In contrast to the West German and American responses to Kinsey, which were forward looking but heterosexually focused, British commentators picked out Kinsey's claims about the frequency of homosexual practices to distance their own nation from these findings. An early response to *Sexual Behavior of the Human Male* published in the *British Medical Journal* in November 1948, for example, was at pains to dissociate British national life from what was implicitly figured as the excessive amount of homosexual occurrence found in the American population. The article noted that the chairman of the British Social Hygiene Council, Fred Grundy, broadly agreed with Kinsey's findings on homosexuality, arguing that "much the same *pattern* would be found in this country [the United Kingdom]" while nevertheless insisting that in Britain "the incidence of homosexual practices would probably be rather less."[29] Ensuring that the point about the lesser frequency of British homosexuality (and its flipside, the greater occurrence of heterosexuality in the country) not be lost, Grundy concluded with the observation that while "Kinsey had brought a fresh breath of realism to the subject of sex behaviour," the same was "perhaps . . . not so much needed over here as it was in the States."[30] This kind of rhetoric is resonant of older discourses about national stereotyping that located homosexuality in the realm of the "foreign" and sometimes ascribed the occurrence of homosexuality to nations that were considered direct political rivals (such as in the French slang term for homosexuality, *le vice allemand*). It also indicates that homosexuality remained a loaded term, the bearer of an unwanted otherness whose subjects continued to be figured as strange to the nation's normal life.

That Hirschfeld's name still had some currency in these debates is indicated by one of the first book-length responses to Kinsey's work. In 1949, London-based Falcon Press published *Sexual Behaviour and the Kinsey Report*, written by two Americans, Morris Leopold Ernst and David Loth. The book shifted the tone of debate from Grundy's defensive position of UK heterosexuality toward a more open attack on the homosexuality of German Nazism. Ernst and Loth were influential figures: Loth was a prolific journalist and writer, and Ernst was a well-known American lawyer, most famous, as the book's jacket proclaims, "for his defence in cases of so called 'obscenity' in books such as Havelock Ellis's *The Psychology of Sex* and James Joyce's *Ulysses*."[31] Ernst's contribution to the publication of these works (which also included, for example, Radclyffe Hall's *The Well of Loneliness*) in the United States is well documented, alongside his somewhat paradoxical involvement in the setting up of the National Civil Liberties Bureau, support for the Federal Bureau of Investigation, and anticommunist stance.[32] Ernst and Loth celebrated Kinsey's work with patriotic pride, claiming that "the Kinsey

Report sets Americans apart. For today Americans are the only nation who have some sound scientific basis for knowing what the sexual behaviour of their men actually is."[33] Yet if Ernst's legal work suggests that he was sympathetic to sexual reform, supportive of the dissociation of sex from moral and other value judgments, the national framing of the discussion makes clear that he and Loth were no neutral observers. They contrast progressive America with an old European world where, as they argue, "the most sensational and widely reported trials for homosexual behavior have been conducted."[34] The examples they give are both from a German context: The first is the Eulenburg-Harden affair of 1907, in which, as I discuss in Chapter 1, a journalist accused members of the entourage of Kaiser Wilhelm II of homosexuality, prompting a series of libel trials that dragged both the issue of homosexuality and Hirschfeld, who acted as an expert witness on the subject, into the German public sphere.[35] The second instance Ernst and Loth mention is what they call "the Munich blood purge of Captain [Ernst] Roehm" in 1934, in which the Nazi founder of the SA was executed. The operation ostensibly aimed to rid the Nazi party of men Hitler distrusted politically, but it also marks the point when the party distanced itself from homosexual members such as Roehm.[36]

Chapter 4 shows that the complex debates about homosexuality and Nazism clearly form part of the distinct national history of Germany and its reception. However, conceptualizing the homosexual as a threat to the nation did not start or end with the Nazi regime. It infamously resurfaced in North America during the McCarthy era with the report "Employment of Homosexuals and Other Sex Perverts in the U.S. Government."[37] This was presented to the U.S. Congress in the winter of 1950 and is considered the motor that drove the persecution of homosexuals in the decade that followed. Ernst and Loth to some extent anticipate these debates, but in a way that implicates both homosexuality generally and Hirschfeld's sexology specifically in Nazism. They write:

> One of the great studies in sexual behaviour was that of Hirschfeld, who early in the century persuaded 10,000 men and women to fill out a questionnaire containing 130 questions. They were what he called "psychobiological" questions, but on the basis of them and of his medical practice, he reached some conclusions about homosexuality in Germany. One of these was that in the Germany of his day, with a population of 62,000,000 there were nearly a million and a half men and women "whose constitutional predisposition is largely or completely homosexual." Just how big a proportion of his estimated million and half German homosexuals found their way into

Nazi uniform is not known, of course. But a good many of them were attracted by the Nazi principles and the society of their fellows in a bond which excluded all women.[38]

The chilling change of direction in the argument, which moves from a description of Hirschfeld's "great" work to the suggestion that "a good many" of Germany's homosexual men would have been "attracted by the Nazi principles," illustrates the ease by which homosexuality was aligned with the abhorrent without needing further explanation. This is not to deny that some Nazis were homosexual but to question the alignment of homosexuality with Nazism, which is a way of rendering it hateful and justifying its persecution and attack.[39] Morris and Loth show how easily Hirschfeld's name could still be invoked as shorthand for an old, "homosexual" sexology, which is implicated in the rise of Nazism despite the fact that many of the early sex researchers, Hirschfeld included, were Jewish and, as in his case, homosexual victims of the Nazi regime.

Hirschfeld's postwar reception shows, then, that homosexuality continued to be disqualified even, or perhaps especially, in projects such as Kinsey's that overtly sought to replace moral assumptions and social norms with an objective scientific approach to sex. If this realization is in many ways unsurprising—critics of both "scientific objectivity" and the history of terms such as *tolerance* have demonstrated the limits of rhetorical movements that speak progress while retaining the status quo—the backward glances of Kinsey and his contemporaries to the early homosexual rights activism nevertheless also indicate the complex allegiances and disavowals that demarcated queer speakability and livability in the 1950s. While Kinsey's work in certain respects seems to continue Hirschfeld's homosexual emancipation project—his observations on the frequency of homosexual practice normalize difference and in so doing seemingly contribute to a move toward greater tolerance of homosexuality within American society—Kinsey's dismissal of Hirschfeld's sexological authority nevertheless shows up the limits of his objectivity. Kinsey's avowedly apolitical, future-oriented science of sex retains older, negative assumptions about homosexuality, as it implies that scientific objectivity is contingent on the heterosexuality of the scientist. It was partly via the popular success of Kinsey's work that these assumptions were then absorbed into postwar culture. If the evidence of the damage perpetuated here is found in brief textual encounters, its reach is much broader. It shows how homophobia was transmitted through the scientific sphere beyond debates around homosexuality itself: Kinsey's rejection of Hirschfeld marks the "straight turn" of sex research in the postwar years.

(Im)Mortal Queer

What is gained, then, from tracking the lines and allegiances that bind queerness to violence, including death? Lesbian and gay historians, literary and cultural critics, writers, and artists have, initially at least, focused specifically on challenging the denials of queer existence by recuperating the past, recovering affirmative evidence of the richness and persistence of queer existence across time. The recent rise of lesbian, queer, and trans historical novels and (graphic) memoirs, for instance—by Sarah Waters, Alison Bechdel, Jewelle Gomez, and Juliet Jacques, to name but a few—has importantly inserted trans and female same-sex lives in dominant narratives about (literary) history and society. Given the pernicious iterations and reemergences of antiqueer attack against people whose bodies and desires do not match social norms and expectations, the importance of such interventions can hardly be overstated. Sometimes in such creative and critical accounts the past is figured as an affective prop whose "queer touch" caresses and lingers with those who feel a connection with historical subjects.[40] During the AIDS crisis of the 1980s, for example, when the epidemic loss of queer life was widely treated with cynicism, contempt, and discrimination, the British novelist Neil Bartlett wrote an imaginative biography, *Who Was That Man?*, that affectively linked Wilde's life and suffering to Bartlett's own existence as a gay man in London in the 1980s.[41] Bartlett's assemblage of historical fragments and autobiographical narrative demonstrates that the figure of Oscar Wilde continues to animate gay lives long after his death. Bringing into queer touch the losses of the AIDS crisis with the iconic death of the man associated with the emergence of the modern homosexual, the novel troubles the heteronormative time of history. At the same time, however, works such as Bartlett's *Who Was That Man?* are also a reminder that modern queer history tends to be told in foundational moments: the trial of Oscar Wilde and the AIDS catastrophe are just two of the defining moments in English and American male same-sex histories.

Yet queer lives across time are only partly graspable via attention to major historical events and transformations. This book examines the violence concealed in queer history, which is often difficult to bring into view. Considering the impact of violence, including death, on the formation of a collective sense of queer existence, I spend time with the dead and the injured. But I also try to signal where the "homosexual cause" is implicated in the racism and sexism that frame whose lives and deaths are apprehensible in modern Western culture and on what terms. My aim here is not to rehearse narratives of victimhood but to reveal both queer suffering and the suffering that remained in the blind spots of early homosexual rights activism. One of the difficulties in discussing violence and death in relation to queer lives is to avoid, on the one hand, oversimplified cause-and-effect narratives about the impact of persecution and social denial. And on the other hand, I try to circumvent the celebratory imagination that figures some queer deaths, including suicide, in heroic and sometimes liberatory terms. This is not to say that certain queer deaths cannot or should not be understood as products of specific, devastating circumstances. Chapter 2 in particular shows that persecution, social attack, and a cruel carceral system can lead to death from physical illness as well as suicide, an insight that does not deny the agency and political potential of some self-staged deaths. But to claim, as I do, that modern queer culture is shaped by—or *through*—death and violence is fraught most of all because it asks that queer history be accountable not only for its dead but for the violence and suffering perpetuated in relation to modern same-sex rights activism.

In their introduction to *Queer Necropolitics*, Jin Haritaworn, Adi Kunstman, and Silvia Posocco have pointed out that "in the place of simple dichotomies of repression versus visibility, or oppression versus rights . . . sexual difference is increasingly absorbed into hegemonic apparatuses, in a way that accelerates death."[42] Citing Jasbir Puar's work they observe "a recent turn in how queer subjects are figured, from those who are left to die, to those that reproduce life," noting, however, that this turn still excludes some gender-non-conforming bodies and that some queer lives "are targeted for killing or left to die" with some queer deaths remaining ungrievable.[43] If Haritaworn, Kunstman, and Posocco are firmly focused on "the present and future(s) including . . . haunted futures," their words nevertheless speak to my concern with violence and death in Magnus Hirschfeld's work. *The Hirschfeld Archives* reveals the limits of queer apprehension at that point in time when homosexual rights activism was first beginning to take shape. The book documents the violence that made some queer lives (feel) unlivable even as it also reveals how a parochial focus on homosexual rights at times obscured other kinds of injustice and suffering, especially in relation to gendered and racial oppression. A testament to the queer dead whose existence left little trace in the historical archive but whose collective suffering nevertheless caused emotional shockwaves that reverberate across time and continue to haunt the present, Hirschfeld's work shows that violence experienced, committed, and ignored is an intrinsic part of modern queer culture.

Notes

INTRODUCTION

1. While, as Laura Doan has shown, not everyone in the early twentieth century defined themselves in terms of sexual identity, during this time the scientific and cultural debates about sexual types and orientations started to gain more widespread traction. See Laura Doan, *Disturbing Practices: History, Sexuality, and Women's Experiences of Modern War* (Chicago: University of Chicago Press, 2013), as well as her previous study, *Fashioning Sapphism: The Origins of a Modern English Lesbian Culture* (New York: Columbia University Press, 2001). For accounts of the influence of sexology on modernist culture, see, e.g., Anna Katharina Schaffner and Shane Weller, eds., *Modernist Eroticisms: European Literature after Sexology* (Basingstoke, UK: Palgrave Macmillan, 2012); Lisa Z. Sigel, *Making Modern Love: Sexual Narratives in Interwar Britain* (Philadelphia: Temple University Press, 2012); and Hugh Stevens and Caroline Howlett, eds., *Modernist Sexualities* (Manchester, UK: Manchester University Press, 2000). For accounts of the emergence of sexology and modern sexuality, see, e.g., Heike Bauer, *English Literary Sexology: Translations of Inversion, 1860–1930* (Basingstoke, UK: Palgrave Macmillan, 2009); Lucy Bland and Laura Doan, eds., *Sexology in Culture: Labelling Bodies and Desires* (Cambridge, UK: Polity, 1998); Joseph Bristow, *Sexuality*, 2nd ed. (New York: Routledge, 2011); Vernon Rosario, ed., *Science and Homosexualities* (New York: Routledge, 1997); Valerie Rohy, *Anachronism and Its Others: Sexuality, Race, Temporality* (Albany: State University of New York Press, 2009); Siobhan B. Somerville, *Queering the Color Line: Race and the Invention of Homosexuality in American Culture* (Durham, NC: Duke University Press, 2000); Ann Laura Stoler, *Race and the Education of Desire: Foucault's History of Sexuality and the Colonial Order of Things* (Durham, NC: Duke University Press, 2005); Robert Deam Tobin, *Peripheral Desires: The German Discovery*

of Sex (Philadelphia: University of Pennsylvania Press, 2015); and Chris Waters, "Sexology," in *Palgrave Advances in the Modern History of Sexuality*, ed. H. G. Cocks and Matt Houlbrook (Basingstoke, UK: Palgrave, 2005), 41–63.

2. See Rainer Herrn, "Vom Traum zum Trauma: Das Institut für Sexualwissenschaft," in *Magnus Hirschfeld: Ein Leben im Spannungsfeld von Wissenschaft, Politik und Gesellschaft*, ed. Elke-Vera Kotowski and Julius Schoeps (Berlin: be.bra, 2004), 175.

3. My account of events is based on Ralf Dose, "Vorbemerkungen," in *Testament: Heft II*, by Magnus Hirschfeld, ed. Ralf Dose (Berlin: Hentrich and Hentrich, 2013), 4–6.

4. Amy L. Stone and Jaime Cantrell, "Introduction: Something Queer at the Archive," in *Out of the Closet, Into the Archives: Researching Sexual Histories*, ed. Amy L. Stone and Jaime Cantrell (Albany: State University of New York Press, 2015), 3.

5. See, for instance, the contributions to two special issues of *Radical History Review*: "Queering Archives: Historical Unravelings," ed. Daniel Marshall, Kevin P. Murphy, and Zeb Tortorici, special issue, *Radical History Review* 2014, no. 120 (2014); and "Queering Archives: Intimate Tracings," ed. Daniel Marshall, Kevin P. Murphy, and Zeb Tortorici, special issue, *Radical History Review* 2015, no. 122 (2015). See also "Archives and Archiving," ed. K. J. Rawson and Aaron Devor, special issue, *TSQ: Transgender Studies Quarterly* 2, no. 4 (2015).

6. Anjali Arondekar, "Queer Archives: A Roundtable Discussion," *Radical History Review* 2015, no. 122 (2015): 216.

7. Daniel Marshall, Kevin P. Murphy, and Zeb Tortorici, "Editors' Introduction," in "Queering Archives: Intimate Tracings," ed. Daniel Marshall, Kevin P. Murphy, and Zeb Tortorici, special issue, *Radical History Review* 2015, no. 122 (2015): 1.

8. Ann Cvetkovich, *An Archive of Feelings: Trauma, Sexuality, and Lesbian Public Culture* (Durham, NC: Duke University Press, 2003), 7.

9. Judith (Jack) Halberstam, *The Queer Art of Failure* (Durham, NC: Duke University Press, 2011), 186–187.

10. Cvetkovich, *An Archive of Feelings*, 3.

11. Michel Foucault, *The History of Sexuality*, vol. 1, *An Introduction*, trans. Robert Hurley (London: Penguin Books, 1990), 68.

12. For an example of this kind of approach, see Jeffrey Weeks's early work on the production of sexuality as a means of control, *Sex, Politics and Society: The Regulations of Sexuality since 1800* (London: Pearson, 1981).

13. See, e.g., Eve Kosofsky Sedgwick's influential *Between Men: English Literature and Male Homosocial Desire* (New York: Columbia University Press, 1985) and her *Epistemology of the Closet* (Berkeley: University of California Press, 1990). See also Carolyn J. Dean, *Sexuality and Modern Western Culture* (New York: Twayne, 1996), and more recent studies such as Janice Irvine, *Disorders of Desire: Sexuality and Gender in Modern American Sexology* (Philadelphia: Temple University Press, 2005); Heather Love, *Feeling Backward: Loss and the Politics of Queer History* (Cambridge, MA: Harvard University Press, 2007); and Joy Damousi, Birgit Lang, and Katie Sutton, eds., *Case Studies and the Dissemination of Knowledge* (New York: Routledge, 2015).

14. For an indication of the breadth of the scholarship, in addition to the studies already cited, see "Nature and Normality in the History of Sexuality," ed. Peter Cryle and Lisa Downing, special issue, *Psychology and Sexuality* 1, no. 3 (2010); and "Feminine Sexual Pathologies," ed. Peter Cryle and Lisa Downing, special issue, *Journal of the*

History of Sexuality 18, no. 1 (2009); Susan Stryker, *Transgender History* (Berkeley, CA: Seal Press, 2008); Sarah Toulahan and Kate Fisher, eds., *The Routledge History of Sex and the Body, 1500 to the Present* (New York: Routledge, 2013); and Omise'eke Natasha Tinsley's *Thiefing Sugar: Eroticism between Women in Caribbean Literature* (Durham, NC: Duke University Press, 2010).

    15. See Lisa Duggan, *Sapphic Slashers: Sex, Violence, and American Modernity* (Durham, NC: Duke University Press, 2000); Günter Grau and Claudia Schoppmann, eds., *Hidden Holocaust: Gay and Lesbian Persecution in Germany, 1933–45* (New York: Routledge, 1995); Dagmar Herzog, ed., *Brutality and Desire: War and Sexuality in Europe's Twentieth Century* (Basingstoke, UK: Palgrave Macmillan, 2009); Gail Mason, *The Spectacle of Violence: Homophobia, Gender and Knowledge* (New York: Routledge, 2002); and Chandan Reddy, *Freedom with Violence: Race, Sexuality, and the U.S. State* (Durham, NC: Duke University Press, 2011).

    16. See, e.g., Anjali Arondekar, *For the Record: On Sexuality and the Colonial Archive in India* (Durham, NC: Duke University Press, 2009); Heike Bauer, ed., *Sexology and Translation: Cultural and Scientific Encounters across the Modern World* (Philadelphia: Temple University Press, 2015); Chiara Beccalossi, *Female Sexual Inversion: Same-Sex Desires in Italian and British Sexology, c. 1870–1920* (Basingstoke, UK: Palgrave Macmillan, 2012); Howard Chiang and Ari Larissa Heinrich, eds., *Queer Sinophone Cultures* (Oxford: Routledge, 2014); Veronika Fuechtner, Douglas Haynes, and Ryan Jones, eds., *Towards a Global History of Sexual Science, 1880–1950* (Berkeley: University of California Press, forthcoming); Sabine Frühstück, *Colonizing Sex: Sexology and Social Control in Modern Japan* (Berkeley: University of California Press, 2003); Robert Kulpa and Joanna Mizielińska, eds., *De-Centring Western Sexualities: Central and Eastern European Perspectives* (Farnham, UK: Ashgate, 2011); Tse-Lan D. Sang, *The Emerging Lesbian: Female Same-Sex Desire in Modern China* (Chicago: University of Chicago Press, 2003); and Saskia Wieringa and Horacio Sivori, eds., *The Sexual History of the Global South: Sexual Politics in Africa, Asia, and Latin America* (London: Zed Books, 2013).

    17. Regina Kunzel, *Criminal Intimacy: Prison and the Uneven History of Modern American Sexuality* (Chicago: Chicago University Press, 2008), 5.

    18. Nancy Scheper-Hughes and Philippe Bourgois, "Introduction: Making Sense of Violence," in *Violence in War and Peace*, ed. Nancy Scheper-Hughes and Philippe Bourgois (Oxford: Blackwell, 2004), 1.

    19. For a discussion of Munich's queer life and its suppression around the time of Hirschfeld's visit, see Laurie Marhoefer, *Sex and the Weimar Republic: German Homosexual Emancipation and the Rise of the Nazis* (Toronto: University of Toronto Press, 2015), 49–51. For a recent discussion of the German history and historiography of sexuality, see Scott Spector, Helmut Puff, and Dagmar Herzog, eds., *After "The History of Sexuality": German Genealogies with and beyond Foucault* (New York: Berghahn, 2012).

    20. "Kill Dr. M. Hirschfeld: Well-Known German Scientist Victim of a Munich Mob," *New York Times*, October 12, 1920, p. 14.

    21. "Deny Professor Hirschfeld Is Dead," *New York Times*, October 15, 1920, p. 4. The incident was less well reported in Britain. One of the only mentions of it I could find in the British press is from the *Western Daily Press*, which published a mere sentence on the matter, stating that "a Munich message contradicts the reported death of Professor Magnus Hirschfeld who was injured in a street attack." Untitled article, *Western Daily Press*, October 13, 1920, p. 3.

22. This statement is from an article published in a right-wing Dresden newspaper, translated by Charlotte Wolff in *Magnus Hirschfeld: A Portrait of a Pioneer in Sexology* (London: Quartet, 1986), 198. Manfred Herzer notes that not all the German press responded in the same way. He points out that the German socialist and communist newspapers "emphasized the attackers' anti-Semitic motive while exercising a peculiar restraint concerning the homosexual aspect of the entire incident." Manfred Herzer, "Communists, Social Democrats, and the Homosexual Movement in the Weimar Republic," in *Gay Men and the Sexual History of the Political Left*, ed. Gert Hekma, Harry Oosterhuis, and James Steakley (Binghampton, NY: Haworth, 1995), 202. The collection "Gay Men and the Sexual History of the Political Left" was also published as a special issue of the *Journal of Homosexuality* 29, no. 2–3 (1995).

23. Hirschfeld, "Autobiographical Sketch," in *Encyclopedia Sexualis: A Comprehensive Encyclopedia-Dictionary of Sexual Sciences*, ed. Victor Robinson (New York: Dingwall-Rock, 1936), 320. Hirschfeld wrote this autobiographical account in the third person.

24. Wolff, *Magnus Hirschfeld*, 198. Wolff's analysis, which is psychoanalytically influenced, and often speculative, is characterized by a dearth of references. However, historical evidence of the event can be found, including in a letter Hirschfeld wrote to the socialist newspaper *Münchener Post*, which was reprinted in his "Aus der Bewegung," *Jahrbuch für sexuelle Zwischenstufen* 20 (1920–1921): 106–142.

25. Love, *Feeling Backward*, 1.

26. The expression is from Elizabeth Stephens, "Bad Feelings," *Australian Feminist Studies* 30, no. 85 (2015): 274.

27. Ibid.

28. See Sara Ahmed, *Willful Subjects* (Durham, NC: Duke University Press, 2014); Sara Ahmed's posts to her blog, *feminist killjoys*, at https://feministkilljoys.com; Judith Butler, *Precarious Life: The Power of Mourning and Violence* (London: Verso, 2006); Ann Cvetkovich, *Depression: A Public Feeling* (Durham, NC: Duke University Press, 2012); and Love, *Feeling Backward*. See also Lauren Berlant's critique of neoliberal positivity, *Cruel Optimism* (Durham, NC: Duke University Press, 2011); and Sianne Ngai, *Ugly Feelings* (Cambridge, MA: Harvard University Press, 2005).

29. Cvetkovich, *An Archive of Feelings*, 16.

30. Love, *Feeling Backward*, 1.

31. Ralf Dose, *Magnus Hirschfeld: The Origins of the Gay Liberation Movement* (New York: Monthly Review Press, 2014); Elena Mancini, *Magnus Hirschfeld and the Quest for Sexual Freedom: A History of the First International Sexual Freedom Movement* (New York: Palgrave Macmillan, 2010); James Steakley, "*Per scientiam ad justitiam*: Magnus Hirschfeld and the Sexual Politics of Innate Homosexuality," in *Science and Homosexualities*, ed. Vernon A. Rosario (New York: Routledge, 1997), 133–154; James Steakley, *The Homosexual Emancipation Movement in Germany* (Salem, NH: Ayer, 1975); Wolff, *Magnus Hirschfeld*.

32. Elizabeth Freeman, "Time Binds; or, Erotohistoriography," *Social Text* 23, nos. 3–4 (2005): 59. See also Freeman's discussion of the issues at stake in Elizabeth Freeman, *Time Binds: Queer Temporalities, Queer Histories* (Durham, NC: Duke University Press, 2010).

33. Carla Freccero, "Queer Spectrality: Haunting the Past," in *A Companion to Lesbian, Gay, Bisexual, Transgender, and Queer Studies*, ed. George E. Haggerty and Molly

McGarty (Oxford: Blackwell, 2007), 195. See also Carla Freccero, *Queer/Early/Modern* (Durham, NC: Duke University Press, 2006).

34. Magnus Hirschfeld, *Die Homosexualität des Mannes und des Weibes* (Berlin: de Gruyter, 1984), 736–737. The book was first published 1914.

35. Freeman, *Time Binds*, 93.

36. Metropolitan Museum of Art, "One Who Understands," available at http://www.metmuseum.org/art/collection/search/489986 (accessed October 7, 2016).

37. Freeman, *Time Binds*, 93.

38. Kimberlé Crenshaw, "Mapping the Margins: Intersectionality, Identity Politics, and Violence against Women of Color," *Stanford Law Review* 43, no. 6 (1991): 1242. Judith Butler opened the debates about what makes lives livable in *Undoing Gender* (New York: Routledge, 2004).

39. For an insight into the different perspectives on the relationship between queer and transgender, see, e.g., Sara Ahmed, "Interview with Judith Butler," *Sexualities* 19, no. 4 (2016): 482–492, which discusses the tensions, as well as possible allegiances, between queer and trans; Judith (Jack) Halberstam's spatiotemporal critique of queer subcultures and "transgenderism" *In a Queer Time and Place: Transgender Bodies, Subcultural Lives* (New York: New York University Press, 2005), 15; and Susan Stryker and Stephen Whittle, eds., *Transgender Studies Reader* (New York: Routledge, 2006). For a discussion of intersex in relation to queer, see, e.g., Lina Eckert's critique of the antisocial turn, "Intersexualization and Queer-Anarchist Futures," in *Queer Futures: Reconsidering Ethics, Activism, and the Political*, ed. Elahe Hashemi Yekani, Eveline Killian, and Beatrice Michaelis (London: Routledge, 2013), 51–66; *Critical Intersex*, ed. Morgan Holmes (Farnham, UK: Ashgate, 2012); and "Intersex and After," ed. Iain Morland, special issue, *GLQ: Journal of Lesbian and Gay Studies* 15, no. 2 (2009).

40. Ahmed, "Interview with Judith Butler," 492.

41. *Oxford English Dictionary*, s.v. "oblivion."

CHAPTER 1

Material in this chapter was previously published in Heike Bauer, "'Race,' Normativity and the History of Sexuality: The Case of Magnus Hirschfeld's Racism and Early-Twentieth-Century Sexology," *Psychology and Sexuality* 1, no. 3 (2010): 239–249 (www.tandfonline.com).

1. Magnus Hirschfeld, *Racism*, trans. Eden and Cedar Paul (London: Victor Gollancz, 1938).

2. Robert Deam Tobin, *Peripheral Desires: The German Discovery of Sex* (Philadelphia: University of Pennsylvania Press, 2015), 136. Tobin pays attention to the different perspectives on German colonialism by various homosexual rights proponents.

3. Sara Ahmed, *Queer Phenomenology* (Durham, NC: Duke University Press, 2006), 37.

4. See Siobhan Somerville, "Scientific Racism and the Emergence of the Homosexual Body," *Journal for the History of Sexuality* 5, no. 2 (1994): 243–266; and Siobhan Somerville, *Queering the Color Line: Race and the Invention of Homosexuality in American Culture* (Durham, NC: Duke University Press, 2000).

5. Ann Cvetkovich, *Depression: A Public Feeling* (Durham, NC: Duke University Press, 2012), 125, 121.

6. For a discussion of the vital implications of the "framing" of public discourses, see Judith Butler, *Frames of War: When Is Life Grievable?* (London: Verso, 2009).

7. Publications in this area are numerous. Path-breaking studies include, in addition to Somerville's work cited above, Anne McClintock, *Imperial Leather: Race, Gender and Sexuality in the Colonial Contest* (New York: Routledge 1995); Roderick Ferguson, *Aberrations in Black: Toward a Queer of Color Critique* (Minneapolis: University of Minnesota Press, 2004); Ann Laura Stoler, *Carnal Knowledge and Imperial Power: Race and the Intimate in Colonial Rule* (Berkeley: University of California Press, 2002); Ann Laura Stoler, *Race and the Education of Desire: Foucault's "History of Sexuality" and the Colonial Order of Things* (Durham, NC: Duke University Press, 2005); Julian Carter, "Normality, Whiteness, Authorship: Evolutionary Sexology and the Primitive Pervert," in *Science and Homosexualities*, ed. Vernon Rosario (New York: Routledge, 1997), 155–176; Valerie Rohy, *Anachronism and Its Others: Sexuality, Race, Temporality* (Albany: State University of New York Press, 2009); and Omise'eke Natasha Tinsley, *Thiefing Sugar: Eroticism between Women in Caribbean Literature* (Durham, NC: Duke University Press, 2010).

8. See "Magnus Hirschfeld Gästebuch," MS 85.451, Deutsches Literaturarchiv Marbach.

9. See *Oxford English Dictionary*, 2nd ed., s.v. "racism." See also Robert Miles, "Apropos the Idea of 'Race' . . . Again," In *Theories of Race and Racism*, ed. Les Back and Jon Solomos (London: Routledge, 2009), 125–143.

10. Hirschfeld, *Racism*, 35.

11. See, e.g., Shelley Baranowski, *Nazi Empire: German Colonialism and Imperialism from Bismarck to Hitler* (Cambridge: Cambridge University Press, 2011); Benjamin Madley, "From Africa to Auschwitz: How German South West Africa Incubated Ideas and Methods Adopted and Developed by the Nazis in Eastern Europe," *European History Quarterly* 35, no. 3 (2005): 429–464; Volker Langbehn and Mohammad Salama, eds., *German Colonialism: Race, the Holocaust, and Postwar Germany* (New York: Columbia University Press, 2011); and David Olusoga and Casper Erichsen, *The Kaiser's Holocaust: Germany's Forgotten Genocide and the Colonial Roots of Nazism* (London: Faber and Faber, 2011).

12. Hirschfeld, *Racism*, 97.

13. Ibid.

14. Ibid., 176.

15. Magnus Hirschfeld, *Naturgesetze der Liebe: Eine gemeinverständliche Untersuchung über den Liebes-Eindruck, Liebes-Drang und Liebes-Ausdruck* (Berlin: Pulvermacher, 1912), 16. All translations from German to English are mine unless otherwise noted.

16. Ibid., 18.

17. Hirschfeld, *Racism*, 162.

18. The word is "Pansexualismus" in the original. See Hirschfeld, *Naturgesetze der Liebe*, 23.

19. Jonathan Katz, *The Invention of Heterosexuality* (Chicago: University of Chicago Press, 1995), discusses the modern history of the concept.

20. Hirschfeld, *Racism*, 150–151.

21. Georges Canguilhem, *On the Normal and the Pathological*, trans. Carolyn R. Fawcett (London: Reidel, 1978), 151.

22. Ibid., 149.

23. Judith Butler, *Precarious Life: The Powers of Mourning and Violence* (London: Verso, 2006), 16.

24. Sara Ahmed, *On Being Included: Racism and Diversity in Institutional Life* (Durham, NC: Duke University Press, 2012), 179. Writing in a different but linked context (i.e., concerned with college students rather than the academics who teach them), Joyce E. King observed what she calls students' "dysconscious racism," which hinders antiracist efforts not by malice but because of a poor grasp of the issues at stake. Joyce E. King, "Dysconscious Racism: Ideology, Identity, and the Miseducation of Teachers," *Journal of Negro Education* 60, no. 2 (1991): 133–146. The journal, founded in 1932 at Howard University, has deliberately kept its name to retain a link to historical debates about the education of black people.

25. See, for instance, Eric Ames, Marcia Klotz, and Lora Wildenthal, eds., *Germany's Colonial Pasts* (Lincoln: University of Nebraska Press, 2005); and Sara Friedrichsmeyer, Sara Lennox, and Susanne Zantop, eds., *The Imperialist Imagination: German Colonialism and Its Legacy* (Ann Arbor: University of Michigan Press, 1998). Sebastian Conradt's *German Colonialism: A Short History* (Cambridge: Cambridge University Press, 2012), provides a summary of major developments. Britta Schilling, in a study of the private memories of colonialism that still exist in present-day Germany, argues that unlike, for example, in the United Kingdom, where the existence of the British Empire is a continuous presence, in Germany the "collective memory of colonialism was at times discontinuous, with gaps, disruptions, changes of emphasis and moments of 'forgetting,' especially after 1945." Britta Schilling, "Imperial Heirlooms: The Private Memory of Colonialism in Germany," *Journal of Imperial and Commonwealth History* 41, no. 4 (2013): 664.

26. In addition to the studies cited in the preceding note and note 11, see Baranowski, *Nazi Empire*; and Michelle R. Moyd, *Violent Intermediaries: African Soldiers, Conquest, and Everyday Colonialism in German East Africa* (Athens: University of Ohio Press, 2014).

27. *Oxford English Dictionary*, 2nd ed., s.v. "progress."

28. Magnus Hirschfeld, "Über Erkrankungen des Nervensystems im Gefolge der Influenza" (Ph.D. diss., Friedrich-Wilhelms-Universität, Berlin, 1892), 1.

29. Hirschfeld senior set up a medical practice in Kolberg, where Hirschfeld was born. It was mainly distinguished by a focus on alternative therapies such as hydrological treatments. A senior figure in the local Jewish community, he also helped introduce a community sewer system. See Dose, *Magnus Hirschfeld: The Origins of the Gay Liberation Movement*, 17–19.

30. Paul Weindling, *Health, Race and German Politics between National Unification and Nazism, 1870–1945* (Cambridge: Cambridge University Press, 1989), 102.

31. See also Pratik Chakrabarti, *Medicine and Empire: 1600–1960* (Basingstoke, UK: Palgrave Macmillan, 2014), especially his discussion of the history of tropical medicine on pages 144–147.

32. Hirschfeld, "Über Erkrankungen des Nervensystems im Gefolge der Influenza," 15, 32.

33. George Dehner, *Influenza* (Pittsburgh, PA: University of Pittsburgh Press, 2012), 37–41. See also Deborah J. Neill, "Germans and the Transnational Community of Tropical Medicine," in *German Colonialism in a Global Age*, ed. Bradley Naranch and Geoff Eley (Durham, NC: Duke University Press, 2014), 74–92.

34. The original phrase is "vom Osten aus alle Culturlaender mit gewaltigen Armen umfasste." Hirschfeld, "Über Erkrankungen des Nervensystems im Gefolge der Influenza," 1.

35. Studies of degeneration are numerous. See, e.g., Daniel Pick's early work *Faces of Degeneration: A European Disorder, c. 1848–c. 1918* (Cambridge: Cambridge University Press, 1989); and Dana Seitler's more recent *Atavistic Tendencies: The Culture of Science in American Modernity* (Minneapolis: University of Minnesota Press, 2008).

36. Margrit Davies, *Public Health and Colonialism: The Case of German New Guinea, 1884–1914* (Wiesbaden, Germany: Otto Harrassowitz, 2002), 14–20.

37. The phrase is "das Naturprinzip der Rassenveredlung" in the original. See Hirschfeld, *Naturgesetze der Liebe*, 132. There has been some debate about whether the support of eugenics by sexual reformers such as Hirschfeld directly contributed to the emergence of Nazism. Rather than such reductive and somewhat far-fetched arguments about a one-way flow of influence from homosexual culture to Nazism, it is more accurate to point out that both sexual reformers and right-wing hatemongers were animated by the scientific positivism of the turn of the nineteenth century. See, e.g., Marhoefer's excellent critique of the debates in *Sex and the Weimar Republic*, 137.

38. Magnus Hirschfeld, *Weltreise eines Sexualforschers*, ed. Hans Christoph Buch (Frankfurt, Germany: Eichborn, 2006), 157–165. This account is discussed more fully in Chapter 5. See also Silvio Marcus de Souza Correa, "'Combatting' Tropical Diseases in the German Colonial Press," trans. Derrick Guy Phillips, *História, Ciêncas, Saúde–Manguinhos*, March 2012, available at http://www.scielo.br/pdf/hcsm/v20n1/en_ahop0313.pdf.

39. "Royal Prussian Ministry of War" in the original German is "königlich preussiches Kriegsministerium." See Hirschfeld, "Über Erkrankungen des Nervensystems im Gefolge der Influenza," 29.

40. See, e.g., Davies, *Public Health and Colonialism*, 14. She also notes that the number of doctors doubled in Germany between 1876 and 1900, leading to a shortage of work, which might have induced some medical doctors to seek work in the colonies (14–15). See also Deborah Brunton, ed., *Health, Disease and Society in Europe, 1800–1930: A Source Book* (Manchester, UK: Manchester University Press, 2004).

41. Robert Deam Tobin, "Widernatürliche Unzucht! Paragraph 175 in Deutsch-Südwestafrika," in *Crimes of Passion: Repräsentationen der Sexualpathologie im frühen 20. Jahrhundert*, ed. Oliver Böni and Jasper Johnstone (Berlin: de Gruyter, 2015), 277–300.

42. See Tobin's compelling discussion of Hirschfeld's involvement in the case in ibid., 288–290.

43. Bradley Naranch, "Introduction: German Colonialism Made Simple," in *German Colonialism in a Global Age*, ed. Geoff Eley and Bradley Naranch (Durham, NC: Duke University Press, 2014), 9.

44. Shannon Sullivan, *Revealing Whiteness: The Unconscious Habits of Racial Privilege* (Bloomington: Indiana University Press, 2006), 6.

45. See, e.g., Rikke Andreassen, *Human Exhibitions: Race, Sexuality, Gender in Ethnic Displays* (London: Routledge, 2016).

46. See Fionnghuala Sweeney, *Frederick Douglass and the Atlantic World* (Liverpool, UK: University of Liverpool Press, 2006), 178–180; Elliott Rudwick and August Meier, "Black Man in the 'White City': Negroes and the Columbian Exposition 1893"

Phylon 26, no. 4 (1965): 356. Douglass gave his famous "Lecture on Haiti" during the dedication ceremonies of the Haitian pavilion at the World's Fair in Jackson Park, Chicago, on January 2, 1893. It is available at http://www2.webster.edu/~corbetre/haiti/history/1844-1915/douglass.htm.

47. Quoted in Barbara J. Ballard, "A People without a Nation," *Chicago History*, Summer 1999, p. 34.

48. Ibid., 36. See also Bridget R. Cooks, "Fixing Race: Visual Representations of African Americans at the World's Columbian Exposition, Chicago, 1893." *Patterns of Prejudice* 41, no. 5 (2007): 435–465.

49. Zakkiyah Jackson, "Animal: New Theorizations of Race and Posthumanism," *Feminist Studies* 39, no. 3 (2014): 669–685.

50. The image was published as part of a satirical poem by Phillip Egerton, under the pseudonym "Gorilla." "Monkeyana," *Punch*, May 18, 1861, p. 206.

51. Charlotte Wolff, *Magnus Hirschfeld: Portrait of a Pioneer in Sexology* (London: Quartet, 1986), 29.

52. The phrase is "in völlig gleicher Weise" in the original. Magnus Hirschfeld, *Die Homosexualität des Mannes und des Weibes* (Berlin: de Gruyter, 1984), 471. The book was first published 1914.

53. Hirschfeld, *Die Homosexualität*, 471.

54. Charlotte Wolff notes that he was at the fair in that capacity in *Magnus Hirschfeld*, 28–30.

55. Fatima El-Tayeb, "Dangerous Liaisons: Race, Nation and German Identity," in *Not So Plain as Black and White: Afro-German Culture and History, 1890–2000*, ed. Patrizia Mazón and Reinhild Steingröver (Rochester, NY: University of Rochester Press, 2005), 37.

56. Magnus Hirschfeld, "Aus Amerika," *Die Aufklärung* 1, no. 4 (1929): 128.

57. See Christa Schwarz, "Europe and the Harlem Renaissance: 2—Berlin," in *Encyclopedia of the Harlem Renaissance, A–J*, ed. Cary D. Wintz and Paul Finkelman (New York: Routledge, 2004), 344–347.

58. See Robin Ellis, "People-Watching: *Völkerschau* Viewing Practices and *The Indian Tomb* (1921)," in *"Es ist seit Rahel uns erlaubt, Gedanken zu haben": Essays in Honor of Heidi Thomann Tewarson*, ed. Steven R. Huff and Dorothea Kaufmann (Würzburg, Germany: Königshausen and Neumann, 2012), 187–206.

59. Jennifer Kopf, "Picturing Difference: Writing the Races in the 1896 Berlin Trade Exposition's Souvenir Album," *Historical Geography* 36 (2008): 112–138; Norbert Schmidt, *Kolonialmetropole Berlin: Zur Funktion der Völkerschau im Rahmen der ersten deutschen Kolonialaustellung in Berlin 1896* (Berlin: GRIN, 2005).

60. Walter Benjamin, "Grandville, or World Exhibitions," in *The Arcades Project*, ed. Rolf Tiedemann, trans. Howard Eiland and Kevin McLaughlin (Cambridge, MA: Belknap, 1999), 7.

61. David Ciarlo, *Advertising Empire: Race and Visual Culture in Imperial Germany* (Cambridge, MA: Harvard University Press, 2011). See also Wulf D. Hund, Michael Pickering, and Anandi Ramamurthy, eds., *Colonial Advertising and Commodity Racism* (Vienna, Austria: Lit, 2013); Volker Langbehn, ed., *German Colonialism, Visual Culture, and Modern Memory* (New York: Routledge, 2010), 3; and Anne McClintock's influential *Imperial Leather*.

62. Wulf D. Hund, "Advertising White Supremacy: Capitalism, Colonialism and Commodity Racism," in Hund, Pickering, and Ramamurthy, *Colonial Advertising and Commodity Racism*, 31.

63. Wulf D. Hund, Michael Pickering, and Anandi Ramamurthy, "Editorial," in Hund, Pickering, and Ramamurthy, *Colonial Advertising and Commodity Racism*, 10.

64. See Anne Dreesback, *Gezähmte Wilde: Die Zurschaustellung "exotischer" Menschen in Deutschland, 1870–1940* (Frankfurt, Germany: Campus, 2005), 251–254.

65. Roslyn Poignant, *Professional Savages: Captive Lives and Western Spectacle* (New Haven, CT: Yale University Press, 2004). Nigel Rothfels discusses the exhibition of humans in the founding of German zoos in *Savages and Beasts: The Birth of the Modern Zoo* (Baltimore: Johns Hopkins University Press, 2002).

66. Sadiah Qureshi, *Peoples on Parade: Exhibitions, Empire, and Anthropology in Nineteenth-Century Britain* (Chicago: University of Chicago Press, 2011).

67. See, e.g., Ellis, "People-Watching," 187–206; and Kopf, "Picturing Difference," 112–138.

68. For an astute analysis of gender and the colonies, see Lora Wildenthal, *German Women for Empire, 1884–1945* (Durham, NC: Duke University Press, 2001).

69. The phrase is "beschämenden Erinnerungen an die Kolonialausstellung von 1896 in Berlin" in the original. "Rassenfragen," *Deutsche Kolonialzeitung*, September 4, 1909, p. 593. See also Deutsches Historisches Museum, "11. Treptow: Die Deutsche Colonial-Ausstellung von 1896 im Treptower Park," available at https://www.dhm.de/ausstellungen/namibia/stadtspaziergang/treptow.htm#59 (accessed October 8, 2016).

70. The phrase is "wo weiße Frauen und Mädchen . . . Negern aus Kamerun und anderen Kolonien nachliefen" in the original. "Rassenfragen," 593. See also Deutsches Historisches Museum, "11. Treptow."

71. The term here means marriage between white Germans and black people, although the same debate also mentions marriage to Jews. See *Reichsprotokolle* 1912/14,3: 1648. See also, e.g., Wildenthal's discussion of "race mixing" in *German Women for Empire*, 79–130.

72. "Mentally deficient" is "geistiger Minderwertigkeit" in the original. Hirschfeld, *Die Homosexualität*, 391. See also his claim that "from the perspective of racial hygiene the marriage of a male or female homosexual always [would be] a precarious undertaking" (vom rassenhygienischen Standpunkt die Ehe eines oder einer Homosexuellen stets ein gewagtes Unternehmen [sei]). Ibid.

73. For a discussion of these debates, see Medardus Brehl, "Rassenmischung als Indiskretion: Textliche Re-Präsentationen des 'Mischlings' in der Deutschen Kolonialliteratur über den Hererokrieg," in *Rassenmischehen, Mischlinge, Rassentrennung: Zur Politik der Rasse im deutschen Kolonialreich*, ed. Frank Becker (Stuttgart, Germany: Franz Steiner, 2004), 254–268.

74. Tobin, *Peripheral Desires*, 160.

75. Magnus Hirschfeld [Th. Ramien, pseud.], *Sappho und Sokrates, oder Wie erklärt sich die Liebe der Männer und Frauen zu Personen des eigenen Geschlechts?* (Leipzig, Germany: Max Spohr, 1896).

76. Spohr claimed that he wanted to support a movement that was of interest to him: "der mich interessierenden Bewegung nützlich sein." Max Spohr, *Erklärung für die Mitglieder des Kommitees* (Leipzig, Germany: März, 1907), MS IX, p. 36, Magnus Hirschfeld Collection, Kinsey Institute, Bloomington, IN. Spohr also played an

important role in publicizing Oscar Wilde's work in Germany. See Yvonne Ivory, "The Trouble with Oscar Wilde's Legacy for the Early Homosexual Rights Movement in Germany," in *Oscar Wilde and Modern Culture: The Making of a Legend*, ed. Joseph Bristow (Athens: Ohio University Press, 2008), 133–153.

77. The phrase is "die Verwaltung verhielt sich nach wie vor den Eingeborenen gegenüber passiv" in the original. See Franz Josef von Bülow, *Deutsch-Südwestafrika: Drei Jahre im Lande Henrik Witboois* (Berlin: Mittler and Sohn, 1897), 67.

78. See, e.g., *Jahrbuch für sexuelle Zwischenstufen* 3 (1901), which includes an article by Hirschfeld, "Sind sexuelle Zwischenstufen zur Ehe geeignet?" (Are sexual intermediaries suitable for marriage?) (37–71), and a longer piece by a Dr. F. Karsch, "Uranismus und Tribadismus under den Naturvölkern" (Uranism and tribadism in primitive people) (72–202).

79. He received some limited public attention in 1897, when he was arrested on a charge of malpractice because, as the London-based publication *Wings*, the successor to the *British Women's Temperance Journal*, reported in an untitled piece, "He had refused to give one of his patients alcohol who was supposed to need it." *Wings*, February 1, 1897, p. 18. Hirschfeld maintained an antialcohol stance throughout his life, publishing, for instance, a critique of the influence of alcoholism on family life, *Alkohol und Familienleben* (Berlin: Fritz Stolt, 1906), and a study of working-class alcohol consumption, *Die Gurgel Berlins* (Berlin: Seemann, 1907).

80. The original petition, "An die gesetzgebenden Körperschaften des Deutschen Reiches" (To the legislative bodies of the German Empire), has been digitized by Humboldt University; see http://digi-alt.ub.hu-berlin.de/viewer/fullscreen/BV042530362/5. It was signed by many influential doctors, lawyers, writers, and artists. They included the psychiatrist Richard von Krafft-Ebing, author of *Psychopathia Sexualis*, whose work had influenced Hirschfeld's ideas and who was a firm believer in the superiority of Christianity over Islam. See Richard von Krafft-Ebing, *Psychopathia Sexualis, with Especial Reference to the Antipathic Sexual Instinct: A Medico-Legal Study*, trans. F. J. Rebman (New York: Eugenics, 1934), 3–4. Also signing the petition was Hirschfeld's professional rival Albert Moll, who famously sought to "cure" homosexuality and who drew a distinction between "primitive" and "civilised" bodies, arguing, for instance, that a "congenital racial peculiarity" forced "races" other than the "civilised European[s]" to enter puberty at an early age. Albert Moll, *The Sexual Life of the Child*, trans. Eden Paul (New York: Macmillan, 1919), 162, 254. See also Robert Beachy's account of the formation of the Scientific Humanitarian Committee in *Gay Berlin: Birth of a Modern Identity* (New York: Vintage, 2014); Laurie Marhoefer, *Sex and the Weimar Republic*, 125–135; and Florence Tamagne, *A History of Homosexuality in Europe*, vols. 1 and 2, *Berlin, London, Paris, 1919–1939* (New York: Algora, 2005), 61.

81. See Dose, *Magnus Hirschfeld: Origins of the Gay Liberation Movement*, 38–39, which notes that Hirschfeld's friend and colleague Kurt Hiller in 1922 nominated Hirschfeld to stand as a candidate for the Social Democrats. It is not clear if Hirschfeld supported the nomination, and nothing came of it.

82. See Tracie Matysik, "In the Name of the Law: The 'Female Homosexual' and the Criminal Code in Fin de Siècle Germany," *Journal of the History of Sexuality* 13, no. 1 (2004): 26–48.

83. The events are documented in MS XV, pp. 96–111, Magnus Hirschfeld Collection, Kinsey Institute.

84. See Isabel Hull, *The Entourage of Kaiser Wilhelm II, 1888–1918* (Cambridge: Cambridge University Press, 1983), 126–128.

85. According to a Hamburg-based newspaper, for example, both the prosecutor and the judge distanced themselves from Hirschfeld, emphasizing that it was not they who invited him "as an expert" (*als Sachverständigen*). Untitled article, *Hamburger Anzeiger*, December 25, 1907, p. 3.

86. "The Prussian Court Scandals: Count Moltke and Herr Harden," *The Times* (London), October 26, 1907, p. 5. Another article claimed that "attention has been called to the extremely reprehensible character of the pseudo-scientific movement associated with the name of a witness at both trials—Dr Magnus Hirschfeld." "The Bülow Libel Case," *The Times* (London), November 8, 1907, p. 7.

87. Hirschfeld's name was used in the antisemitic propaganda of *L'Action Française*, the daily newspaper, published by Léon Daudet, of a right-wing political movement that was increasingly gathering support. Untitled article, *L'Action Française*, October 5, 1912, p. 5.

88. This was published in the right-wing paper *Germania*, while leaflets distributed outside Hirschfeld's home proclaimed, "Dr Hirschfeld—A Public Danger. The Jews Are Our Undoing." Quoted in Wolff, *Magnus Hirschfeld*, 73–74.

89. The phrase is "alles mühevoll Errungene wieder in Zweifel stellte'" in the original. See Magnus Hirschfeld, "Der Kampf um den § 175," *Aufklärung* 1, no. 10 (1929): 291. See also Wolff, *Magnus Hirschfeld*, 71.

90. Eve Kosofsky Sedgwick, *Between Men: English Literature and Male Homosocial Desire* (New York: Columbia University Press, 1985), 89. See also Edward Kempf, "The Psychopathology of the Acute Homosexual Panic: Acute Pernicious Dissociation Neuroses," in *Psychopathology*, by Edward Kempf (St. Louis, MO: C. V. Mosby, 1920), 477–515.

91. Magnus Hirschfeld, "Sexual Hypochondria and Morbid Scrupulousness," in *Sexual Truths*, ed. William J. Robinson (Hoboken, NJ: American Biological Society, 1919), 226.

92. Ibid., 222.

93. Ibid., 221.

94. Ibid.

95. The phrase is "un rapide movement de la langue at des lèvres" in the original. Léo Taxil, *La Corruption Fin-de-Siècle* (Paris: Librairie Nilsson, 1894), 263.

96. The sentence is "C'est le signe conventionnel, adopté entres tribades, pour dire: 'Je suis pour femme'" in the original. Ibid., 263.

97. Hirschfeld, "Sexual Hypochondria and Morbid Scrupulousness," 221. The American physician William D. Robinson claimed in his editorial footnote accompanying Hirschfeld's claims that the homosexual paranoia of the early Weimar Republic could not occur in America because "only an insignificant fraction of the [American] people know that there is such a thing as homosexuality," a disclaimer that suggests that there is a link between sexual knowledge and behavior even as it also signals Robinson's attempt to dissociate America from homosexuality.

98. Magnus Hirschfeld, *Sexualpsychologie und Volkspsychologie: Eine epikritische Studie zum Harden-Prozess* (Leipzig, Germany: Georg H. Wigand, 1908), 5.

99. George Weinberg, *Society and the Healthy Homosexual* (New York: St Martin's Press, 1992), 149.

100. See, e.g., Elizabeth Cramer, *Addressing Homophobia and Heterosexism on College Campuses* (New York: Routledge, 2014); Andy Harvey, "Regulating Homophobic Hate Speech: Back to the Basics about Language and Politics?" *Sexualities* 15, no. 2 (2012): 191–206; and David B. A. Murray, ed., *Homophobias: Lust and Loathing across Time and Space* (Durham, NC: Duke University Press, 2009). The analytical uses of *homophobia* have been criticized more recently in the context of debates about homonationalism, in which a focus on homophobia obscures racialized and colonial violence.

101. The phrase is "schwere nervöse Störungen nach Malaria und Schwarzwasserfieber in Verbindung mit angeborener Sexualanomalie" in the original. See Hirschfeld, *Sexualpsychologie und Volkspsychologie*, 9.

102. Ibid.

103. See, e.g., Isabel Hull, *Absolute Destruction: Military Culture and the Practices of War in Imperial Germany* (Ithaca, NY: Cornell University Press, 2005); Madley, "From Africa to Auschwitz," 429–464; David Olusoga and Casper Erichsen, *The Kaiser's Holocaust: Germany's Forgotten Genocide and the Colonial Roots of Nazism* (London: Faber and Faber, 2011); Dominic J. Schaller, "Genocide in Colonial South-West Africa: The German War against the Herero and Nama, 1904–1907," in *Genocide of Indigenous Peoples: A Critical Bibliographic Review*, ed. Samuel Totten and Robert K. Hitchcock (New Brunswick, NJ: Transaction, 2011), 37–60; and Helmut Walser Smith, *The Continuities of German History: Nation, Religion, and Race across the Long Nineteenth Century* (Cambridge: Cambridge University Press, 2008).

104. The phrase is "bestialische Graumsamkeit" in the original. See Curt Rudolf Kreuschner, "Die Herero," *Freiburger Zeitung*, January 17, 1904, p. 1.

105. See Michael F. O'Riley, "Postcolonial Haunting: Anxiety, Affect, and the Situated Encounter," *Postcolonial Text* 3, no. 4 (2007), available at http://www.postcolonial.org/index.php/pct/article/view/728/496.

106. Tobin, "Widernatürliche Unzucht!"

107. Heinrich Ploss, Max Bartels, and Paul Bartels, *Woman: An Historical, Gynaecological and Anthropological Compendium*, ed. Eric John Dingwall (London: W. Heinemann, 1935).

108. The phrase is "der eingeborenen afrikanischen Urbevölkerung" in the original. Hirschfeld, *Die Homosexualität*, 559.

109. The phrase is "das Verschiedenartige erscheint ganz geringfügig gegenüber dem Gemeinsamen" in the original. Hirschfeld, *Die Homosexualität*, 527.

110. Anna Katharina Schaffner, *Modernism and Perversion: Sexual Deviance in Sexology and Literature, 1850–1930* (Basingstoke, UK: Palgrave Macmillan, 2011), 118. Schaffner presents an excellent discussion of the scientific assumptions that underpin Hirschfeld's conception of sexuality on pages 112–121.

111. For a fuller discussion of this case, see Heike Bauer, "Measurements of Civilization: Non-Western Female Sexuality and the Fin-De-Siècle Social Body," in *Sexuality at the Fin de Siècle: The Making of a "Central Problem,"* ed. Peter Cryle and Christopher E. Forth (Cranbury, NJ: University of Delaware Press, 2008), 93–108.

112. The phrase is "es [handelt] sich bei der Frau in Algerien um Kolonialverhältnisse" in the original short review, "Die Frau in Algerien," which does not include an author or publication details, in MS XIV, p. 91, Magnus Hirschfeld Collection, Kinsey Institute.

113. The phrase is "Kaiserlicher Bezirksleiter" in the original. Adam Mischlich, *Wörterbuch der Hausasprache* (Berlin: Georg Reimer, 1906), title page. See also Adam Mischlich, *Lehrbuch der Hausasprache* (Berlin: Georg Reimer, 1911).

114. For a discussion of the role of language and colonial power in southern Africa, see Rachael Gilmour, *Grammars of Colonialism: Representing Languages in Colonial South Africa* (Basingstoke, UK: Palgrave Macmillan, 2006).

115. The original reads, "Als . . . das geeinte junge Deutschland mächtig erstärkte und immer mehr Bedeutung in der Welt gewann, sahen die erstaunten alten europäischen Nachbarsvölker diesen Umschwung und Aufschwung nicht gleichgültig, sondern affektbetont an. . . . Lieben konnten die Völker den Emporkömmling nicht . . . darum hassen sie ihn." Magnus Hirschfeld, *Warum Hassen uns die Völker? Eine Kriegspsychologische Betrachtung* (Bonn, Germany: Marcus and Weber, 1915), 35.

116. See, e.g., Sigmund Freud, "Femininity," in *The Standard Edition of the Complete Psychological Works of Sigmund Freud*, vol. 22, *"New Introductory Lectures on Psycho-Analysis" and Other Works*, trans. and ed. James Strachey (London: Hogarth, 1933), 111–135. For a discussion of these debates, see, e.g., Esther D. Rothblum and Lynne A. Bond, eds., *Preventing Heterosexism and Homophobia* (Thousand Oaks, CA: Sage, 1996); and Barry D. Adams, "Theorizing Homophobia," in *Sexualities: Critical Concepts in Sociology*, ed. Kenneth Plummer (London: Routledge, 2002), 170–187.

117. The original phrase is "'Vandalen,' 'wilde Horden,' 'reisende Tiere,' oder, wie eine amerikanische Zeitung sich auszudrücken beliebte, 'die Apachen unter den Völkern.'" Hirschfeld, *Warum Hassen uns die Völker?* 9.

118. The phrase is "Missgunst gegen die Entwicklung und Größe des jungen Deutsche Reichs" in the original. Ibid., 7.

119. "Hatred of the Hun: The Pathology of It Explained," *Manchester Courier*, July 5, 1915, p. 8.

120. Charlotte Wolff, *Magnus Hirschfeld: A Portrait of a Pioneer in Sexology* (London: Quartet, 1986), 161.

121. The original is "Kampf gegen Torheit, Grausamkeit und Mißverstehn . . . ohne Menschenfurcht und Hassen hat er gekämpft—und keinen je verlassen" in Sophie Hoechstetter, "Dr Magnus Hirschfeld," *Vierteljahresberichte des Wissenschaftlich-humanitäres Kommitee während der Kriegszeit: Zum 50: Geburtstag von Dr Magnus Hirschfeld, 14 Mai 1818* 18, nos. 2–3 (1918): 11.

122. The phrase is "Gefahr und Angriff" in the original. Ibid., 12.

123. The phrase is "ein Volk [dass] den Frieden und die Arbeit liebte [und] Greuel und Grausamkeit verabscheute" in ibid.

124. Hirschfeld, *Warum Hassen uns die Völker?* 3.

125. Mancini, *Magnus Hirschfeld and the Quest for Sexual Freedom*, 111.

126. Gilles Tréhel, "Magnus Hirschfeld (1868–1935) et la femme soldat," *L'Esprit du Temps*, no. 125 (2013–2014): 125–137. See also Gilles Tréhel, "Magnus Hirschfeld, Helene Deutsch, Sigmund Freud et les trois femmes combatants," *Psychothérapies* 35, no. 4 (2015): 267–274.

127. The phrase is "übermenschlich gross" in the original. See Magnus Hirschfeld, *Kriegspsychologisches* (Bonn, Germany: Marcus and Webers, 1916), 4.

128. "Psychology of War: Notable German Statement," *Hawera and Normanby Star* (New Zealand), May 1, 1917, p. 2.

129. Ibid.

130. Magnus Hirschfeld and Andreas Gaspar, eds., *Sittengeschichte des Weltkriegs* (Leipzig, Germany: Sexualwissenschaft Schneider, 1930). The first English translation was published as Magnus Hirschfeld and Andreas Gaspar, eds., *The Sexual History of the World War* (New York: Panurge Press, 1934).

131. The phrase is "Interregnum des Gemeinschaftslebens" in the original. Hirschfeld and Gaspar, *Sittengeschichte des Weltkriegs*, x.

132. Marhoefer, *Sex and the Weimar Republic*, 14.

133. For a recent analysis of the liberatory impact of modern gay culture, see Gregory Woods, *Homintern: How Gay Culture Liberated the Modern World* (New Haven, CT: Yale University Press, 2016).

134. Stoler, *Race and the Education of Desire*, 7, 206.

135. Jasbir Puar, "Rethinking Homonationalism," *International Journal of Middle East Studies* 45, no. 2 (2013): 336, 337. See also Jasbir Puar, *Terrorist Assemblages: Homonationalism in Queer Times* (Durham, NC: Duke University Press, 2010); the discussions of race and sexual rights politics in Chandan Reddy, *Freedom with Violence: Race, Sexuality and the U.S. State* (Durham, NC: Duke University Press, 2011); and Cynthia Weber, *Queer International Relations* (Oxford: Oxford University Press, 2016), esp. 47–71. In addition to debates about the deployment of sexual rights discourse by certain nation-states, a huge and varied body of scholarship exists on same-sex-rights activism and visibility across the contemporary world. For an indication of the issues at stake, see, for instance, Naisargi N. Dave, *Queer Activism in India: A Story in the Anthropology of Ethics* (Durham, NC: Duke University Press, 2012); Prince Karakire Guma, "Revisiting Homophobia in Times of Solidarity and Visibility in Uganda," *Rupkatha Journal on Interdisciplinary Studies in Humanities* 6, no. 1 (2014): 97–107; and Lucetta Yip Lo Kam, "Desiring T, Desiring Self: 'T-Style' Pop Singers and Lesbian Culture in China," *Journal of Lesbian Studies* 18, no. 3 (2014): 252–265.

CHAPTER 2

Material in this chapter was previously published in Heike Bauer, "Suicidal Subjects: Translation and the Affective Foundations of Magnus Hirschfeld's Sexology," in *Sexology and Translation: Cultural and Scientific Encounters across the Modern World, 1880–1930*, ed. Heike Bauer (Philadelphia: Temple University Press, 2015), 233–252.

1. For studies on the intersections of violence, sexuality, and the persecution of queer women and men, see, e.g., Gail Mason, *The Spectacle of Violence: Homophobia, Gender and Knowledge* (New York: Routledge, 2002); Carolyn J. Dean, *The Frail Social Body: Pornography, Homosexuality and Other Fantasies in Interwar France* (Berkeley: University of California Press, 2000); Lisa Duggan, *Sapphic Slashers: Sex, Violence and American Modernity* (Durham, NC: Duke University Press, 2000); Günter Grau and Claudia Schoppmann, eds., *Hidden Holocaust: Gay and Lesbian Persecution in Germany, 1933–45* (New York: Routledge, 1995); Dagmar Herzog, ed., *Sexuality and German Fascism* (Oxford: Berghahn, 2005); and David K. Johnson, *The Lavender Scare: The Cold War Persecution of Gays and Lesbians in the Federal Government* (Chicago: University of Chicago Press, 2004). For an analysis of present-day experiences of homophobic violence, see Douglas Victor Janoff, *Pink Blood: Homophobic Violence in Canada* (Toronto: University of Toronto Press, 2005).

2. Ann Cvetkovich, *An Archive of Feelings: Trauma, Sexuality and Lesbian Public Cultures* (Durham, NC: Duke University Press, 2003), 3.

3. The expression "different from the others" is a translation of the title of the early prohomosexual movie *Anders als die Andern* (1919), which includes a cameo appearance by Hirschfeld.

4. See, e.g., Julia Briggs, *Virginia Woolf: An Inner Life* (Orlando, FL: Harcourt, 2005), 395–402, which discusses Woolf's suicide and contrasts it with the suicides of exiled writers such as Walter Benjamin. A diagnostic approach marks Thomas Caramagno's *The Flight of the Mind: Virginia Woolf's Art and Manic-Depressive Illness* (Berkeley: University of California Press, 1992). Esther Leslie's *Walter Benjamin* (London: Reaktion, 2007) discusses his suicide and the range of responses to it since.

5. Jose Muñoz, *Cruising Utopia: The Then and There of Queer Futurity* (New York: New York University Press, 2009).

6. Ibid., 148, 167.

7. Reiner Herrn, conversation with the author, "Humanities Institute 2013: Towards a Global History of Sexual Science" seminar, Dartmouth College, July 2, 2013.

8. Affirmative Anglo-American histories of same-sex sexuality that challenge this negative stereotyping include John D'Emilio and Estelle B. Freedman, *Intimate Matters: A History of Sexuality in America* (New York: Harper and Row, 1988); Laura Doan, *Fashioning Sapphism: The Origins of Modern English Lesbian Culture* (New York: Columbia University Press, 2001); Noreen Giffney, Michelle Sauer, and Diane Watt, eds., *The Lesbian Premodern* (New York: Palgrave Macmillan, 2011); Amanda Littauer, *Bad Girls: Young Women, Sex, and Rebellion before the Sixties* (Chapel Hill: University of North Carolina Press, 2015); and Martha Vicinus, *Intimate Friends: Women Who Love Women, 1778–1928* (Chicago: University of Chicago Press, 2004). See also the growing body of work in other national and transnational contexts—for example, Leila Rupp, *Sapphistries: A Global History of Love between Women* (New York: New York University Press, 2009); Tse-Lan Sang, *The Emerging Lesbian: Female Same-Sex Desire in Modern China* (Chicago: University of Chicago Press, 2003); Michiko Suzuki, *Becoming Modern Women: Love and Female Identity in Prewar Japanese Literature and Culture* (Stanford, CA: Stanford University Press, 2010); and Ruth Vanita, ed., *Queering India: Same-Sex Love and Eroticism in Indian Culture and Society* (New York: Routledge, 2002).

9. Heather Love, *Feeling Backward: Loss and the Politics of Queer History* (Cambridge, MA: Harvard University Press, 2007), 1.

10. Magnus Hirschfeld, "Autobiographical Sketch," in *Encyclopedia Sexualis: A Comprehensive Encyclopedia-Dictionary of Sexual Sciences*, ed. Victor Robinson (New York: Dingwall-Rock, 1936), 318.

11. Magnus Hirschfeld, "Die Gründung des WhK und seine ersten Mitglieder," in *Von Einst bis Jetzt: Geschichte einer homosexuellen Bewegung, 1897–1922*, ed. Manfred Herzer and James Steakley (Berlin: Rosa Winkel, 1986), 48.

12. Andreas Bähr, "Between 'Self-Murder' and 'Suicide': The Modern Etymology of Self-Killing," *Journal of Social History* 46, no. 3 (2013): 620–632.

13. See, for example, Émile Durkheim, *Suicide: A Study in Sociology*, ed. George Simpson, trans. John A. Spaulding and George Simpson (New York: Free Press, 1979), 326–360. More recent studies include Richard Bell, *We Shall Be No More: Suicide and Self-Government in the Newly United States* (Boston: Harvard University Press, 2012);

Howard Kushner, *American Suicide* (New Brunswick, NJ: Rutgers University Press, 1991); Irina Paperno, *Suicide as a Cultural Institution in Dostoevsky's Russia* (Ithaca, NY: Cornell University Press, 1997); Kevin Grauke, "'I Cannot Bear to Be Hurted Anymore': Suicide as Dialectical Ideological Sin in Nineteenth-Century American Realism," in *Representations of Death in Nineteenth-Century US Writing and Culture*, ed. Lucy Frank (Aldershot, UK: Ashgate, 2007), 77–88; Helmut Thome, "Violent Crime (and Suicide) in Imperial Germany, 1883–1902," *International Criminal Justice Review* 20, no. 1 (2010): 5–34; and Thomas Joiner, *Myths about Suicide* (Boston: Harvard University Press, 2010).

14. For an overview of English suicide laws and their Christian underpinnings, see Norman St. John-Stevas, *Life, Death and the Law: Law and Christian Morals in England and the United States* (Washington, DC: Beard Books, 2002), 233–241. Also relevant are Barbara Gates, *Victorian Suicide: Mad Crimes and Sad Histories* (Princeton, NJ: Princeton University Press, 1988); Olive Anderson, *Suicide in Victorian and Edwardian England* (Oxford: Clarendon, 1987); and Ron Brown's analysis of the changing discourses about suicide in *The Art of Suicide* (London: Reaktion, 2001), 146–193. In Jewish history the mass suicide at Masada is seen as a formative, if controversial, event.

15. Henry Romilly Fedden, *Suicide: A Social and Historical Study* (London: Peter Davies, 1938), 247–248.

16. The phrases in the original are "die Kraft," "die Wahrheit," and "gegen die an sich nicht das mindeste einzuwenden war." Hirschfeld, "Die Gründung des WhK und seine ersten Mitlglieder," 48.

17. The phrase is "was mir fast that Herz abdrücken wollte" in the original. Ibid., 48.

18. Friedrich Nietzsche, *Also Sprach Zarathustra? Ein Buch für Alle und Keinen* (Chemnitz, Germany: Ernst Schmeitzner, 1883).

19. The phrase is "den freien Tod, der mir kommt, weil ich will" in the original. Ibid., 109.

20. The phrase is "der mindestens theoretisch volles Verständnis für die homosexuelle Liebe besaß" in the original. Magnus Hirschfeld, *Die Homosexualität des Mannes und des Weibes* (Berlin: de Gruyter, 1984), 421. The book was first published 1914.

21. The phrase and sentence are "Aufschrei eines Elenden" and "Der Gedanke, daß Sie dazu beitragen könnten, daß auch das deutsche Vaterland über uns gerechter denkt, verschönt meine Sterbestunde" in the original. Hirschfeld, "Die Gründung des WHK und seine ersten Mitlglieder," 48 (emphasis added).

22. Katrina Jaworski, "The Author, Agency and Suicide," *Social Identities* 16, no. 5 (2010): 677.

23. Ibid.

24. Cvetkovich, *An Archive of Feelings*, 7.

25. Sigmund Freud, letter to C. G. Jung, February 25, 1908, in *The Freud/Jung Letters: The Correspondence between Sigmund Freud and C. G. Jung*, ed. William McGuire, trans. Ralph Mannheim and R.F.C. Hull (London: Hogarth, 1974), 125–127.

26. Hirschfeld, "Autobiographical Sketch," 319.

27. Elena Mancini renders this notoriously difficult-to-translate name as "The Community of the Self-Owned." Elena Mancini, *Magnus Hirschfeld and the Quest for Sexual Freedom: A History of the First International Sexual Freedom Movement* (New York: Palgrave Macmillan, 2010), 181. I prefer my own translation—Community of

the Autonomous—because I think it captures better the anarchist political leanings of the group.

28. See, e.g., Yvonne Ivory, "The Urning and His Own: Individualism and the Fin-de-Siècle Invert," *German Studies Review* 26, no. 2 (2003): 333–352, esp. 338; and Robert Deam Tobin, *Peripheral Desires: The German Discovery of Sex* (Philadelphia: University of Pennsylvania Press, 2015).

29. They complained that Hirschfeld already had too many other commitments to dedicate himself fully to the leadership of the WhK. However, Hirschfeld ignored opposition and refused to give up the reins. See MS X, p. 40, Magnus Hirschfeld Collection, Kinsey Institute, Bloomington, IN.

30. Ibid.

31. Cathy Caruth, preface to Cathy Caruth, ed., *Trauma: Explorations in Memory* (Baltimore: Johns Hopkins University Press, 1995), vii.

32. Hirschfeld, "Autobiographical Sketch," 317–321.

33. Hirschfeld, "Die Gründung des WhK und seine ersten Mitglieder," 48 (emphasis added).

34. The cultural historian Peter Cryle, in an extensive survey of eighteenth- and nineteenth-century French literature, has shown that male anxieties about the wedding night are deeply entrenched in the cultural imagination. Peter Cryle, *The Telling of the Act: Sexuality as Narrative in Eighteenth- and Nineteenth-Century France* (London: Associated University Press, 2001).

35. Hirschfeld, "Autobiographical Sketch," 318.

36. Victor Robinson, *The Story of Medicine* (New York: New Home Library, 1943), 1.

37. Karma Lochrie, *Heterosyncracies: Female Sexuality When Normal Wasn't* (Minneapolis: University of Minnesota Press, 2005), 24–25.

38. Ibid.

39. See, e.g., Janice M. Irvine's excellent dissection of the issues at stake in *Disorders of Desire: Sexuality and Gender in Modern American Sexology* (Philadelphia: Temple University Press, 2005).

40. Hirschfeld, "Die Gründung des WhK und seine ersten Mitlglieder," 49.

41. Magnus Hirschfeld [Th. Ramien, pseud.], *Sappho und Sokrates, oder Wie erklärt sich die Liebe der Männer und Frauen zu Personen des eigenen Geschlechts?* (Leipzig, Germany: Max Spohr, 1896).

42. Émile Durkheim, *Le Suicide* (Paris, 1897).

43. See Ian Marsh, *Suicide: Foucault, History and Truth* (New York: Cambridge University Press, 2010), 77–192; and Robert D. Goldney, Johann A. Schioldann, and Kirsten I. Dunn, "Suicide before Durkheim," *Health and History* 10, no. 2 (2008): 73–93.

44. Karl Marx, "Peuchet on Suicide," trans. Eric A. Plaut, Gabrielle Edgcomb, and Kevin Anderson, in *Marx on Suicide*, ed. Eric A. Plaut and Kevin Anderson (Evanston, IL: Northwestern University Press, 1999), 51.

45. The expression the "act whose author is also the sufferer" is from Durkheim's *Suicide: A Study in Sociology*, 42.

46. Hubert Kennedy traces their antihomosexuality in "Johann Baptist von Schweitzer: The Queer Marx Loved to Hate," *Journal of Homosexuality* 29, nos. 2–3 (1995): 69–96.

47. Friedrich Engels, letter to Karl Marx, June 22, 1869, in *Marx and Engels Collected Works*, vol. 43, ed. Jack Cohen et al. (London: Lawrence and Wishard, 2010), 295. The translation of the French sentence captures the older connotations of *cons*, which is derived from the Latin *cunnus* and was used in de Sade's work with the sense and force of *cunt*. Its strength was eroded in the course of the nineteenth and twentieth centuries as it became a common disparaging expression for stupid people. I am grateful to Peter Cryle for explaining the linguistic change to me.

48. See Heike Bauer, *English Literary Sexology: Translations of Inversion, 1860–1939* (Basingstoke, UK: Palgrave Macmillan, 2009), 23–29.

49. The original sentence reads, "Daß eine große Anzahl Homosexueller sich im Zusammenhange mir ihrer geschlechtlichen Eigenart veranlaßt sieht, ihrem Leben ein freiwilliges Ende zu bereiten, steht außer Zweifel." Hirschfeld, *Homosexualität des Mannes und des Weibes*, 902.

50. Ibid., 913.

51. The passage is "Paare die sich gemeinsam töteten . . . ziehen die Todesgemeinsamkeit der Lebenseinsamkeit, Vereinigung im Sterben der sozialen und gesetzlich gebotenen Trennung vor" in the original. Ibid., 905.

52. Quoted in Kevin Anderson, "Marx on Suicide in the Context of His Other Writings on Alienation and Gender," in *Marx on Suicide*, ed. Eric A. Plaut and Kevin Anderson (Evanston, IL: Northwestern University Press, 1999), 7.

53. The passage is "Die Homosexuellen leiden nicht an der Homosexualität, sondern an ihrer unrichtigen Beurteilung durch sich und andere" in the original. Hirschfeld, "Die Gründung des WHK und seine ersten Mitlglieder," 49.

54. The phrase is "draußen niemand mehr etwas von ihm wissen wollte" in the original. Hirschfeld, *Homosexualität des Mannes und des Weibes*, 906.

55. The phrase is "selbst im Falle seiner Verurteilung" in the original. Ibid.

56. Ibid., 903.

57. Ibid., 902.

58. Ibid.

59. Ibid., 913.

60. The original reads, "Bitte, nach den Motiven unserer Tat nicht zu forschen." Ibid., 914.

61. Adrienne Rich, "Compulsory Heterosexuality and Lesbian Existence," *Signs* 5, no. 4 (1980): 649.

62. Ibid.

63. For a good analysis of the film in historical context, see James Steakley, "Cinema and Censorship in the Weimar Republic: The Case of *Anders als die Andern*," *Film History* 11, no. 2 (1999): 181–203. For a critique of the film's commercialization of sexuality, see Jill Suzanne Smith, *Berlin Coquette: Prostitution and the New Woman, 1890–1930* (Ithaca, NY: Cornell University Press, 2013).

64. MS XIII, p. 68, Magnus Hirschfeld Collection, Kinsey Institute.

65. Hirschfeld, *Homosexualität des Mannes und des Weibes*, 899.

66. I discuss the episode more fully in Heike Bauer, "Staging Un/Translatability: Magnus Hirschfeld Encounters Philadelphia," in *Un/Translatables: New Maps for Germanic Literatures*, ed. Bethany Wiggin and Catriona MacLeod (Evanston, IL: Northwestern University Press, 2016), 193–202.

67. See Paula Bennett and Vernon Rosario, eds., *Solitary Pleasures: The Historical, Literary and Artistic Discourses of Autoeroticism* (New York: Routledge, 1995), 1–19.

68. Andrew Scull, *Social Order/Mental Disorder: Anglo-American Psychiatry in Historical Perspective* (Berkeley: University of California Press, 1989), 96–118; Jennifer Terry, *An American Obsession: Science, Homosexuality and Medicine in Modern Society* (Chicago: University of Chicago Press, 1999).

69. The full passage is as follows: "Der Arzt, den er in Philadelphia seiner homosexuellen Leiden halber um Rat gefragt habe, ihm geantworted hätte: 'es gäbe für ihn nur drei Möglichkeiten: Selbstbefriedigung (use his right hand), freiwilliger Aufenthalt in einer Irrenanstalt (place himself in a madhouse) oder Selbstmord (or better, commit suicide).'" Hirschfeld, *Homosexualität des Mannes und des Weibes*, 899.

70. See, e.g., Joseph Bristow, ed., *Oscar Wilde and Modern Culture: The Making of a Legend* (Athens: University of Ohio Press, 2008); Ed Cohen, *Talk on the Wilde Side* (New York: Routledge, 1993); Michèle Mendelssohn, *Henry James, Oscar Wilde and Aesthetic Culture* (Edinburgh: Edinburgh University Press, 2007), esp. 197–239; Kerry Powell, *Acting Wilde: Victorian Sexuality, Theatre, and Oscar Wilde* (Cambridge: Cambridge University Press, 2011); and Alan Sinfield, *The Wilde Century: Effeminacy, Oscar Wilde, and the Queer Moment* (New York: Columbia University Press, 1994).

71. For example, Melissa Knox, in her psychoanalysis of Wilde's life, *A Long and Lovely Suicide* (New Haven, CT: Yale University Press, 1996), goes back to Wilde's childhood for the basis of her claim that Wilde was driven by a self-destructive heroism. In a more recent study, *Salome's Modernity: Oscar Wilde and the Aesthetics of Transgression* (Ann Arbor: University of Michigan Press, 2011), Petra Dierkes-Thrun argues that the eponymous heroine of Wilde's popular play was widely understood as Wilde's alter ego and made even more famous after his death in Richard Strauss's opera adaptation, a reception that drew attention away from Wilde's own lonely death (78).

72. Richard Ellmann, *Oscar Wilde* (London: Vintage, 1988); Arthur Ransome, *Oscar Wilde: A Critical Study* (New York: Mitchell Kennerly, 1912), 199.

73. Ellmann, *Oscar Wilde*, 92, 581–582.

74. See, e.g., Joseph Bristow, "Introduction," in *Wilde Discoveries: Traditions, Histories, Archives*, ed. Joseph Bristow (Toronto: University of Toronto Press, 2013), 1–45; and Carol Lorraine Carano, "Mad Lords and Irishmen: Representations of Lord Byron and Oscar Wilde since 1967 (Ph.D. diss., University of Missouri–Kansas City, 2008), 223.

75. Ashley H. Robins and Sean L. Sellars, "Oscar Wilde's Terminal Illness: Reappraisal after a Century," *The Lancet* 356 (November 2000): 1841–1843.

76. Stefano Evangelista, ed., *The Reception of Oscar Wilde in Europe* (New York: Continuum, 2010), provides a detailed study of Wilde's impact. It includes a chapter by Victoria Reid, "André Gide's 'Hommage à Oscar Wilde' or 'The Tale of Judas'" (96–107), which examines the impact of Wilde's death on Gide. See also Bristow, *Oscar Wilde and Modern Culture*; Uwe Böker, Richard Corballis, and Julie Hibbard, eds., *The Importance of Reinventing Oscar: Versions of Wilde during the Last 100 Years* (Amsterdam: Rodopi, 2002); and Nancy Erber, "The French Trials of Oscar Wilde," *Journal of the History of Sexuality* 6, no. 4 (1996): 549–588.

77. The phrase is "Hölle der Homosexuellen" in the original. Magnus Hirschfeld, "Oscar Wilde," in *Von Einst bis Jetzt: Geschichte einer homosexuellen Bewegung, 1897–1922*, ed. Manfred Herzer and James Steakley (Berlin: Rosa Winkel, 1986), 65.

78. Yvonne Ivory, "The Trouble with Oscar: Wilde's Legacy for the Early Homosexual Rights Movement in Germany," in Bristow, *Oscar Wilde and Modern Culture*, 146.
79. Hirschfeld, "Autobiographical Sketch," 318.
80. The latter phrase is "schämte sich des väterlichen Namens" in the original. Hirschfeld, "Oscar Wilde," 66.
81. The phrase is "wie ein unaständiges Wort, bei dessen Aussprache Homosexuelle schamhaft eröteten, Frauen die Augen niederschlugen und normale Männer sich empörten" in the original. Ibid., 66.
82. According to Hirschfeld, they attached the number J.3.3. Ibid., 67. He might have misread the young men's signs, because Wilde's actual prisoner number in Reading was C.3.3.
83. The phrase is "den markerschütterndsten Aufschrei, den jemals eine geknechtete Seele über ihre und der Menschheit Qual ausgestoßen hat" in the original. Ibid.
84. The phrase is "still(e) Freud und Ergriffenheit" in the original. Ibid.
85. Ann E. Kaplan, *Trauma Culture: The Politics of Loss and Terror in Media and Literature* (New York: Rutgers University Press, 2005), 2.
86. Judith Butler, *Undoing Gender* (New York: Routledge, 2004), 219.

CHAPTER 3

1. The category sexual abuse of children was introduced into West German law in 1973, the same year that it was recognized by the U.S. Supreme Court. East Germany had already introduced a similar law in §149 in the 1960s, and the United Kingdom covered "offences against children under 13" in the 1956 Sexual Offences Act. For an overview of key debates, see Jennifer Brown and Sandra L. Walklate eds., *Handbook on Sexual Violence* (Abingdon, UK: Routledge, 2012).
2. This is despite, as Robert Deam Tobin has shown, that as early as the 1860s, when the modern vocabulary of same-sex sexuality first started to emerge, the Hungarian Karl Maria Kertbeny, who coined the term *homosexuality* in 1869, had already attempted "to reassure his readers that homosexuals are not sexually attracted to children." See Robert Deam Tobin, *Peripheral Desires: The German Discovery of Sex* (Philadelphia: University of Pennsylvania Press, 2015), 123.
3. The phrases he used are "Notzucht" (an older term for rape), "Nötigung" (coercion), "Schändung" (which can mean both violation and desecration), and "sexuelle[s] Sebstverfügungsrecht," in Magnus Hirschfeld, "Sexualeingriffe," *Die Aufklärung* 1, no. 7 (1929): 201, 202.
4. Ibid., 202.
5. Louise Jackson, *Child Sexual Abuse in Victorian England* (London: Routledge, 2000). Jackson notes that while the category of sexual abuse in the modern sense was not yet firmly established—Victorians used euphemisms such as "immorality," "tampering," and "ruining"—the existence of such abuse was nevertheless widely known and understood and it was prosecuted in the courts as "indecent assault, rape, unlawful carnal knowledge or its attempt" (3). See also, e.g., Monika Flegel, *Conceptualizing Cruelty to Children in Nineteenth-Century England: Literature, Representation and the NSPCC* (Farnham, UK: Ashgate, 2009); Tanja Hommen, *Sittlichkeitsverbrechen: Sexuelle Gewalt im Kaiserreich* (Frankfurt, Germany: Campus, 1999); Rachel Fuchs, *Abandoned Children: Foundlings and Child Welfare in Nineteenth-Century France* (Albany: State

University of New York Press, 1984); and John E. B. Myers, "A Short History of Child Protection in America," *Family Law Quarterly* 42, no. 3 (2008): 449–463.

6. Shani D'Cruze, "Sexual Violence since 1750," in *The Routledge History of Sex and the Body*, ed. Kate Fisher and Sarah Toulahan (Abingdon, UK: Routledge, 2013), 444–460.

7. In a thought-provoking collection of essays on contemporary child-law debates, Jo Bridgeman and Daniel Monk point out the shift in focus from "social and political concern for *children* [to] the importance of *childhood* as a category of cultural and governmental significance for society as a whole." Jo Bridgeman and Daniel Monk, "Introduction: Reflections on the Relationship between Feminism and Child Law," in *Feminist Perspectives on Child Law*, ed. Jo Bridgeman and Daniel Monk (London: Cavendish, 2000), 1 (emphasis in original).

8. W. T. Stead, "The Maiden Tribute of Modern Babylon," *Pall Mall Gazette*, July 1885. The main four articles on the investigation were published July 6, 7, 8, and 10, respectively; they were preceded and followed by articles framing the discussion. For an early analysis of the case, see Judith Walkowitz, *City of Dreadful Delight: Narratives of Sexual Danger in Late-Victorian London* (Chicago: University of Chicago Press, 1992).

9. See, e.g., Joseph Bristow, "Wilde, *Dorian Gray* and Gross Indecency," in *Sexual Sameness: Textual Difference in Lesbian and Gay Writing*, ed. Joseph Bristow (Abingdon, UK: Routledge, 2014), 44–62; and Matt Cook, *London and the Culture of Homosexuality, 1885–1914* (Cambridge: University of Cambridge Press, 2003), 45.

10. Jackson, *Child Sexual Abuse in Victorian England*, 4–5.

11. See, e.g., Lucy Bland, *Banishing the Beast: Sexuality and the Early Feminists* (London: Penguin, 1995); Kate Lawson and Lynn Shakinovsky, *The Marked Body: Domestic Violence in Mid-Nineteenth-Century Literature* (Albany: State University of New York Press, 2002); Elena Mancini, *Magnus Hirschfeld and the Quest for Sexual Freedom: A History of the First International Sexual Freedom Movement* (New York: Palgrave Macmillan, 2010); and Chris Weedon, *Gender, Feminism, and Fiction in Germany, 1840–1914* (New York: Peter Lang, 2006).

12. Jana Funke, "'We Cannot Be Greek Now': Age Difference, Corruption of Youth and the Making of *Sexual Inversion*," *English Studies* 94, no. 2 (2013): 139–153; Jackson, *Child Sexual Abuse in Victorian England*. See also Laura Doan's discussion of debates about predatory older lesbians in *Fashioning Sapphism: The Origins of a Modern Lesbian Culture* (New York: Columbia University Press, 2001), 31–63; and Montgomery Hyde, *The Other Love: A Historical and Contemporary Survey of Homosexuality in Britain* (London: Mayflower, 1972).

13. Richard von Krafft-Ebing, *Psychopathia Sexualis with Especial Reference to the Antipathic Sexual Instinct: A Medico-Legal Study*, trans. F. J. Rebman (New York: Eugenics, 1934), 555. He discusses four cases on pages 555–558. See also Steven Angelides, "The Emergence of the Paedophile in the Late Twentieth Century," *Australian Historical Studies* 36, no. 126 (2005): 272–295.

14. See Sigmund Freud, "The Aetiology of Hysteria," in *The Standard Edition of the Complete Psychological Works of Sigmund Freud*, vol. 3, *Early Psycho-Analytic Publications*, trans. and ed. James Strachey (London: Hogarth, 1978), 187–221. Jeffrey Masson famously argued that Freud himself suppressed knowledge of child abuse. See Jeffrey Masson, *The Assault on Truth: Freud's Suppression of the Seduction Theory* (New York: Farrar, Straus, and Giroux, 1984).

15. See, e.g., Wilhelm Stekel, *Die Geschlechtskälte der Frau* (Berlin: Urban and Schwarzenberg, 1921); and Wilhelm Stekel, *Peculiarities of Behaviour: Wandering Mania, Dipsomania, Cleptomania, Pyromania and Allied Impulsive Acts*, vol. 1, trans. James S. van Teslaar (London: Williams Norgate, 1925). See also Tobin, *Peripheral Desires*, esp. 72; and Lutz D. H. Sauerteig, "Loss of Innocence: Albert Moll, Sigmund Freud, and the Invention of Childhood Sexuality around 1900," *Medical History* 56, no. 2 (2012): 156–183.

16. Auguste Ambroise Tardieu, "Etude médico-légale sur les sévices et mauvais traitements exercés sur des enfants," *Annales d'hygiène publique et de médecine légale* 12 (1860): 361–398. See also Jean Labbé, "Ambroise Tardieu: The Man and His Work on Child Maltreatment a Century before Kempe," *Child Abuse and Neglect* 29 (2005): 311–324; Vernon A. Rosario, *The Erotic Imagination: French Histories of Perversity* (Oxford: Oxford University Press, 1997); and Lisa DeTora, "Recognizing the Trauma: Battering and the Discourse of Domestic Violence," in *Gender Scripts in Medicine and Narrative*, ed. Marcelline Block and Angela Laflen (Cambridge: Cambridge Scholars, 2010), 238–268.

17. He discussed what he called, for example, "d'attentats commis sur les enfants" (attacks on children). Auguste Ambroise Tardieu, *Étude Médico-Légale sur les Attentats aux Mœurs* (Paris: Charpentier, 1857), 8. See also Ivan Crozier, "All the Appearances Were Perfectly Normal: The Anus and the Sodomite in Nineteenth-Century Medical Discourse," in *Body Parts: Critical Explorations in Corporeality*, ed. Christopher E. Forth and Ivan Crozier (Lanham, MD: Lexington, 2005), 65–84.

18. Linda Dowling's *Hellenism and Homosexuality in Victorian Oxford* (Ithaca, NY: Cornell University Press, 1994) provides a detailed discussion of this development including in relation to representations of boys in work of famous men who loved men, such as John Addington Symonds and Oscar Wilde.

19. See, e.g., Stefano Evangelista, "'Lovers and Philosophers at Once': Aesthetic Platonism in the Victorian Fin de Siècle," *Yearbook of English Studies* 36, no. 2 (2006): 203–244; and the materials on boy love gathered by Chris White, ed., *Nineteenth-Century Writings on Homosexuality: A Sourcebook* (London: Routledge, 1999), 317–325.

20. See, for instance, William Johnson's *Ionica*, which includes poems such as "A Study of Boyhood" (61–64) and was published as William Cory, *Ionica* (London: George Allen, 1905). See also Dowling, *Hellenism and Homosexuality*, 114.

21. Martha Vicinus, "The Adolescent Boy: Fin-de-Siècle Femme Fatale?," in *Victorian Sexual Dissidence*, ed. Richard Dellamora (Chicago: University of Chicago Press, 1999), 84.

22. Ibid.

23. Funke, "We Cannot Be Greek Now," 139–153.

24. John Addington Symonds, *The Memoirs of John Addington Symonds*, ed. Phyllis Grosskurth (London: Hutchinson, 1984), 16. See also Funke, "We Cannot Be Greek Now," 149.

25. See Heike Bauer, *English Literary Sexology: Translations of Inversion, 1860–1930* (Basingstoke, UK: Palgrave Macmillan, 2009), 64.

26. John Francis Bloxham [X, pseud.], "The Priest and the Acolyte," *The Chameleon* 1, no. 1 (1894): 29–47.

27. Lisa Hamilton, "Oscar Wilde, New Women and the Rhetoric of Effeminacy," in *Wilde Writings: Contextual Conditions*, ed. Joseph Bristow (Toronto: University of Toronto Press, 2003), 242.

28. Bloxham, "The Priest and the Acolyte," 47.

29. Chris White claims that Wilde called the work "disgusting, perfect twaddle." See White, *Nineteenth-Century Writings on Homosexuality*, 353n41.

30. Jackson, *Child Sexual Abuse in Victorian England*, 3.

31. Magnus Hirschfeld, "Aus England," *Die Aufklärung* 1, no. 3 (1929): 3.

32. Magnus Hirschfeld, *Die Homosexualität des Mannes und des Weibes* (Berlin: de Gruyter, 1984), 669. The book was first published 1914, with an introduction by E. J. Haeberle.

33. He mentions that the missionary's account was published in a May 1910 issue of the *Peking Daily News*. While other issues of this paper still exist in libraries in China, North America, and England, this particular issue seems curiously to have gone missing. I am grateful to Leon Rocha and Liying Sun for helping me with my search.

34. The phrase is "zu allem erbötig" in Hirschfeld, *Die Homosexualität des Mannes und des Weibes*, 616.

35. The original passage reads, "Wie wenig das Volk im Grunde genommen an homosexuellem Verkehre Anstoβ nimmt, lehrt wohl am besten die Tatsache, daβ die Eltern selbst sowohl Töchter als Söhne oft schon in jugendlichem Alter an öffentliche Häuser abgeben, weil sie glauben, ihnen so eine bessere Zukunft zu sichern, als sie selbst sie ihnen bieten vermögen." Ibid., 617.

36. For a discussion of how adolescence was defined at the time, see Don Romesburg, "Making Adolescence More or Less Modern," in *The Routledge History of Childhood in the Western World*, ed. Paula S. Fass (New York: Routledge, 2013), 236–238.

37. Quoted in Harry Oosterhuis and Hubert Kennedy, eds., *Homosexuality and Male Bonding in Pre-Nazi Germany: The Youth Movement, the Gay Movement and Male Bonding before Hitler's Rise; Original Transcripts from "Der Eigene," the First Gay Journal in the World* (Binghampton, UK: Haworth, 2011), 121.

38. Tobin, *Peripheral Desires*, 123.

39. Hirschfeld, *Die Homosexualität des Mannes und des Weibes*, 590.

40. See, e.g., Edward Ross Dickinson, *The Politics of German Child Welfare from the Empire to the Federal Republic* (Cambridge, MA: Harvard University Press, 1996), 18–30; and Rachel Fuchs, *Gender and Poverty in Nineteenth-Century Europe* (Cambridge: Cambridge University Press, 2005), 159.

41. Karl Heinrich Ulrichs, *Forschungen über das Rätsel der mannmänlichen Liebe* (Leipzig, Germany: Selbstverlag des Verfassers, 1864).

42. See, e.g., Karl Heinrich Ulrichs, *Memnon: Die Geschlechtsnatur des mannliebenden Urnings* (Schleiz, Germany: Hugo Benn, 1868).

43. The German reads, 'Kreuzige, kreuzige!" Karl Heinrich Ulrichs, *Gladius furens: Das Naturräthsel der Urningsliebe und der Irrtum des Gesetzgebers*, ed. Wolfram Setz (1868; Munich: Forum Homosexualität, 2000), 7. See also Bauer, *English Literary Sexology*, 23–29.

44. According to observers Virchow used the term in a parliamentary speech in 1873. See, e.g., Thilo Rauch, *Die Ferienkoloniebewegung: Zur Geschichte der privaten Fürsorge im Kaiserreich* (Wiesbaden, Germany: Springer, 1992), 79. See also Mancini, *Magnus Hirschfeld and the Quest for Sexual Freedom*, 21; and Marsha Morton, *Max*

Klinger and Wilhelmine Culture: On the Threshold of German Modernism (Farnham, UK: Ashgate, 2014), 100–101.

45. Sonja Weinberg has pointed out, for example, the antisemitism at the heart of many Catholic responses to liberalism in *Pogroms and Riots: German Press Responses to Anti-Jewish Violence in Germany* (Frankfurt, Germany: Peter Lang, 2010).

46. Wilhelm Reich, *Die Sexualität im Kulturkampf: Zur sozialistischen Umstrukturierung des Menschen*, 2nd ed. (Berlin: Sexualpolitik, 1936).

47. See Magnus Hirschfeld, "New Morals for Old in Soviet Russia," *Illustrated London News*, April 6, 1929, p. 586.

48. For a fuller discussion of the article, see Bauer, *English Literary Sexology*, 46–47.

49. Hirschfeld, "New Morals for Old in Soviet Russia," 586–587.

50. Ibid., 586.

51. Ibid.

52. Magnus Hirschfeld, "Das Russische Strafrecht," *Die Aufklärung* 1, no. 8 (1929): 225–227.

53. The full text of the 1794 code is available (in German) via the free online legal repository OpinoIuris, at http://opinioiuris.de/quelle/1621.

54. The phrase is "geeignete Zuchtmittel" in the original. See Die Geprügelte Generation, "Die Rolle der Justiz," available at http://gepruegelte-generation.de/hintergrundinformationen/die-rolle-der-justiz (accessed October 10, 2016).

55. The law was reworded in 1958 to give the "carer" the right to castigate the child. It was abolished in 2000 when a child's right to be raised without violence (*gewaltfreie Erziehung*) was enshrined in the German civil code.

56. See Marjory Lamberti, "Radical Schoolteachers and the Origins of the Progressive Education Movement in Germany, 1900–1914," *History of Education Quarterly* 40, no. 1 (2000): 22–48.

57. Lynn Abrams, "Crime against Marriage? Wife-Beating, the Law and Divorce in Nineteenth-Century Hamburg," in *Gender and Crime in Modern Europe*, ed. Meg Arnot and Cornelie Usborne (London: UCL Press, 2001), 120.

58. Magnus Hirschfeld and Ewald Bohm, *Sexualerziehung: Der Weg durch Natürlichkeit zur neuen Moral* (Berlin: Universitas, 1930). See also Ewald Bohm, *Lehrbuch der Rorschach-Psychodiagnostik* (Zurich, Switzerland: Huber, 1957).

59. Magnus Hirschfeld, *Das urnische Kind* (Berlin: Urban and Schwarzenberg, 1903). For an overview of the historical debates, see R. Danielle Egan and Gail Hawkes, *Theorizing the Sexual Child in Modernity* (Basingstoke, UK: Palgrave Macmillan, 2010), esp. 75–97.

60. Hirschfeld, *Das urnische Kind*, 6, 8.

61. Albert Moll, *Das Sexualleben des Kindes* (Leipzig, Germany: Vogel, 1908); and Albert Moll, *The Sexual Life of the Child*, trans. Eden Paul (New York: Macmillan, 1912). See also Egan and Hawkes, *Theorizing the Sexual Child*, 92. Eden Paul, sometimes together with Cedar Paul, translated many of Hirschfeld's works into English.

62. The original text reads, "Die meisten Selbstmorde . . . haben sexuelle Motive." Hirschfeld and Bohm, *Sexualerziehung*, 12.

63. Ibid., 11.

64. Ibid., 232, 230.

65. The phrase is "echt von unecht unterscheiden," which literally translates as "real from false." Ibid., 234.

66. Magnus Hirschfeld, *Sexualität und Kriminalität* (Berlin: Renaissance, 1924).

67. For an excellent discussion of the gendered history of child sexual abuse, see Andrea Josipovic, "Secret Things and the Confinement of Walls: 'The Private Sphere' in Crimes of Child Sexual Abuse Perpetrated by Women," *Australian Feminist Studies* 30, no. 85 (2015): 252–272.

68. Hirschfeld, *Sexualität und Kriminalität*, 12.

69. Ibid.

70. Friedemann Pfaefflin, "The Surgical Castration of Detained Sex Offenders Amounts to Degrading Treatment," *Sexual Offender Treatment* 5, no. 2 (2010), available at http://www.sexual-offender-treatment.org/86.html. The practice is highly controversial and regularly discussed in German and Anglophone media. For a brief English summary of the German castration law, see Tade Matthias Spanger, *Medical Law in Germany* (Alphen, Netherlands: Kluwer, 2011), 118; and Florence Tamagne, *A History of Homosexuality in Europe*, vols. 1 and 2, *Berlin, London, Paris, 1919–1939* (New York: Algora, 2006), 400–401. For accounts of the castration of homosexuals under the Nazi regime, see Geoffrey J. Giles, "'The Most Unkindest Cut of All': Castration, Homosexuality, and Nazi Justice," *Journal of Contemporary History* 27, no. 1 (1992): 41–61; and Stefan Micheler, "Homophobic Propaganda and the Denunciation of Same-Sex Desiring Men under National Socialism," trans. Patricia Szobar, in *Sexuality and German Fascism*, ed. Dagmar Herzog (London: Berghahn, 2005), 95–135. From a different critical angle—and with a focus on Asian men in North America—David L. Eng's *Racial Castration: Managing Masculinity in Asian America* (Durham, NC: Duke University Press, 2001) is useful for thinking through the racialized and sexualized fantasies that support castration practices.

71. Details are on the initiative's website, in both English and German, at https://www.dont-offend.org.

72. The phrase is "gewaltsamen Verstümmelungen" in Hirschfeld, *Sexualität und Kriminalität*, 13.

73. The original phrase is "ob sie den Verlust ihrer Freiheit oder den Verlust ihrer Geschlechtsdrüsen vorziehen." Ibid.

74. The original phrase is "gemeingefährliche Triebstörung." Ibid.

75. The original phrase is "um mit dem Gesetz nicht in Konflikt zu kommen." Ibid.

76. The full original sentence reads, "Bei intersexuellen Männern und Frauen beispielsweise, die gelengentlich aus eigenem Entschluss diesen Eingriff an sich vornehmen lassen, um mit dem Gesetz nicht in Konflikt zu kommen, have ich ein völliges Erlöschen ihrer Triebrichtung nicht beobachten können" (In intersexual men and women, for example, who occasionally made the decision to have the procedure to avoid conflict with the law, I observed no complete cessation of the sexual drive). Ibid.

77. The phrase is "sie wünschen, dass man alles versuche, um ihre körperliche Beschaffenheit mit ihrer seelischen anzupassen" in ibid., 35. That many of Hirschfeld's transvestite patients experienced their body as "problematic" is discussed further in Rainer Herrn, *Schnittmuster des Geschlechts: Transvestitismus und Transsexualität in der frühen Sexualwissenschaft* (Giessen, Germany: Psychosozial, 2005), 103–105.

78. Hirschfeld, *Sexualität und Kriminalität*, 32–33.

79. For critiques of the medicalization and mutilation of intersex bodies, see, e.g., Georgiann Davis, *Contesting Intersex: The Dubious Diagnosis* (New York: New York University Press, 2015); Morgan Holmes, ed., *Critical Intersex* (Farnham, UK: Ashgate, 2012); Iain Morland, ed., "Intersex and After," special issue, *GLQ: Journal of Lesbian*

and Gay Studies 15, no. 2 (2009); Elizabeth Reis, *Bodies in Doubt: An American History of Intersex* (Baltimore: Johns Hopkins University Press, 2010); Katrina Roen, "Queer Kids: Toward Ethical Clinical Interactions with Intersex People," in *Ethics of the Body: Postconventional Challenges*, ed. Margrit Shildrick and Roxanne Mykitiuk (Cambridge, MA: MIT Press, 2005), 259–278; and Del La Grace Volcano, "The Herm Portfolio," *GLQ: Journal of Lesbian and Gay Studies* 15, no. 2 (2009): 261–265. See also Del La Grace Volcano's "gender abolitionist" photography at http://www.dellagracevolcano.com/statement.html.

80. Magnus Hirschfeld, *Übergänge zwischen dem männlichen und weiblichen Geschlecht* (Leipzig, Germany: Malende, 1904), 14.

81. Magnus Hirschfeld, "Was eint und trennt das Menschengeschlecht?" *Die Aufklärung* 1, nos. 11–12 (1929): 321.

82. Hirschfeld, *Sexualität und Kriminalität*, 13.

83. The phrase is "psychosexueller Infantilismus." Ibid.

84. Sigmund Freud, "Totem and Taboo," in *The Standard Edition of the Complete Psychological Works of Sigmund Freud*, vol. 13, *"Totem and Taboo" and Other Works*, trans. and ed. James Strachey (London: Hogarth, 1933), 16.

85. The original passage reads, "Zur Ehre der Menschheit sei es gesagt, dass die meisten Kinderschänder bei gewissenhafter Untersuchung sich nicht als willkürliche, bösartige Verbrecher erweisen, sondern als geistig, körperlich und genital zurückgebliebene Menschen." Hirschfeld, *Sexualität und Kriminalität*, 14.

86. Magnus Hirschfeld, "Die Bestrafung sexueller Triebabweichungen," in *Zur Reform des Sexualstrafrechts* (Bern, Switzerland: Bircher, 1926), 159.

87. Lisa Downing, *The Subject of Murder: Gender, Exceptionality, and the Modern Killer* (Chicago: University of Chicago Press, 2013).

88. Hirschfeld and Bohm, *Sexualerziehung*, 13–14.

89. Ibid.

90. Ibid., 9.

91. Hirschfeld sets out the case for sexology's reform potential in his foreword to Felix Halle, *Geschlechtsleben und Strafrecht* (Berlin: Mopr Verlag, 1931), ix–xii.

92. Magnus Hirschfeld, "Prügelpädagogen," *Die Aufklärung* 1, no. 4 (1929): 97.

93. Ibid.

94. See "Ammon, Therese," *Weblexikon der Wiener Sozialdemokratie*, available at http://www.dasrotewien.at/ammon-therese.html (accessed October 10, 2016).

95. "Die Kinderhölle in Mariaquell," *Die Unzufriedene: Eine unabhängige Wochenschrift für alle Frauen* 7, no. 12 (1929): 1–12.

96. Ibid., 1.

97. The phrase is "fromme Kinderfreunde" in Hirschfeld, "Prügelpädagogen," 97.

98. Ute Thyen and Irene Johns, "Recognition and Prevention of Child Sexual Abuse in Germany," in *Child Abuse in Europe*, ed. Corinne May-Chahal and Maria Herzog (Strasbourg, France: Council of Europe, 2003), 80.

99. UN Human Rights, "Convention on the Rights of the Child," 1990, available at http://www.ohchr.org/en/professionalinterest/pages/crc.aspx.

100. Karen Wells and Heather Montgomery, "Everyday Violence and Social Recognition," in *Childhood, Youth and Violence in Global Context: Research and Practice in Dialogue*, ed. Karen Wells, Erica Burman, Heather Montgomery, and Alison Watson (Basingstoke, UK: Palgrave Macmillan, 2014), 8.

101. Ibid., 11.

102. The phrase is "der einem Kinde von 13 Jahren gegenüber zärtlich geworden ist" in Hirschfeld, "Prügelpädagogen," 97.

103. The original passage reads, "Wir sind gewiss für weitgehenden Jugendschutz, aber wir besitzen die Kühnheit, offen auszusprechen, dass dieses Messen mit ungleichem Mass, wenn es sich um einen Schlag und wenn es sich um einen Kuss auf die Backe handelt, auch eine der vielen Ungereimtheiten ist, die einer aufgeklärten Zeit kaum noch verständlich sein werden." Ibid., 97.

104. Volkmar Sigusch, ed., *Personenlexikon der Sexualforschung* (Frankfurt, Germany: Campus, 2009), 389.

105. The phrase is "flüchtige, impulsiv, unvorbereitete" in Hirschfeld, "Prügelpädagogen," 98.

106. The original phrase is "sich nicht auf die Geschlechtsteile erstreckte." Ibid., 98.

107. Antu Soreinen, "Cross-Generational Relationships before 'the Lesbian': Female Same-Sex Sexuality in 1950s Rural Finland," in *Queer 1950s: Rethinking Sexuality in the Postwar Years*, ed. Heike Bauer and Matt Cook (Basingstoke, UK: Palgrave Macmillan, 2012), 77–93.

108. For a discussion of the politics of empathy, see Carolyn Dean, *The Fragility of Empathy after the Holocaust* (Ithaca, NY: Cornell University Press, 2004).

CHAPTER 4

Material in this chapter was previously published in Heike Bauer, "Burning Sexual Subjects: Books, Homophobia and the Nazi Destruction of the Institute of Sexual Sciences in Berlin," in *Book Destruction from the Medieval to the Contemporary*, ed. Gill Partington and Adam Smyth (Basingstoke, UK: Palgrave Macmillan, 2014), 17–33.

1. Ralf Dose, for instance, in a short biography of Hirschfeld, presents an all-male cast of what he calls "important" medical members of the institute without indicating how their work intersected with feminist work of the time. Ralf Dose, *Magnus Hirschfeld: The Origins of the Gay Liberation Movement* (New York: Monthly Review Press, 2014), 53–55. Laurie Marhoefer's *Sex and the Weimar Republic: German Homosexual Emancipation and the Rise of the Nazis* (Toronto: University of Toronto Press, 2015) considerably expands the focus by resituating the work of the institute in the context of the broader political movements and cultural debates of the Weimar Republic.

2. Magnus Hirschfeld Society, "Founders of the Institute," available at http://www.magnus-hirschfeld.de/institute-for-sexual-science-1919–1933/personnel/founders-of-the-institute (accessed October 10, 2016). In general, the online exhibition of the Magnus Hirschfeld Society provides an excellent overview of the institute's history; see http://www.hirschfeld.in-berlin.de/institut/en/ifsframe.html.

3. Margaret Sanger, *An Autobiography* (New York: Norton, 1938), 280–281. For a discussion of Sanger's transatlantic connections, see Layne Parish Craig, *When Sex Changed: Birth Control and Literature between the World Wars* (New Brunswick, NJ: Rutgers University Press, 2013), esp. 5–8.

4. Sanger, *An Autobiography*, 280–281.

5. Margaret Sanger, *The Pivot of Civilization* (New York: Brentano's, 1922), 81 and esp. "The Fertility of the Feeble-Minded," 80–104. See also Angela Franks, *Margaret Sanger's Eugenics Legacy: The Control of Female Fertility* (Jefferson, NC: McFarland, 2005).

6. The tensions at the institute between homosexual reformers and the feminist movement are addressed by Atina Grossmann, "Magnus Hirschfeld, Sexualreform und die Neue Frau: Das Institut für Sexualwissenschaft und das Weimarer Berlin," in *Magnus Hirschfeld: Ein Leben im Spannungsfeld von Wissenschaft, Politik und Gesellschaft*, ed. Elke-Vera Kotowski and Julius Schoeps (Berlin: be.bra, 2004), 201–216.

7. He wrote in the dedication to his book *Die Gurgel Berlins* that "[sich] vieles verbindet" (there are many connections) with Franziska. Magnus Hirschfeld, *Die Gurgel Berlins*, 2nd ed. (Berlin: Seemann, 1908).

8. Her original phrasing is "Ich freue mich, dass die Natur mir in Dir, lieber Magnus, den Freund im Bruder gab." Franziska Mann, "Ich freue mich" (a note written for her sixtieth birthday), June 9, 1919, MS AR 2980, Leo Baeck Institute, New York. Mann published several books, including an impressionistic take on the bildungsroman, *Der Schäfer: Eine Geschichte aus der Stille* (Berlin: Axel Juncker 1919), and the epistolary novel *Die Stufe: Fragment einer Liebe* (Berlin: Mosaik, 1922), which tells the story of the love between an older woman and a younger man.

9. Magnus Hirschfeld and Franziska Mann, *Was jede Frau vom Wahlrecht wissen muß!* (Berlin: A. Pulvermacher, 1918), 7. For an analysis of the historical context, see Kathleen Canning, "Gender and the Imaginary of Revolution in Germany," in *Germany 1916–23: A Revolution in Context*, ed. Klaus Weinhauer, Anthony McElligott, and Kirsten Heinsohn (Bielefeld, Germany: Transcript, 2015), 103–126.

10. For nuanced discussions of the birth control and abortion reform movements, see Atina Grossmann, *Reforming Sex: The German Movement for Birth Control and Abortion Reform, 1920–1950* (Oxford: Oxford University Press, 1995); and Cornelie Usborne, *Cultures of Abortion in Weimar Germany* (New York: Berghahn, 2007).

11. For a thorough discussion of Stöcker's eugenicist views in the context of the history and historiography of German sex reform debates around the turn of the nineteenth century, see Jill Suzanne Smith, *Berlin Coquette: Prostitution and the New Woman, 1890–1930* (Ithaca, NY: Cornell University Press, 2013). For an excellent critique of the racial binds of Stöcker's views—or rather, the role of "cultural Othering" in her work—see Kirsten Leng, "Culture, Difference, and Sexual Progress in Turn-of-the-Century Europe: Cultural Othering and the German League for the Protection of Mothers and Sexual Reform, 1905–1914," *Journal of the History of Sexuality*, 25, no. 1 (2016): 62–82.

12. See "Hirschfeld, Magnus, *Jahrbuch für sexuelle Zwischenstufen, Heft 5*," *Mutterschutz* 3 (1907): 217.

13. Iwan Bloch, "Liebe und Kultur," *Mutterschutz* 3, no. 1 (1905): 26–32; Iwan Bloch, *Das Sexualleben unserer Zeit in seinen Beziehungen zur modernen Kultur* (Berlin: Louis Marcus, 1907). The first English translation of the sixth edition of this book was published two years after the German publication. See Iwan Bloch, *The Sexual Life of Our Time in Its Relations to Modern Civilization*, trans. Eden Paul (London: Rebman, 1909).

14. Havelock Ellis, "Die Bedeutung der Schwangerschaft," *Mutterschutz* 1, no. 6 (1905): 213–216.

15. Havelock Ellis, "Ursprung and Entwicklung der Prostitution," *Mutterschutz* 3 (1907): 13–23.

16. See Tracie Matysik, "In the Name of the Law: The 'Female Homosexual' and the Criminal Code in Fin de Siècle Germany," *Journal of the History of Sexuality* 13, no. 1 (2004): 26–48. See also Elena Mancini, *Magnus Hirschfeld and the Quest for Sexual*

Freedom: A History of the First International Sexual Freedom Movement (New York: Palgrave Macmillan, 2010), 15.

17. See Rainer Herrn, "Vom Traum zum Trauma: Das Institut für Sexualwissenschaft," in *Magnus Hirschfeld: Ein Leben im Spannungsfeld von Wissenschaft, Politik und Gesellschaft*, ed. Elke-Vera Kotowski and Julius Schoeps (Berlin: be.bra, 2004), 173–199.

18. He acted as a consultant to the film *Sündige Mütter* (Sinful mothers), directed by Richard Oswald and released in German cinemas in 1918, which was part of the series of sexual education films that also included *Anders als die Andern* (Different from the others). See Cornelie Usborne, *Cultures of Abortion in Weimar Germany* (New York: Berghahn, 2007), 31.

19. Magnus Hirschfeld and Richard Linsert, *Empfängnisverhütung: Mittel and Methoden* (Berlin: Neuer Deutscher, 1928).

20. Helene Stöcker, *Verkünder und Verwirklicher: Beiträge zum Gewaltproblem nebst einem zum erstem Male in deutschen Sprache veröffentlichten Briefe Tolstois* (Berlin: Neue Generation, 1928). See also Walter Schücking, Helene Stöcker, and Elisabeth Rotten, *Durch zum Rechtsfrieden* (Berlin: Neues Vaterland, 1919).

21. Kirsten Leng, "The Personal Is Scientific: Women, Gender, and the Production of Sexological Knowledge in Germany and Austria, 1900–1931," *History of Psychology* 18, no. 3 (2015): 238–251.

22. See Dose, *Magnus Hirschfeld: The Origins of the Gay Liberation Movement*, 57.

23. See Walter Benjamin, *Gesammelte Schriften*, vol. 4.1, ed. Tillmann Rexroth (Frankfurt, Germany: Suhrkamp, 1972), 257–260. I am grateful to Esther Leslie for bringing this account to my attention. See also Dose, *Magnus Hirschfeld: The Origins of the Gay Liberation Movement*, 54.

24. Dianne Chisholm, "Benjamin's Gender, Sex, and Eros," in *A Companion to the Work of Walter Benjamin*, ed. Rolf G. Goebel (Rochester, NY: Camden House, 2009), 252.

25. Dose, *Magnus Hirschfeld: The Origins of the Gay Liberation Movement*, 57.

26. Babette Gross, *Willi Münzenberg: Eine Politische Biographie* (Stuttgart, Germany: Deutsche Verlags-Anstalt, 1967), 202.

27. See Magnus Hirschfeld, "New Morals for Old in Soviet Russia," *Illustrated London News*, April 6, 1929, p. 586; Magnus Hirschfeld, *Verstaatlichung des Gesundheitswesens* (Berlin: Neues Vaterland, 1919).

28. Gross, *Willi Münzenberg*, 202.

29. The original phrases are "vielgeliebter Papa" and "Lebens-und Arbeitsbundes." MS XVI, 146, Magnus Hirschfeld Collection, Kinsey Institute, Bloomington, IN.

30. Alexandra Ripa, "Hirschfeld privat: Seine Haushaelterin erinnert sich," in Kotowski and Schoeps, *Magnus Hirschfeld: Im Spannungsfeld*, 68.

31. Gross, *Willi Münzenberg*, 202.

32. Ibid.

33. Rosie Cox, *The Servant Problem: The Home Life of a Global Economy* (London: Tauris, 2006).

34. Alison Light, *Mrs. Woolf and the Servants* (London: Penguin, 2008). See also, e.g., Antoinette Fauve-Chamoux, ed., *Domestic Service and the Formation of European Identity: Understanding the Globalization of Domestic Work, 16th–21st Centuries* (Bern, Switzerland: Peter Lang, 2004); and Victoria K. Haskins and Claire Lowrie, eds.,

Colonization and Domestic Service: Historical and Contemporary Perspectives (New York: Routledge, 2015).

35. Edith Lees Ellis, *Attainment* (London: Alston Rivers, 1909).

36. See, e.g., Francis Turville-Petre, "Excavations in the Mugharet El-Kebarah," *Journal of the Royal Anthropological Institute of Great Britain and Ireland* 62 (1932): 271–276. See also Ofer Bar-Yosef and Jane Callender, "A Forgotten Archaeologist: The Life of Francis Turville-Petre," *Palestine Exploration Quarterly* 129, no. 1 (1997): 2–18.

37. Christopher Isherwood, *Christopher and His Kind* (London: Vintage, 1976), 93.

38. Mia Spiro's *Anti-Nazi Modernism: Challenges of Resistance in 1930s Fiction* (Evanston, IL: Northwestern University Press, 2012) provides a thought-provoking assessment of Isherwood's writing in the historical and cultural context of the time.

39. Isherwood, *Christopher and His Kind*, 92.

40. Magnus Hirschfeld Society, "Institute Employees and Domestic Personnel," available at http://www.magnus-hirschfeld.de/institute-for-sexual-science-1919–1933/personnel/institute-employees-and-domestic-personnel (accessed October 10, 2016).

41. Cross-class relationships played a sometimes romanticized role in modern male homosexual culture formation. E. M. Forster's *Maurice*, written in 1913–1914 but not published until 1971, for example, famously depicts a happy ending for Maurice's relationship with the gamekeeper Scudders.

42. Magnus Hirschfeld, *Die Transvestiten: Eine Untersuchung über den erotischen Verkleidungstrieb* (Berlin: Medicinischer, 1910). See also Katie Sutton, "Sexological Cases and the Prehistory of Transgender Identity Politics in Interwar Germany," in *Case Studies and the Dissemination of Knowledge*, ed. Joy Damousi, Birgit Lang, and Katie Sutton (New York: Routledge, 2015), 85–103.

43. K. J. Rawson, "Introduction: 'An Inevitably Political Craft,'" *Transgender Studies Quarterly* 2, no. 4 (2015): 544. See also the discussion of terminology in Vernon Rosario, "Studs, Stems and Fishy Boys: Adolescent Latino Gender Variance and the Slippery Diagnosis of Transsexuality," in *Transgender Experience: Place, Ethnicity and Visibility*, ed. Chantal Zabus and David Coab (New York: Routledge, 2014).

44. Rawson, "Introduction," 545.

45. Susan Stryker, *Transgender History* (Berkeley, CA: Seal Press, 2008), 1.

46. Magnus Hirschfeld, *Die Transvestiten*.

47. Stryker, *Transgender History*, 39.

48. Geertje Mak, "'Passing Women': Im Sprechzimmer von Magnus Hirschfeld; Warum der Begriff 'Transvestit' nicht für Frauen in Männerkleidern eingeführ wurde," trans. Mirjam Hausmann, *Österreichische Zeitschrift für Geschichtswissenschaften* 9, no. 3 (1998): 384, 396. See also Katie Sutton, *The Masculine Woman in Weimar Germany* (New York: Berghahn, 2011), 116–121.

49. Mak, "Passing Women"; Darryl B. Hill, "Sexuality and Gender in Hirschfeld's *Die Transvestiten*: A Case of the 'Elusive Evidence of the Ordinary,'" *Journal of the History of Sexuality* 14, no 3 (2005): 316–332.

50. Judith (Jack) Halberstam, *Female Masculinity* (Durham, NC: Duke University Press, 1998).

51. Ina Linge, "Gender and Agency between 'Sexualwissenschaft' and Autobiography: The Case of N.O. Body's *Aus eines Mannes Mädchenjahren*," *German Life and Letters* 68, no. 3 (2015): 388.

52. The most detailed study of this is Rainer Herrn, *Schnittmuster des Geschlechts: Transvestitismus und Transsexualität in der frühen Sexualwissenschaft* (Giessen, Germany: Psychosozial, 2005).

53. Ludwig Levy-Lenz, *Discretion and Indiscretion: Memoirs of a Sexologist* (New York: Cadillac, 1954). See also Robert Beachy's account of Levy-Lenz's contribution to the institute's gender alignment surgeries in *Gay Berlin: Birth of a Modern Identity* (New York: Vintage, 2014), 276–278.

54. Levy-Lenz, *Discretion and Indiscretion*, 54.

55. Isherwood, *Christopher and His Kind*, 16.

56. Herrn, *Schnittmuster*, esp. 65–69.

57. Levy-Lenz, *Discretion and Indiscretion*.

58. Katie Sutton, "'We Too Deserve a Place in the Sun': The Politics of Transvestite Identity in Weimar Germany," *German Studies Review* 35, no. 2 (2012): 344.

59. See ibid., 339. The English sexologist Havelock Ellis coined the term *eonism* to describe cross-dressing in his *Studies in the Psychology of Sex*, vol. 7, *Eonism and Other Supplementary Studies* (Philadelphia: F. A. Davies, 1928).

60. Joanne Meyerowitz, *How Sex Changed: A History of Transsexuality in the United States* (Cambridge, MA: Harvard University Press, 2002), 19–20. See also Richard Mühsam "Chirurgische Eingriffe bei Anomalien des Sexuallebens," *Therapie der Gegenwart* 67 (1926): 451–455. In contrast to Dorchen and others, Lili Elbe, whose life has been fictionalized and recently turned into a Hollywood movie, *The Danish Girl* (2015; dir. Tom Hooper), underwent her sex change operations not in Berlin but in Dresden. Niels Hoyer, ed., *Man into Woman: An Authentic Record of a Change of Sex* (London: Jarrolds, 1933). See also, e.g., Herrn, *Schnittmuster*, 204–211; Sabine Meyer, *"Wie Lili zu einem richtigen Mädchen wurde": Lili Elbe: Zur Konstruktion von Geschlecht und Identität zwischen Medialisierung, Regulierung und Subjektivierung* (Bielefeld, Germany: Transcript, 2015), esp. 312–331; and Joanne Meyerowitz, "Sex Change and the Popular Press: Historical Notes on Transsexuality in the United States, 1930–1955," *GLQ: A Journal of Lesbian and Gay Studies* 4, no. 2 (1998): 159–187.

61. See Beachy, *Gay Berlin*, and the German edition of the book, *Das Andere Berlin: Die Erfindung der Homosexualität* (Munich, Germany: Siedler, 2015).

62. Richard Weiss, "Modern Rejuvenation," *Malayan Saturday Post*, April 13, 1929, p. 30. For an account of Shapiro's work, see G. Bogwardt, "Bernard Shapiro: An Orthodox Jew as an Early Andrologist in the 20th Century," *Sudhoffs Archiv* 86, no. 2 (2002): 181–197.

63. See Herrn, "Vom Traum zum Trauma," 173–199.

64. See Christian Pross, "Nazi Doctors, German Medicine, and Historical Truth," in *The Nazi Doctors and the Nuremberg Code: Human Rights in Human Experimentation*, ed. George J. Annas and Michael A. Grodin (Oxford: University of Oxford Press, 1992), 36.

65. Felix Abraham, "Genitalumwandlungen an zwei männlichen Transvestiten," *Zeitschrift für Sexualwissenschaft and Sexualpolitik*, no. 18 (1931): 223–226.

66. The phrase is "eine Art Luxusoperation mit spielerischem Charakter" in ibid., 225.

67. Ibid., 226.

68. Herrn, *Schnittmuster*, 181.

69. In addition to the writings about her and photographs of her naked body as part of case studies, there also exist pictures of her in her maid uniform, and a photograph in which she is wearing a fancy dress costume is reprinted in Herrn, *Schnittmuster*, 181.

70. See Magnus Hirschfeld, *Berlins Drittes Geschlecht* (Leipzig, Germany: Seeman, 1904). In addition to the *Jahrbuch für sexuelle Zwischenstufen*, see also, for instance, Magnus Hirschfeld, *Sexualpathologie: Ein Lehrbuch für Ärzte und Studierende*, vol. 2, *Sexuelle Zwischenstufen* (Bonn, Germany: Marcus and Webers, 1922).

71. Magnus Hirschfeld, *Die Homosexualität des Mannes und des Weibes* (Berlin: de Gruyter, 1984). The book was first published 1914.

72. See, e.g., the discussion of the "Sexualapparat" (genitals) in ibid., 125–132.

73. The phrase is "unendlich variables Mischungsverhältnis" in Hirschfeld, *Die Transvestiten*, 4. See also his early work *Geschlechts-Übergänge* (Leipzig, Germany: Malende, 1905).

74. See, e.g., Volker Weiss, . . . *mit ärztlicher Hilfe zum Geschlecht?* (Hamburg, Germany: Männerschwarm, 2009).

75. See Sutton, "We Too Deserve a Place in the Sun," 330–340, for an account of the growth of transvestite organizations and publicity.

76. Judith Butler, *Frames of War: When Is Life Grievable?* (London: Verso, 2009).

77. The English expression shown in the figure is "sexual transitions," but "sexual intermediaries" became the more commonly used term by Hirschfeld and his colleagues.

78. For accounts of the role of photography in the classification of humans, see, e.g., Peter Becker, "The Standardized Gaze: The Standardization of the Search Warrant in Nineteenth-Century Germany," in *Documenting Individual Identity: The Development of State Practices in the Modern World*, ed. Jane Kaplan and John Torpley (Princeton, NJ: Princeton University Press, 2001), 139–163; Amos Morris-Reich, *Race and Photography: Racial Photography as Scientific Evidence, 1876–1980* (Cambridge, MA: Harvard University Press, 2016); and Molly Rogers, *Delia's Tears: Race, Science and Photography in Nineteenth-Century America* (New Haven, CT: Yale University Press, 2010).

79. *Anders als die Andern* (dir. Richard Oswald) is the title of a film about homosexual blackmail released in German cinemas in 1919 in which Hirschfeld makes a guest appearance.

80. For a discussion of medical practice today, see S. Creighton, J. Alderson, S. Brown, and C. L. Minto, "Medical Photography: Ethics, Consent, and the Intersex Patient," *BJU International* 89, no. 1 (2002): 67–71.

81. The perspectives brought to this history are varied. See, e.g., Georgiann Davis, *Contesting Intersex: The Dubious Diagnosis* (New York: New York University Press, 2015); Alice Dreger, *Hermaphrodites and the Medical Invention of Sex* (Cambridge, MA: Harvard University Press, 2009); Terry Goldie, *The Man Who Invented Gender: Engaging the Ideas of John Money* (Vancouver, British Columbia: UCB Press, 2014), 39–66; Katarina Karkazis, *Fixing Sex: Intersex, Medical Authority, and Lived Experience* (Durham, NC: Duke University Press, 2008); Geertje Mak, *Doubting Sex: Inscriptions, Bodies, Selves in Nineteenth-Century Case Histories* (Manchester, UK: Manchester University Press, 2012); Elizabeth Reis, *Bodies in Doubt: An American History of Intersex* (Baltimore: Johns Hopkins University Press, 2010); and Katrina Roen, "Queer Kids: Toward Ethical Clinical Interactions with Intersex People," in *Ethics of the Body: Postconventional*

Challenges, ed. Margrit Shildrick and Roxanne Mykitiuk (Cambridge, MA: MIT Press, 2005), 259–278.

82. David James Prickett, "Magnus Hirschfeld and the Photographic (Re)Invention of the 'Third Sex,'" in *Visual Culture in Twentieth-Century Germany: Text as Spectacle*, ed. Gail Finney (Bloomington: Indiana University Press, 2006), 116.

83. Katie Sutton, "Representing the 'Third Sex': Cultural Translations of the Sexological Encounter in Early Twentieth-Century Germany," in *Sexology and Translation: Cultural and Scientific Encounters across the Modern World*, ed. Heike Bauer (Philadelphia: Temple University Press, 2015), 54.

84. Ibid., 55.

85. Harry Benjamin, "Reminiscences," *Journal of Sex Research* 6, no. 1 (1970): 4.

86. Magnus Hirschfeld, *Berlins Drittes Geschlecht*, 9th ed., ed. Manfred Herzer (Berlin: Rosa Winkel, 1991), 187.

87. Susan Stryker discusses Hirschfeld's role in *Transgender History* (Berkeley, CA: Seal Press, 2008), 38–41.

88. Sanger, *An Autobiography*, 280.

89. For a discussion of Serge Voronoff, see Henry Rubin, "The Logic of Treatment," in *The Transgender Reader*, ed. Susan Stryker and Stephen Whittle (New York: Routledge, 2006), 485; and Chandak Sengoopta, *The Most Secret Quintessence of Life: Sex, Glands, and Hormones, 1850–1950* (Chicago: University of Chicago Press, 2006), 95–97.

90. Sanger, *An Autobiography*, 280.

91. Isherwood, *Christopher and His Kind*, 16.

92. Ibid., 16–17.

93. Influential studies in English of the book burnings include Leonidas E. Hill, "The Nazi Attack on 'Un-German' Literature, 1933–1945," in *The Holocaust and the Book*, ed. Jonathan Rose (Amherst: University of Massachusetts Press, 2001), 9–46; J. M. Ritchie, "The Nazi Book-Burning," *Modern Language Review* 83, no. 3 (1988): 627–643; and George Mosse and James Jones, "Bookburning and the Betrayal of German Intellectuals," *New German Critique*, no. 31 (1984): 143–155. For accounts of the contemporary UK and U.S. reception of the book burnings, see Matthew Fishburn, "Books Are Weapons: Wartime Responses to the Nazi Bookfires of 1933," *Book History* 10 (2007): 223–251; and Guy Stern, "The Burning of the Books in Nazi Germany, 1933: The American Response," *Simon Wiesenthal Center Annual* 2, available at http://motlc.wiesenthal.com/site/pp.asp?c=gvKVLcMVIuG&b=395007 (accessed October 10, 2016).

94. The events have been discussed in studies of the histories of homosexuality, Nazism, and the Nazi book burnings more specifically. See, for instance, Herrn, "Vom Traum zum Trauma"; Rebecca Knuth, *Burning Books and Leveling Libraries: Extremist Violence and Cultural Destruction* (Westport, CT: Praeger, 2006), 101–120; and James Steakley, *The Homosexual Emancipation Movement*, 103–105. See also Charlotte Wolff, *Magnus Hirschfeld: Portrait of a Pioneer in Sexology* (London: Quartet, 1986), 376–379.

95. See, e.g., John C. Fout, "Sexual Politics in Wilhelmine Germany: The Male Gender Crisis and Moral Purity and Homophobia," in *Forbidden History: The State, Society, and the Regulation of Sexuality in Modern Europe*, ed. John C. Fout (Chicago: University of Chicago Press, 1992), 259–292; and Richard Plant, *The Pink Triangle: The Nazi War against Homosexuals* (New York: Holt, 1986).

96. Rüdiger Lautmann, "The Pink Triangle: The Persecution of Homosexual Males in Concentration Camps in Nazi Germany," in *The Gay Past: A Collection of Historical Essays*, ed. Salvatore J. Licata and Robert P. Petersen (New York: Routledge, 2013), 141–160.

97. Quoted in Erwin J. Haeberle, "Swastika, Pink Triangle, and Yellow Star: The Destruction of Sexology in Nazi Germany," in *Hidden from History: Reclaiming the Gay and Lesbian Past*, ed. Martin Duberman, Martha Vicinus, and George Chauncey Jr. (London: Penguin, 1991), 369.

98. See, for example, Matthew Fishburn, *Burning Books* (Basingstoke, UK: Palgrave Macmillan, 2008), 41–43; and Steakley, *The Homosexual Emancipation Movement*, 103. For a discussion of Jewishness and sexology, see David Baile, "The Discipline of *Sexualwissenschaft* Emerges in Germany, Creating Divergent Notions of European Jewry," in *Yale Companion to Jewish Writing and Thought in German Culture, 1096–1996*, ed. Sander L. Gilman and Jack Zipes (New Haven, CT: Yale University Press, 1997), 273–279; and Christina von Braun, "Ist die Sexualwissenschaft eine 'jüdische' Wissenschaft?" in Kotowski and Schoeps, *Magnus Hirschfeld*, 255–269. For a discussion of the debates about homosexuality and Nazism, see, e.g., Andrew Hewitt, *Political Inversions, Homosexuality, Fascism and the Modernist Imaginary* (Stanford, CA: Stanford University Press, 1996), which tracks, and to some extent reclaims, the history of masculine men who desired other men and whose lives were lived outside emancipatory sexual subcultures. Hewitt argues that we pay attention to homosexual involvement in the Nazi regime to better understand "what homosexuality was (and is) for" (81). Jack Halberstam in turn, while disagreeing with the Oedipal framework of Hewitt's analysis, nevertheless also observes that "the erasure of the masculinist gay movement indicates an unwillingness to grapple with difficult historical antecedents and a desire to impose a certain kind of identity politics on history . . . a universalizing and racially specific history of homosexuality." Judith (Jack) Halberstam, *The Queer Art of Failure* (Durham, NC: Duke University Press, 2011), 158 (and see her discussion of Hewitt on pages 156–158). See also Elizabeth D. Heineman, "Sexuality and Nazism: The Doubly Unspeakable?," in *Sexuality and German Fascism*, ed. Dagmar Herzog (Oxford: Berghahn, 2005), 22–66; and Christiane Wilke's study of the memorialization of Nazi victims with complex identities such as Hirschfeld's, "Remembering Complexity? Memorials for Nazi Victims in Berlin," *International Journal of Transitional Justice* 7, no. 1 (2013): 136–156.

99. Reiner Herrn, "Sex brennt: Magnus Hirschfeld, sein Institut für Sexualwissenschaft und die Bücherverbrennung," available at https://gedenkort.charite.de/file admin/user_upload/microsites/ohne_AZ/sonstige/gedenkort/ausstellung_sex-brennt/ Sex-brennt_Hirschfeld.pdf (accessed December 30, 2016). Herrn gives an excellent overview of the event.

100. World Committee for the Victims of Fascism, *The Brown Book of the Hitler Terror* (New York: Alfred A. Knopf, 1938), 158–161. See also Steakley, *The Homosexual Emancipation Movement*, 103–105.

101. The date is derived from Hirschfeld's own account in *Die Homosexualität des Mannes und des Weibes*, published in 1914, in which he claims to have first drafted the questionnaire "vor 14 Jahren" (fourteen years ago). Hirschfeld, *Die Homosexualität des Mannes und des Weibes*, 239–240. Elena Mancini, in contrast, claims that Hirschfeld developed the questionnaire in 1902 with his friend Hermann von Teschenberg. See Mancini, *Magnus Hirschfeld and the Quest for Sexual Freedom*, 174n109.

102. Benjamin, "Reminiscences," 5. See also Herzog, *Sexuality and German Fascism*.

103. Haeberle, "Swastika, Pink Triangle and Yellow Star," 274 (emphasis added).

104. Wolff, *Magnus Hirschfeld*, 376; Haeberle, "Swastika, Pink Triangle and Yellow Star," 270–287. Haeberle republished *Die Homosexualität des Mannes und des Weibes* in 1984 with a substantial new introduction that made Hirschfeld's contribution better known among historians of sexuality.

105. A sample questionnaire is included in Hirschfeld, *Die Homosexualität des Mannes und des Weibes*, 240–263.

106. Ibid., 262.

107. Butler, *Frames of War*, 61.

108. See, for instance, Robert Gellately, *Backing Hitler: Consent and Coercion in Nazi Germany* (Oxford: Oxford University Press, 2001), 60–63.

109. Sharon Patricia Holland, *The Erotic Life of Racism* (Durham, NC: Duke University Press, 2012), 107 (emphasis in original).

110. Stefan Micheler, "Homophobic Propaganda and the Denunciation of Same-Sex Desiring Men under National Socialism," trans. Patricia Szobar, in *Sexuality and German Fascism*, ed. Dagmar Herzog (London: Berghahn, 2005), 98.

111. "In Germany Today," *Palestine Post*, October 26, 1934, p. 5.

112. Fishburn, "Books Are Weapons," 236.

113. Ibid., 227.

114. For instance, a Hirschfeld caricature featured prominently on the cover of *Der Stürmer* 7, no. 8 (1929). Sander Gilman discusses antisemitic stereotyping in *The Jew's Body* (New York: Routledge, 1992). See also Robert Deam Tobin, "Preface," in Robert Deam Tobin, *Warm Brothers: Queer Theory and the Age of Goethe* (Philadelphia: University of Pennsylvania Press, 2000), vii–x; and Linda Mizejewski's discussion of the "contradictory and edgy" attitudes to homosexuality during the Weimar Republic in *Divine Decadence: Fascism, Female Spectacle, and the Makings of Sally Bowles* (Princeton, NJ: Princeton University Press, 1992), 27.

115. Magnus Hirschfeld, "Autobiographical Sketch," in *Encyclopedia Sexualis: A Comprehensive Encyclopedia-Dictionary of Sexual Sciences*, ed. Victor Robinson (New York: Dingwall-Rock, 1936), 317–321.

116. "Wir wählen Hindenburg! Wir wählen Hitler!" poster, 1932, ID no. 2005.A40, Museum of Jewish Heritage, New York, available at http://collection.mjhnyc.org/index.php?g=detail&action=search&object_id=6168.

117. Dagmar Herzog, *Sex after Fascism: Memory and Mortality in Twentieth-Century Germany* (Princeton, NJ: Princeton University Press, 2005), 23.

118. See Hirschfeld's own account of events in Wolff, *Magnus Hirschfeld*, 379.

119. Quoted in J. M. Ritchie, "The Nazi Book-Burning," 630.

120. Magnus Hirschfeld, *Tagebuch*, ed. Rolf Dose (Berlin: Hentrich and Hentrich, 2013), 84.

121. See "Books Burn as Goebbels Speaks," May 10, 1933, United States Holocaust Memorial Museum, available at http://www.ushmm.org/wlc/en/media_fi.php?ModuleId=10005852&MediaId=158.

122. Mosse and Jones, "Bookburning and the Betrayal of German Intellectuals," 144.

123. Maryanne Dever, "Papered Over," in *Out of the Closet, Into the Archives: Researching Sexual Histories*, ed. Amy L. Stone and Jaime Cantrell (Albany: State University of New York Press, 2015), 86.
124. Ibid.

CHAPTER 5

1. See, e.g., Cindy Patton and Benigno Sánchez-Eppler, eds., *Queer Diaspora* (Durham, NC: Duke University Press, 2000).
2. Sara Ahmed, *Strange Encounters: Embodied Others in Post-coloniality* (London: Routledge, 2000), 82. See also, e.g., Gayatri Gopinath's work on the queer South Asian diaspora, which tracks how "queerness becomes a way to challenge nationalist ideologies" but is simultaneously rooted in and exceeding the local, *Impossible Desires: Queer Diasporas and South Asian Cultures* (Durham, NC: Duke University Press, 2005), 11; and Meg Wesling, "Why Queer Diaspora?," *Feminist Review*, 90 (2008): 30–47.
3. Heather Love, "Forced Exile: Walter Pater's Queer Modernism," in *Bad Modernisms*, ed. Douglas Mao and Rebecca L. Walkowitz (Durham, NC: Duke University Press, 2006), 26.
4. Magnus Hirschfeld, *Die Weltreise eines Sexualforschers* (Brugg, Switzerland: Bözberg, 1933); Magnus Hirschfeld, *Men and Women: The World Journey of a Sexologist*, trans. Oliver P. Green (New York: G. P. Putnam's, 1935).
5. Veronika Fuechtner, "Indians, Jews, and Sex: Magnus Hirschfeld and Indian Sexology," in *Imagining Germany, Imagining Asia: Essays in Asian-German Studies*, ed. Veronika Fuechtner and Mary Riehl (Rochester, NY: Camden House, 2013), 111–130; Jana Funke, "Navigating the Past: Sexuality, Race, and the Uses of the Primitive in Magnus Hirschfeld's *The World Journey of a Sexologist*," in *Sex, Knowledge and Receptions of the Past*, ed. Kate Fisher and Rebecca Langlands (Oxford: Oxford University Press, 2015), 111–134; Mark Johnson, "Transgression and the Making of a 'Western' Sexual Science," in *Transgressive Sex: Subversion and Control in Erotic Encounters*, ed. Hastings Donnan and Fiona Magowan (New York: Berghahn, 2009), 167–189; Birgit Lang, "Sexualwissenschaft auf Reisen: Zur antikolonialen Mimikry in Magnus Hirschfeld's *Die Weltreise eines Sexualforschers* (1933)," *Österreichische Zeitschrift für Geschichtswissenschaften* 22, no. 1.9 (2011): n.p.
6. Sara Ahmed, "Making Feminist Points," *feministkilljoys* (blog), September 11, 2013, available at http://feministkilljoys.com/2013/09/11/making-feminist-points (emphasis in original).
7. Magnus Hirschfeld, *Testament: Heft II*, ed. Ralf Dose (Berlin: Hentrich and Hentrich, 2013), 4–8.
8. Ibid., 9–10.
9. Ibid., 18.
10. Ibid., 16.
11. The phrase is "so lange wie möglich" in ibid., 36.
12. After World War II, Benjamin became so famous for his work on transsexualism that he is sometimes credited with the term's invention; however, it was coined by Hirschfeld in 1923. See Magnus Hirschfeld, "Die Intersexuelle Konstitution," *Jahrbuch für sexuelle Zwischenstufen*, no. 23 (1923): 3–27. Despite distinguishing here between

intersex, transsexual, and homosexuality, Hirschfeld continued to focus primarily on "sexual intermediaries" and the related categories of transvestism and homosexuality that preoccupied him throughout his life.

13. Harry Benjamin, *The Transsexual Phenomenon* (New York: Julian Press, 1966), 12.

14. Erwin Haeberle uncovered letters in which Benjamin, Hirschfeld, and a German émigré to the United States known under his adopted name, Ernest Elmhurst, discuss setting up an American homosexual organization. See Erwin J. Haeberle, "A Movement of Inverts: An Early Plan for an Organisation of Inverts in the United States," *Journal of Homosexuality* 10, nos. 1–2 (1984): 127–135.

15. Magnus Hirschfeld, *Weltreise eines Sexualforschers im Jahre 1931/32*, ed. Hans Christoph Buch (Frankfurt, Germany: Eichborn, 2006), 23.

16. See, e.g., "Die Befreiung des Menschen von Leiden, Not und Schaden ist Dr Magnus Hirschfelds Bestimmung," *New Yorker Volkszeitung*, December 5, 1930; "Neuer Magnus Hirschfeld Vortrag am Sonntag," *New Yorker Volkszeitung*, December 15, 1930; "Dr Magnus Hirschfeld am Sonntag im Labor Temple," *New Yorker Volkszeitung*, December 16, 1930.

17. Ralf Dose, *Magnus Hirschfeld: The Origins of the Gay Liberation Movement* (New York: Monthly Review Press, 2014), 92.

18. "German Expert, 62, Will Study Marriage Here," *New York Times*, November 23, 1930, p. 5. The circulation figures are taken from Funding Universe, "The New York Times Company History," available at http://www.fundinguniverse.com/company-histories/the-new-york-times-company-history (accessed October 10, 2016).

19. For more on the *New Yorker Volkszeitung*, see Karl John Richard Arndt and May E. Olson, *The German Language Press of the Americas: 1732–1956* (Munich, Germany: K. G. Saur, 1973), 464; and Dorothee Schneider, *Trade Unions and Community: The German Working Class in New York, 1870–1900* (Urbana: University of Illinois Press, 1994), 47.

20. "Dr Magnus Hirschfeld Spricht am Sonntag über 'Naturgesetze der Liebe,'" *New Yorker Volkszeitung*, December 25, 1930.

21. Love, "Forced Exile," 40.

22. Ibid., 26.

23. Magnus Hirschfeld, "Choosing Mate a Science under Guidance of German 'Love Clinic,'" interview by George Viereck, *Milwaukee Sentinel*, November 30, 1930, p. 1.

24. Ibid.

25. Hirschfeld, *Testament*, 56, 58.

26. The phrase is "Sehr behindert" in ibid., 72.

27. Quoted in Dose, *Magnus Hirschfeld*, 60.

28. See Hirschfeld, *Testament*, 20n5; Charlotte Wolff, *Magnus Hirschfeld: A Portrait of a Pioneer in Sexology* (London: Quartet, 1986), 223.

29. The phrases are "Zerrüttete Nerven" and "Sexuelle Schwäche" in the Titus Pearls advertisement, *Die Ehe* [Marriage] 5, no. 2 (1930). See Magnus Hirschfeld Society, "Das Institut und die Pharmaindustrie," available at http://www.hirschfeld.in-berlin.de/institut/de/ifsframe.html?theorie/theo_19.html (accessed October 10, 2016).

30. Titus Pearls advertisement, *Sherbrooke Telegram*, September 8, 1932, p. 10.

31. See, e.g., Titus Pearls advertisement, *Muncie Post-Democrat*, November 18, 1932, p. 4; Titus Pearls advertisement, *Bowie Booster*, August 18, 1931, p. 6.

32. See also Fuechtner's discussion about the sale of the Titus Pearls in India in "Indians, Jews, and Sex," 116, 129n10.

33. Magnus Hirschfeld, "'Dr. Einstein of Sex' Not So Favorably Impressed by U.S.," interview by George Viereck, *Milwaukee Sentinel*, February 2, 1931.

34. Hirschfeld, *Testament*, 40.

35. See "Advertisement for a Lecture by Dr. Magnus Hirschfeld, 1931," Dill Pickle Club Records, Box 1, Folder 23, Newberry Library, Chicago.

36. Hirschfeld, *Testament*, 40.

37. The German title literally translates as "humans behind bars" but was changed in the English to reflect the film's content. For an excellent account of the European avant-garde's relationship to Hollywood, see Esther Leslie, *Hollywood Flatlands: Animation, Critical Theory and the Avant-Garde* (London: Verso, 2002).

38. See Magnus Hirschfeld, *Alkohol im Familienleben* (Berlin: Fritz Stolt, 1906); and, for instance, Magnus Hirschfeld, *Sexualität und Kriminalität* (Berlin: Renaissance, 1924), and Magnus Hirschfeld, "Vorwort" (Foreword) to *Geschlechtsleben und Strafrecht*, by Felix Halle (Berlin: Mopr, 1931), ix–xii.

39. For a fuller historical account of the case, see, e.g., Fowler V. Harper, "The Cases of Mooney and Billings," *Oregon Law Review* 8, no. 4 (1929): 374–376; and John C. Ralston, *Fremont Older and the 1916 San Francisco Bombing: A Tireless Crusade for Justice* (Charleston, SC: History Press, 2013).

40. The full phrase is "Opfer einer durch Kriegseregnung gesteigerten politischen Angstneurose," which roughly translates as "victims of a political fear neurosis that was incited by the excitement of the war." Magnus Hirschfeld, letter to Herrn Schlör (president of Internationale Hilfsvereininung), March 12, 1932, Box XII, p. 66, Magnus Hirschfeld Collection, Kinsey Institute, Bloomington, IN.

41. See, for instance, the cover of the journal *Earth*, March 1931, Dill Pickle Club Records, Box 3, Folder 273, Newberry Library.

42. See Fuechtner, "Indians, Jews, and Sex"; Funke, "Sexuality, Race, and the Uses of the Primitive"; and Lang, "Sexualwissenschaft auf Reisen."

43. Liat Kozma, "The Silence of the Pregnant Bride: Non-marital Sex in Middle Eastern Societies," in *Untold Histories of the Middle East: Recovering Voices from the 19th and 20th Centuries*, ed. Amy Singer, Christoph K. Neumann, and Selçuk Akşin Somel (London: Routledge, 2011), 76.

44. Anjali Arondekar and Geeta Patel, "Area Impossible: Notes Toward an Introduction," *GLQ: Journal of Lesbian and Gay Studies* 22, no. 2 (2016): 152.

45. Ibid.

46. Ibid., 153.

47. I put "Euro-" in parentheses because while Arondekar and Patel refer to a European as well as American focus in queer studies, the scholarship they discuss with one exception—the germane *Queer in Europe: Contemporary Case Studies*, edited by Lisa Downing and Robert Gillett (Farnham, UK: Ashgate, 2011)—comes specifically from American and British contexts. Homogenizing "European" queer studies in this way is itself problematic because it obscures national specificities as well as, for instance, the distinct histories of communist Europe or the Nordic countries. For a look at the diversity of scholarship relating to modern sexual histories in Europe, see, e.g., Matt Cook and Jennifer Evans, eds., *Queer Cities, Queer Cultures: Europe since 1945* (London:

Bloomsbury, 2014); Chiara Beccalossi, *Female Sexual Inversion: Same-Sex Desires in Italian and British Sexology, c. 1870–1920* (Basingstoke, UK: Palgrave Macmillan, 2012); and Robert Kulpa and Joanna Mizielińska, *De-Centring Western Sexualities: Central and Eastern European Perspectives* (Farnham, UK: Ashgate, 2011).

48. "Review of 'The Journey of a Sexologist,'" *Canadian Jewish Chronicle*, May 17, 1935, p. 13.

49. Hirschfeld, *Die Weltreise eines Sexualforschers* (Brugg, Switzerland: Böyzberg, 1933); Magnus Hirschfeld, *Men and Women*; Magnus Hirschfeld, *Women East and West: Impressions of a Sex Expert*, trans. Oliver P. Green (London: W. Heinemann, 1935).

50. Hermann Heinrich Ploss, Max Bartels, and Paul Bartels, *Woman: An Historical, Gynæcological and Anthropological Compendium*, ed. Eric John Dingwall (London: W. Heinemann, 1935).

51. Homi Bhabha, *The Location of Culture* (New York: Routledge, 1990), 201.

52. Hirschfeld, *Weltreise eines Sexualforschers im Jahre 1931/32*, 24.

53. See, e.g., Nicholas Matte, "International Sexual Reform and Sexology in Europe, 1897–1933," *Canadian Bulletin of Medical History/Bulletin canadien d'histoire de la medecine* 22, no. 2 (2005): 253–270.

54. His given name was Li Shiu Tong, but Hirschfeld called him Tao Li.

55. Hirschfeld, *Weltreise eines Sexualforschers im Jahre 1931/32*, 98.

56. Ibid., 99.

57. Ibid.; untitled article, *Wiener Allgemeine Zeitung*, April 2, 1932, n.p. See also MS IV, Part 1, p. 9, Magnus Hirschfeld Collection, Kinsey Institute.

58. The original reads, "Jedenfalls sind die 400 bis 500 Millionen Chinesen individuell genauso differenziert wie die hundert Millionen Deutsche oder fünfzig Millionen Engländer." Hirschfeld, *Weltreise eines Sexualforschers im Jahre 1931/32*, 100.

59. For an account of Hirschfeld's visit to China and how it relates to debates about homosexuality there, see Tse-Lan D. Sang, *The Emerging Lesbian: Female Same-Sex Desire in Modern China* (Chicago: University of Chicago Press, 2003), 100–101.

60. Keizō Dohi, *Beiträge zur Geschichte der Syphilis in Ostasien* (Leipzig, Germany: Akademische Verlagsgesellschaft, 1923). See also Deutsches Institut für Japanstudien, "Gakken Bunko (Dohi Keizō)," available at http://tksosa.dijtokyo.org/?page=collection_detail.php&p_id=311 (accessed October 10, 2016); Hirschfeld, *Weltreise eines Sexualforschers im Jahre 1931/32*, 23, 44–45.

61. For a detailed discussion of sexology in Japan, see Sabine Frühstück, *Colonizing Sex: Sexology and Social Control in Modern Japan* (Berkeley: University of California Press, 2003).

62. Funke, "Navigating the Past," 134.

63. They were George Straub and Eric Fennel. Hirschfeld, *Weltreise*, 41. The practice Straub founded still exists today.

64. Hirschfeld calls him F. O. Holleman, and Funke calls him an "Indonesian ethnologist." See Hirschfeld, *Weltreise eines Sexualforschers im Jahre 1931/32*, 179; Funke, "Navigating the Past," 124.

65. Hirschfeld, *Weltreise eines Sexualforschers im Jahre 1931/32*, 50. The German Institute for Japan Studies still exists in Tokyo today. As far as I have been able to ascertain from the institute's holdings, Grundert, who published several books on issues relating to Japan including a comparison between Japan and Germany, did not mention his encounter with Hirschfeld.

66. Ibid., 71. For a discussion of Iwaya, whose given name was Sueo, see Annette Joff, "Iwaya Sazanami: Berliner Tagebuch, November–Dezember 1900" (master's thesis, Humboldt University, Berlin, 2007), 42–44.

67. Iwaya Suyewo, "Nan sho 'k: Päderastie in Japan," *Jahrbuch für sexuelle Zwischenstufen* 5 (1902): 265–271. Note that Iwaya here uses his given name, Sueo, spelled "Suyewo."

68. Hirschfeld, *Weltreise eines Sexualforschers im Jahre 1931/32*, 72.

69. The reference is most likely to Maria Piper, *Die Schaukunst der Japaner* (Berlin: de Gruyter, 1927).

70. Hirschfeld, *Weltreise eines Sexualforschers im Jahre 1931/32*, 73.

71. Ibid., 74.

72. Ibid., 53. Here too Hirschfeld gets names wrong: "Shidzue Ishimoto" was known as Katō Shidzue, and the poet's name was Ikuta Hanayo. For a discussion of feminist debates in Japan at the time, see Michiko Suzuki, *Becoming Modern Women: Love and Female Identity in Prewar Japanese Literature and Culture* (Stanford, CA: Stanford University Press, 2010); and Michiko Suzuki, "The Translation of Edward Carpenter's *The Intermediate Sex* in Early Twentieth-Century Japan," in *Sexology and Translation: Cultural and Scientific Encounters across the Modern World*, ed. Heike Bauer (Philadelphia: Temple University Press, 2015), 197–215.

73. Hirschfeld, *Weltreise eines Sexualforschers im Jahre 1931/32*, 345. It is likely that "Hoda Charaoni" refers to Huda Sha'arawi, a leading Egyptian feminist. See, e.g., Sania Sharawi Lanfranchi, *Casting Off the Veil: The Life of Huda Shaarawi, Egypt's First Feminist* (London: I. B. Tauris, 2012). For a detailed discussion of debates about female sexuality in nineteenth-century Egypt, see Liat Kozma, *Policing Egyptian Women: Sex, Law, and Medicine in Khedival Egypt* (New York: Syracuse University Press, 2011).

74. The word is "Frauentypus" in Hirschfeld, *Weltreise eines Sexualforschers im Jahre 1931/32*, 345.

75. For a discussion of Ma Huo Quintang, see Adelyn Lim; *Transnational Feminism and Women's Movements in Post-1997 Hong Kong: Solidarity beyond the State* (Hong Kong: Hong Kong University Press, 2015), 25.

76. D. M. Bose, S. N. Sen, and B. V. Subbarayappa, eds., *A Concise History of Sexual Science in India* (Delhi: Indian National Science Academy, 1971).

77. The phrase is "indische Liebeskunst" in Magnus Hirschfeld, "Geleitwort," in *Liebe im Orient: Das Kamasutram des Vatsyayana*, by Ferdinand Leiter and Hans H. Thal (Lindau, Germany: Rudolph, 1929), v. See also Magnus Hirschfeld, "Geleitwort," in *Liebe im Orient: Anangaranga, Die Bühne des Liebesgottes*, by Ferdinand Leiter and Hans H. Thal (Vienna, Austria: Schneider, 1929), ix–xiii.

78. Fuechtner, "Indians, Jews, and Sex," 111, 127.

79. Hirschfeld, *Weltreise eines Sexualforschers im Jahre 1931/32*, 160.

80. The influential psychiatrist Richard von Krafft-Ebing argued, for instance, that "the higher the development of the race, the stronger [the] contrasts between men and women" in *Psychopathia Sexualis with Especial Reference to the Antipathic Sexual Instinct: A Medico-Legal Study*, trans. F. J. Rebman (New York: Eugenics, 1934), 42. For critical discussions of the nineteenth-century debates about sex, race, and climate and their histories, see, e.g., Londa Schiebinger, *The Mind Has No Sex? Women in the Origins of Modern Science* (Cambridge, MA: Harvard University Press, 1991), 161–170; and Cheryl A. Logan's more recent discussion of race and climate in *Hormones, Heredity, and*

Race: Spectacular Failure in Interwar Vienna (New Brunswick, NJ: Rutgers University Press, 2013), 64–88.

81. Hirschfeld, *Weltreise eines Sexualforschers im Jahre 1931/32*, 161–162.

82. For an account that is both a critique of Dutch colonialism in Indonesia and an excellent study of the issue at stake in retrieving and assessing this history, see Ann Laura Stoler, *Along the Archival Grain: Epistemic Anxieties and Colonial Common Sense* (Princeton, NJ: Princeton University Press, 2010).

83. Loose items, Magnus Hirschfeld Collection, Kinsey Institute.

84. Ahluwalia refers to the emerging birth control movement in India. Sanjam Ahluwalia, "Demographic Rhetoric and Sexual Surveillance: Indian Middle-Class Advocates of Birth Control, 1902–1940s," in *Confronting the Body: The Politics of Physicality in Colonial and Post-colonial India*, ed. James H. Mills and Satadru Sen (London: Anthem, 2004), 188. See also Sanjam Ahluwalia, *Reproductive Restraints: Birth Control in India, 1877–1947* (Chicago: University of Illinois Press, 2008).

85. The original reads, "Die indische Führerschicht, aus der ich nun schon viele persönlich kennenzulernen das Glück hatte, ist nach Charakter und Wissen vollkommen befähigt, die Lenkung ihres Staates selbst zu besorgen." Hirschfeld, *Weltreise eines Sexualforschers im Jahre 1931/32*, 301.

86. According to Robert Jütte, Nehru had visited Hirschfeld's Berlin institute. See Robert Jütte, "Einleitung," in *Handwörterbuch der Sexualwisschenschaft*, by Max Marcuse (Berlin: de Gruyter, 2001), viii.

87. Hirschfeld, *Weltreise eines Sexualforschers im Jahre 1931/32*, 270.

88. The original reads, "Seit 50 Jahren bin ich ein Anhänger der Freiheit Indiens. . . . [Ich empfinde] es als seine der größten politischen Ungerechigkeiten in der Welt, daβ eines der ältesten Kulturländer . . . nicht frei über sich schalten und walten darf." Ibid., 300.

89. Lang, "Sexualwissenschaft auf Reisen."

90. Hirschfeld, *Weltreise eines Sexualforschers im Jahre 1931/32*, 254–255. See also loose items, Magnus Hirschfeld Collection, Kinsey Institute.

91. Mrinalini Sinha, Introduction to *Mother India*, by Katherine Mayo, ed. Mrinalini Sinha (Ann Arbor: University of Michigan Press, 2000), 3–4.

92. For an overview of the debates, see ibid., 1–41. See also Srirupa Prasad's critique of Gandhi in *Cultural Politics of Hygiene in India, 1890–1940: Contagions of Feeling* (Basingstoke, UK: Palgrave Macmillan, 2015), 43–59.

93. The phrase is "Ein Sexuelles Zerrbild" in Hirschfeld, *Weltreise eines Sexualforschers im Jahre 1931/32*, 245.

94. Ibid., 246–247.

95. Ibid.

96. Fuechtner, "Indians, Jews, and Sex," 115.

97. Havelock Ellis, Preface to *The Sexual Life of Savages in North-Western Melanesia*, by Bronislaw Malinowski (New York: Harvest, 1929), ix.

98. Bronislaw Malinowski, *Sex and Repression in Savage Society* (London: Routledge and Kegan Paul, 1927); Bronislaw Malinowski, *The Sexual Life of Savages in North-Western Melanesia* (New York: Eugenics, 1929).

99. The phrases are "Die Verachtung der Witwe" (266) and "Tempelfrauen" (242) in Hirschfeld, *Weltreise eines Sexualforschers im Jahre 1931/32*.

100. The most famous British doctor in India was Margaret Balfour. I have not been able to find information on N. J. Balfour.

101. Nehru argued that improving the role of women and including them in political life was vital for the future of India. See, e.g., Jawaharlal Nehru, *The Essential Writings of Jawaharlal Nehru*, ed. Sarvepalli Gopal and Uma Iyengar (Oxford: Oxford University Press, 2003). For a critique of women's role in India before and after independence, see, e.g., Partha Chatterjee and Pradeep Jeganathan, eds., *Community, Gender and Violence* (London: Hurst, 2000); Geraldine Forbes, *Women in Modern India* (Cambridge: Cambridge University Press, 2004); and Vrinda Narain, *Reclaiming the Nation: Muslim Women and the Law in India* (Toronto: University of Toronto Press, 2008), esp. 34–79.

102. Gayatri Chakravorty Spivak, "Can the Subaltern Speak?" in *Marxism and the Interpretation of Culture*, ed. Cary Nelson and Lawrence Grossberg (Basingstoke, UK: Macmillan, 1988), 275.

103. Padma Anagol, *The Emergence of Feminism in India, 1850–1920* (Farnham, UK: Ashgate, 2005), 6.

104. Hirschfeld, *Weltreise eines Sexualforschers im Jahre 1931/32*, 304.

105. Ibid., 300.

106. Ibid., 262.

107. Ahmed, "Making Feminist Points."

108. The original text reads, "Einer der größten Gewinne meiner Reise war Tao Li." Hirschfeld, *Testament*, 126.

109. The phrases are "Seine unerschütterliche Treue u. Anhänglichkeit" and "Ich glaube, dass ich in ihm den lange gesuchten Schüler gefunden habe." Ibid., 126.

110. Ibid.

111. Nishant Shahani, *Queer Retrosexualities: The Politics of Reparative Return* (Bethlehem, PA: Lehigh University Press, 2012), 1.

112. Hirschfeld, *Testament*, 134.

113. Liat Kozma, "'We, the Sexologists . . .': Arabic Medical Writing on Sexuality, 1879–1943," *Journal of the History of Sexuality* 22, no. 3 (2013): 431–432. See also Liat Kozma, "Translating Sexology, Writing the Nation: Sexual Discourse and Practice in Hebrew and Arabic in the 1930s," in *Sexology and Translation: Cultural and Scientific Encounters across the Modern World*, ed. Heike Bauer (Philadelphia: Temple University Press, 2015), 135–153.

114. For a sense of the different kinds of debates, see, e.g., Hibba Abugideiri, *Gender and the Making of Modern Medicine in Colonial Egypt* (Farnham, UK: Ashgate, 2010); Kozma, *Policing Egyptian Women*; Hanan Kholoussy, "Monitoring and Medicalising Male Sexuality in Semi-colonial Egypt," *Gender and History* 22, no. 2 (2010): 677–691; and Wilson Chacko Jacob, *Working Out Egypt: Effendi Masculinity and Subject Formation in Colonial Modernity, 1870–1940* (Durham, NC: Duke University Press, 2011).

115. Kholoussy, "Monitoring and Medicalising Male Sexuality in Semi-colonial Egypt," 677.

116. Kozma, "We, the Sexologists," 444.

117. Hirschfeld, *Weltreise eines Sexualforschers im Jahre 1931/32*, 346–347.

118. Ibid., 356.

119. Hirschfeld's notes, extra folder, Magnus Hirschfeld Collection, Kinsey Institute.

120. The phrase is "eine Krankheit" in Hirschfeld, *Weltreise eines Sexualforschers im Jahre 1931/32*, 351. Pasha, who also acted as the personal physician of King Fuad, established, for instance, the Egyptian Association for the Blind and the Egyptian Museum of Health. See Lesley Kitchen Lababidi with Nadia El-Arabi, *Silent No More: Special Needs People in Egypt* (Cairo: American University Press, 2002), 9; and Lanfranchi, *Casting Off the Veil*, 184.

121. The original text reads, "Ich betrachte die sexuelle Triebabweichung als eine Krankheit, die aufmerksame Beachtung der Ärtzte und vorbeugende Maßnahmen erfordert, um eine gesunde neue Generation zu erzielen." Hirschfeld, *Weltreise*, 352.

122. The original reads, "Hinsichtlich der Ägypter ist es für much fraglos, daßihr sittliches und geistiges Durchschnittsniveau dem der europäischen Völker nicht nachsteht." Hirschfeld, *Weltreise eines Sexualforschers im Jahre 1931/32*, 391.

123. The phrase is "indisches Hotel," also referred to as a "nicht europäisch geleitetes Hotel" (not-European-managed hotel), in ibid., 301.

124. The phrases are "Illusionen," "Glaube," and "Phantasie" in ibid., 396.

125. The original reads, "Ich gestehe, daß ich mich auf meiner Weltreise von keiner Stätte so schwer losgerissen habe wie von Jerusalem, daß mir von keinem Lande der Abschied so schwer fiel wie von Palästina." Ibid., 393.

126. Ibid., 395–396.

127. Ibid.

128. Ibid., 397.

129. The phrases are "Die herzerfrischende Bewegtheit und herzerfrischende Natürlichkeit dieser urgesunden jungen Leute, die sich stolz 'Chaluzim,' d.h. 'Pioniere' nennen" in ibid., 398.

130. The phrase is "die einzige einheitlich jüdische Stadt der Gegenwart" in ibid., 400.

131. The phrase is "Erfolg" in ibid., 402.

132. The original reads, "Wie sollte es denn auch unter den Weißen 'reine' Rassen geben, wenn man berücksichtigt, daß jedes Individuum eine Ahnenreihe von Vätern und Müttern besitzt und in sich verbindet, die Tausende, vielleicht sogar Hunderttausende von Generationen umfaßt." Ibid., 402. Hirschfeld emphasizes whiteness in his critique of "pure races."

133. For a discussion of the antibourgeois underpinnings of the protokibbutz movement, see Ofer Nur, *Eros and Tragedy: Jewish Male Fantasies and the Masculine Revolution of Zionism* (Boston: Academic Studies Press, 2013).

134. See Liat Kozma, "Sexology in the Yishuv: The Rise and Decline of Sexual Consultation in Tel Aviv, 1930–1939," *International Journal of Middle East Studies* 42 (2010): 231–249. See also, e.g., Nur's account in *Eros and Tragedy* of the establishment of an "erotic community" of Jewish settlers in Palestine in the early 1920s, which, characterized by a concern with sexual reform, anticipated the kibbutz movement; and Eran Rolnik's analysis of the psychoanalytic movement's contribution to Jewish identity formation in Palestine, *Freud in Zion: Psychoanalysis and the Making of Modern Jewish Identity* (London: Karnac, 2012).

135. Hirschfeld, *Weltreise im Jahre 1931/32*, 399. For an account of Matmon's work—and an excellent comparative study of sexology in Egypt and Palestine—see Kozma, "Translating Sexology, Writing the Nation, 135–153.

136. Hirschfeld, *Weltreise im Jahre 1931/32*, 411–412.

137. Ibid., 411.
138. The phrase is "Geschlechtssorgen" in ibid.
139. Ibid., 398, 419.
140. See, e.g., Judith Butler, *Parting Ways: Jewishness and the Critique of Zionism* (New York: Columbia University Press, 2013); and Jacqueline Rose, *The Question of Zionism* (Princeton, NJ: Princeton University Press, 2005). For a historical account of modern Palestinian identity and politics, see, e.g., Rashid Khalidi, *Palestinian Identity: The Construction of Modern National Consciousness* (New York: Columbia University Press, 2010).
141. Hirschfeld, *Weltreise im Jahre 1931/32*, 426.
142. See Gudrun Krämer, *A History of Palestine: From the Ottoman Empire to the Founding of the State of Israel*, trans. Graham Harman and Gudrun Krämer (Princeton, NJ: Princeton University Press 2011), 256.
143. The phrase is "ein jüdisches Land" in Hirschfeld, *Weltreise im Jahre 1931/32*, 427.
144. The phrase is "100,000 Zionisten" in ibid., 428.
145. The phrases are "die nicht zu unterschätzende Größe der Gefahr, die von dieser Seite dem Zionismus droht," "mutig, fröhlich und zuversichtlich," and "Pioniere" in ibid.
146. Ibid., 429–430.
147. The words are "Panhumanismus," "Kosmopolitismus," and "Menschenliebe" in ibid., 436.
148. Ibid., 432.
149. See, e.g., Ahmad H. Sa'di and Lila Abu-Lughod, eds., *Nakba: Palestine, 1948, and the Claims of Memory* (New York: Columbia University Press, 2007).
150. The word "Freund" can mean both friend and boyfriend.
151. Hirschfeld, *Weltreise, im Jahre 1931/32* 350–352.
152. The phrases are "die alte Hetze" and "die Situation für mich in der Heimat nur noch grauenhafter" in Hirschfeld, *Testament*, 136.
153. The phrase is "Ich kann es kaum fassen" in ibid., 138.
154. Ibid., 142.
155. Ibid.
156. Dr. E. Elkan, letter to Mrs. Howard, October 12, 1971, SA/FPA, World League for Sexual Reform 1929, Wellcome Library, London.
157. See Atina Grossmann, "'Satisfaction Is Domestic Happiness': Mass Working-Class Sex Reform Organizations in Weimar Germany," in *Towards the Holocaust: Anti-Semitism and German Fascism in Weimar Germany*, ed. Michael Dobowski and Isidor Wallimann (Westport, CT: Greenwood Press, 1983), 293n69.
158. The phrase is "heimlich" in Hirschfeld, *Testament*, 170.
159. The phrases are "ein unglückliches Verhängnis" and "nichtssagende Bagatelle" in ibid., 179–180.
160. The phrase is "Badeanstaltsaffäire" in ibid., 178n456.
161. Magnus Hirschfeld, letter to Norman Haire, June 6, 1933, PSY/WOL/6/8/4, File 1, Wellcome Library.
162. At the time of Hirschfeld's death, his two main beneficiaries were abroad, Tao Li in Zurich and Karl Giese in Vienna.
163. Matthew Burroughs Price has argued that detachment is part of queer culture in which it functions as a "balancing act between engagement with and withdrawal from

history." See Matthew Burroughs Price, "A Genealogy of Queer Detachment," *PMLA* 130, no. 3 (2015): 649.

164. Arondekar and Patel, "Area Impossible," 152.

CODA

Material in this chapter was previously published in Heike Bauer, "Sexology Backward: Hirschfeld, Kinsey and the Reshaping of Sex Research in the 1950s," in *Queer 1950s: Rethinking Sexuality in the Postwar Years*, ed. Heike Bauer and Matt Cook (Basingstoke, UK: Palgrave Macmillan, 2012), 133–149.

1. Sara Ahmed, *Queer Phenomenology* (Durham, NC: Duke University Press, 2004), 179.

2. Ibid.

3. I have discussed Kinsey's take on Hirschfeld in more detail in Heike Bauer, "Sexology Backward: Hirschfeld, Kinsey and the Reshaping of Sex Research in the 1950s," in *Queer 1950s: Rethinking Sexuality in the Postwar Years*, ed. Heike Bauer and Matt Cook (Basingstoke, UK: Palgrave Macmillan, 2012), 133–149. For analyses of Kinsey's work in America, Britain, and Germany, see, e.g., Miriam G. Reumann's *Sexual Character: Sex, Gender, and National Identity in the Kinsey Reports* (Berkeley: University of California Press, 2005); Liz Stanley, *Sex Surveyed, 1949–1994: From Mass-Observation's "Little Kinsey" to the National Survey and the Hite Reports* (London: Taylor and Francis, 1995); and Sybille Steinbacher, *Wie der Sex nach Deutschland kam: Der Kampf um Sittlichkeit und Anstand in der frühen Bundesrepublik* (Munich, Germany: Siedler, 2011). Donna J. Drucker reexamines Kinsey's methodology in an altogether more affirmative manner in *The Classification of Sex: Alfred Kinsey and the Organization of Knowledge* (Pittsburgh: Pittsburgh University Press, 2013); Peter Hegarty resituates Kinsey's work in the context of the history of psychology in *A Gentleman's Disagreement: Alfred Kinsey, Lewis Terman, and the Sexual Politics of Smart Men* (Chicago: University of Chicago Press, 2013).

4. Regina Markell Morantz, "The Scientist as Sex Crusader: Alfred C. Kinsey and American Culture," *American Quarterly* 29, no. 5 (1977): 564.

5. Roy Cain, "Disclosure and Secrecy among Gay Men in the United States and Canada: A Shift in Views," in *American Sexual Politics: Sex, Gender, and Race since the Civil War*, ed. John C. Fout and Maura Shaw Tantillo (Chicago: University of Chicago Press, 1993), 292.

6. Lillian Faderman, *Odd Girls and Twilight Lovers: A History of Lesbian Life in Twentieth-Century America* (New York: Penguin, 1992), 140.

7. Janice M. Irvine, *Disorders of Desire: Sexuality and Gender in Modern American Sexology* (Philadelphia: Temple University Press, 2005), 20.

8. Studies of the German and North American histories of sexuality and sex research include Vern L. Bullough, ed., *Before Stonewall: Activists for Gay and Lesbian Rights in Historical Context* (Binghampton, UK: Haworth, 2002); John D'Emilio and Estelle B. Freedman, *Intimate Matters: A History of Sexuality in America* (New York: Harper and Row, 1988); Irvine, *Disorders of Desire*; and Robert Deam Tobin, *Peripheral Desires: The German Discovery of Sex* (Philadelphia: Pennsylvania University Press, 2015). Anna Katharina Schaffner provides an astute comparative analysis of the development of "European" sexology via close attention to German, French, and British

contexts in her *Modernism and Perversion: Sexual Deviance in Sexology and Literature, 1850–1930* (Basingstoke, UK: Palgrave Macmillan, 2011).

9. Steinbacher, *Wie der Sex nach Deutschland kam*, 154.

10. Alfred C. Kinsey, Wardell B. Pomeroy, and Clyde E. Martin, *Sexual Behavior in the Human Male* (Philadelphia: W. B. Saunders, 1948), 3.

11. Alfred C. Kinsey, Wardell B. Pomeroy, Clyde E. Martin, and Paul H Gebhard, *Sexual Behavior in the Human Female* (Philadelphia: W. B. Saunders, 1953), 469.

12. The expression is used by Eve Kosofsky Sedgwick in *Epistemology of the Closet* (Berkeley: University of California Press, 1990), 11, in an argument about the difficulties of working through "the entire cultural network of normative definitions" attached to the binary opposition of homosexuality and heterosexuality.

13. Kinsey, Pomeroy, and Martin, *Sexual Behavior in the Human Male*, 620.

14. Ibid.

15. Ibid.

16. Ibid., 4, 34.

17. Ibid., 620.

18. Harriet Mowrer, "Sex and Marital Adjustment: A Critique of Kinsey's Approach," *Social Problems* 1, no. 4 (1954): 147.

19. Kinsey, Pomeroy, and Martin, *Sexual Behavior in the Human Male*, 623–659.

20. Wardell B. Pomeroy, *Dr. Kinsey and the Institute for Sex Research* (London: Thomas Nelson and Sons, 1972), 69.

21. Ibid.

22. Quoted in Terence Kissack, ed., "Alfred Kinsey and Homosexuality in the '50s: Recollections of Samuel Morris Steward as told to Len Evans," *Journal of the History of Sexuality*, 9, no. 4 (2000): 477.

23. Ibid., 478.

24. Ibid., 476.

25. Heather Love, *Feeling Backward: Loss and the Politics of Queer History* (Cambridge, MA: Harvard University Press, 2007), 9.

26. Kinsey, Pomeroy, Martin, and Gebhard, *Sexual Behavior in the Human Female*, 21.

27. See, for instance, Leo P. Crespi and Edmund A. Stanley Jr., "Youth Looks at the Kinsey Report," *Public Opinion* 12, no. 4 (1948–1949): 687–696; Erdman Palmore, "Published Reactions to the Kinsey Reports," *Social Forces* 31, no. 2 (1952): 165–172; and W. Allen Wallis, "Statistics of the Kinsey Report," *Journal of the American Statistical Association* 44, no. 248 (1949): 463–484. For more information on Kinsey's impact on young women, see Amanda Littauer's excellent *Bad Girls: Young Women, Sex, and Rebellion before the Sixties* (Chapel Hill: University of North Carolina Press, 2015).

28. Steinbacher, *Wie der Sex nach Deutschland kam*, 154.

29. "Sex Behaviour of the Male: Discussion on the Kinsey Report," *British Medical Journal* 2, no. 4584 (1948): 872 (emphasis added).

30. Ibid.

31. Morris Leopold Ernst and David Loth, *Sexual Behaviour and the Kinsey Report* (London: Falcon Press, 1949).

32. See, for instance, Morris Ernst's own "Reflections on the *Ulysses* Trial and Censorship," *James Joyce Quarterly* 3, no. 1 (1965): 3–11; and Lesley A. Taylor, "'I Made

Up My Mind to Get It': The American Trial of *The Well of Loneliness*, New York City, 1928–1929," *Journal of the History of Sexuality* 10, no. 2 (2001): 250–286.

33. Ernst and Loth, *Sexual Behaviour and the Kinsey Report*, 172.

34. Ibid., 169.

35. For an account of the Eulenburg affair, see Isabel V. Hull, *The Entourage of Kaiser Wilhelm II, 1888–1918* (Cambridge: Cambridge University Press, 1982), 109–145.

36. For the complex debates about homosexuality and Nazism, see, e.g., Elizabeth D. Heineman, "Sexuality and Nazism: The Doubly Unspeakable?," in *Sexuality and German Fascism*, ed. Dagmar Herzog (Oxford: Berghahn, 2005), 22–66; Stefan Micheler, "Homophobic Propaganda and the Denunciation of Same-Sex-Desiring Men under National Socialism," trans. Patricia Szobar, in *Sexuality and German Fascism*, ed. Dagmar Herzog (Oxford: Berghahn, 2005), 95–130; and Matthew Burroughs Price, "A Genealogy of Queer Detachment," *PMLA* 130, no. 3 (2015): 648–665.

37. "Employment of Homosexuals and Other Sex Perverts in the U.S. Government: Interim Report Submitted to the Committee on Expenditures in the Executive Departments," 81st Congress, no. 241, December 15 (legislative day November 27), 1950, available at https://ecf.cand.uscourts.gov/cand/09cv2292/evidence/PX2337.pdf. See also Mark Blasius and Shane Phelan, eds., *We Are Everywhere: A Historical Sourcebook of Gay and Lesbian Politics* (New York: Routledge, 1997).

38. Ernst and Loth, *Sexual Behaviour and the Kinsey Report*, 170.

39. Chapter 4 discusses the complex debates that link homosexuality and Nazism, both during the Nazi reign and in postwar assessments of the origin and rise of German fascism. For a good discussion of the issues at stake, see, e.g., Dagmar Herzog, "Hubris and Hypocrisy, Incitement and Disavowal: Sexuality and German Fascism," in *Sexuality and German Fascism*, ed. Dagmar Herzog (Oxford: Berghahn, 2005), 1–21; and Dagmar Herzog, *Sex after Fascism: Memory and Morality in Twentieth-Century Germany* (Princeton, NJ: Princeton University Press, 2007).

40. Much of the scholarship on queer touch is indebted to Carolyn Dinshaw's discussion in *Getting Medieval: Sexualities and Communities, Pre- and Postmodern* (Durham, NC: Duke University Press, 1999). She writes that "queerness knocks signifiers loose, ungrounding bodies, making them strange, working in this way to provoke perceptual shifts and subsequent corporeal response in those touched" (151).

41. Neil Bartlett, *Who Was That Man? A Present for Mr. Oscar Wilde* (London: Serpent's Tail, 1988), xix.

42. Jin Haritaworn, Adi Kunstman, and Silvia Posocco, "Introduction," in *Queer Necropolitics*, ed. Jin Haritaworn, Adi Kunstman, and Silvia Posocco (New York: Routledge, 2014), 1.

43. Ibid., 2.

Bibliography

ARCHIVAL SOURCES

Deutsches Literaturarchiv Marbach [German Literature Archive Marbach]
Dill Pickle Club Records, Newberry Library, Chicago
Leo Baeck Institute, New York
Magnus Hirschfeld Collection, Kinsey Institute, Bloomington, Indiana
Museum of Jewish Heritage, New York
Wellcome Library, London

PRINTED AND ELECTRONIC SOURCES

Abraham, Felix. "Genitalumwandlungen an zwei männlichen Transvestiten." *Zeitschrift fuer Sexualwissenschaft and Sexualpolitik*, no. 18 (1931): 223–226.
Abrams, Lynn. "Crime against Marriage? Wife-Beating, the Law and Divorce in Nineteenth-Century Hamburg." In *Gender and Crime in Modern Europe*, edited by Meg Arnot and Cornelie Usborne, 118–136. London: UCL Press, 2001.
Abugideiri, Hibba. *Gender and the Making of Modern Medicine in Colonial Egypt*. Farnham, UK: Ashgate, 2010.
Adams, Barry D. "Theorizing Homophobia." In *Sexualities: Critical Concepts in Sociology*, edited by Kenneth Plummer, 170–187. London: Routledge, 2002.
Ahluwalia, Sanjam. "Demographic Rhetoric and Sexual Surveillance: Indian Middle-Class Advocates of Birth Control, 1902–1940s." In *Confronting the Body: The Politics of Physicality in Colonial and Post-colonial India*, edited by James H. Mills and Satadru Sen, 183–202. London: Anthem, 2004.

———. *Reproductive Restraints: Birth Control in India, 1877–1947.* Chicago: University of Illinois Press, 2008.
Ahmed, Sara. "Interview with Judith Butler." *Sexualities* 19, no. 4 (2016): 482–492.
———. "Making Feminist Points." *feministkilljoys* (blog), September 11, 2013. Available at https://feministkilljoys.com/2013/09/11/making-feminist-points.
———. *On Being Included: Racism and Diversity in Institutional Life.* Durham, NC: Duke University Press, 2012.
———. *Queer Phenomenology.* Durham, NC: Duke University Press, 2004.
———. *Strange Encounters: Embodied Others in Post-coloniality.* London: Routledge, 2000.
———. *Willful Subjects.* Durham, NC: Duke University Press, 2014.
———. "You Are Oppressing Me!" *feministkilljoys* (blog), February 17, 2016. Available at https://feministkilljoys.com/2016/02/17/you-are-oppressing-me.
Ames, Eric, Marcia Klotz, and Lora Wildenthal, eds. *Germany's Colonial Pasts.* Lincoln: University of Nebraska Press, 2005.
"Ammon, Therese." *Weblexikon der Wiener Sozialdemokratie.* Available at http://www.dasrotewien.at/ammon-therese.html (accessed October 10, 2016).
Anagol, Padma. *The Emergence of Feminism in India, 1850–1920.* Farnham, UK: Ashgate, 2005.
Anderson, Olive. *Suicide in Victorian and Edwardian England.* Oxford: Clarendon, 1987.
Andreassen, Rikke. *Human Exhibitions: Race, Sexuality, Gender in Ethnic Displays.* London: Routledge, 2016.
Angelides, Steven. "The Emergence of the Paedophile in the Late Twentieth Century." *Australian Historical Studies* 36, no. 126 (2005): 272–295.
Arndt, Karl John Richard, and May E. Olson. *The German Language Press of the Americas: 1732–1956.* Munich, Germany: K. G. Saur, 1973.
Arondekar, Anjali. *For the Record: On Sexuality and the Colonial Archive in India.* Durham, NC: Duke University Press, 2009.
———. "Queer Archives: A Roundtable Discussion." *Radical History Review* 122 (2015): 211–232.
Arondekar, Anjali, and Geeta Patel. "Area Impossible: Notes Toward an Introduction." *GLQ: Journal of Lesbian and Gay Studies* 22, no. 2 (2016): 151–171.
Back, Les, and Jon Solomos. "Racism and Anti-Semitism." In *Theories of Race and Racism: A Reader*, edited by Les Back and Jon Solomos, 257–259. London: Routledge, 2000.
Bähr, Andreas. "Between 'Self-Murder' and 'Suicide': The Modern Etymology of Self-Killing." *Journal of Social History* 46, no. 3 (2013): 620–632.
Baile, David. "The Discipline of *Sexualwissenschaft* Emerges in Germany, Creating Divergent Notions of European Jewry." In *Yale Companion to Jewish Writing and Thought in German Culture, 1096–1996*, edited by Sander L. Gilman and Jack Zipes, 273–279. New Haven, CT: Yale University Press, 1997.
Ballard, Barbara J. "A People without a Nation." *Chicago History*, Summer 1999, pp. 27–45.
Baranowski, Shelley. *Nazi Empire: German Colonialism and Imperialism from Bismarck to Hitler.* Cambridge: Cambridge University Press, 2011.
Bartlett, Neil. *Who Was That Man? A Present for Mr Oscar Wilde.* London: Serpent's Tail, 1988.

Bar-Yosef, Ofer, and Jane Callender. "A Forgotten Archaeologist: The Life of Francis Turville-Petre." *Palestine Exploration Quarterly* 129, no. 1 (1997): 2–18.

Bauer, Heike. *English Literary Sexology: Translations of Inversion, 1860–1930*. Basingstoke, UK: Palgrave Macmillan, 2009.

———. "Measurements of Civilization: Non-Western Female Sexuality and the Fin-De-Siècle Social Body." In *Sexuality at the Fin de Siècle: The Making of a "Central Problem,"* edited by Peter Cryle and Christopher E. Forth, 93–108. Cranbury, NJ: University of Delaware Press, 2008.

———, ed. *Sexology and Translation: Cultural and Scientific Encounters across the Modern World*. Philadelphia: Temple University Press, 2015.

———. "Sexology Backward: Hirschfeld, Kinsey and the Reshaping of Sex Research in the 1950s." In *Queer 1950s: Rethinking Sexuality in the Postwar Years*, edited by Heike Bauer and Matt Cook, 133–149. Basingstoke, UK: Palgrave Macmillan, 2012.

———. "Staging Un/Translatability: Magnus Hirschfeld Encounters Philadelphia." In *Un/Translatables: New Maps for Germanic Literatures*, ed. Bethany Wiggin and Catriona MacLeod, 193–202. Evanston, IL: Northwestern University Press, 2016.

Beachy, Robert. *Das Andere Berlin: Die Erfindung der Homosexualität*. Munich, Germany: Siedler, 2015.

———. *Gay Berlin: Birth of a Modern Identity*. New York: Vintage, 2014.

Beccalossi, Chiara, *Female Sexual Inversion: Same-Sex Desires in Italian and British Sexology, c. 1870–1920*. Basingstoke, UK: Palgrave Macmillan, 2012.

Becker, Peter. "The Standardized Gaze: The Standardization of the Search Warrant in Nineteenth-Century Germany." In *Documenting Individual Identity: The Development of State Practices in the Modern World*, edited by Jane Kaplan and John Torpley, 139–163. Princeton, NJ: Princeton University Press, 2001.

Bell, Richard. *We Shall Be No More: Suicide and Self-Government in the Newly United States*. Boston: Harvard University Press, 2012.

Benjamin, Harry. "Reminiscences." *Journal of Sex Research* 6, no. 1 (1970): 3–9.

———. *The Transsexual Phenomenon*. New York: Julian Press, 1966.

Benjamin, Walter. *Gesammelte Schriften*. Vol. 4.1, edited by Tillmann Rexroth. Frankfurt, Germany: Suhrkamp, 1972.

———. "Grandville, or World Exhibitions." In *The Arcades Project*, by Walter Benjamin, edited by Rolf Tiedemann, translated by Howard Eiland and Kevin McLaughlin, 7–8. Cambridge, MA: Belknap, 1999.

Bennett, Paula, and Vernon Rosario, eds. *Solitary Pleasures: The Historical, Literary and Artistic Discourses of Autoeroticism*. New York: Routledge, 1995.

Berlant, Lauren. *Cruel Optimism*. Durham, NC: Duke University Press, 2011.

Bhabha, Homi. *The Location of Culture*. New York: Routledge, 1990.

Bland, Lucy. *Banishing the Beast: Sexuality and the Early Feminists*. London: Penguin, 1995.

Bland, Lucy, and Laura Doan, eds. *Sexology in Culture: Labelling Bodies and Desires*. Cambridge: Polity, 1998.

Blasius, Mark, and Shane Phelan, eds. *We Are Everywhere: A Historical Sourcebook of Gay and Lesbian Politics*. New York: Routledge, 1997.

Bloch, Iwan. *Das Sexualleben unserer Zeit in seinen Beziehungen zur modernen Kultur*. Berlin: Louis Marcus, 1907.

———. "Liebe und Kultur." *Mutterschutz* 3 (1905): 26–32.

———. *The Sexual Life of Our Time in Its Relations to Modern Civilization.* Translated by Eden Paul. London: Rebman, 1909.

Bloxham, John Francis [X, pseud.]. "The Priest and the Acolyte." *The Chameleon*, December 1894, pp. 30–47.

Bogwardt, G. "Bernard Shapiro: An Orthodox Jew as an Early Andrologist in the 20th Century." *Sudhoffs Archiv* 86, no. 2 (2002): 181–197.

Bohm, Ewald. *Lehrbuch der Rorschach-Psychodiagnostik.* Zurich, Switzerland: Huber, 1957.

Böker, Uwe, Richard Corballis, and Julie Hibbard, eds. *The Importance of Reinventing Oscar: Versions of Wilde during the Last 100 Years.* Amsterdam: Rodopi, 2002.

Bose, D. M., S. N. Sen, and B. V. Subbarayappa, eds. *A Concise History of Sexual Science in India.* Delhi: Indian National Science Academy, 1971.

Braun, Christina von. "Ist die Sexualwissenschaft eine 'jüdische' Wissenschaft?" In *Magnus Hirschfeld: Ein Leben im Spannungsfeld von Wissenschaft, Politik und Gesellschaft*, edited by Elke-Vera Kotowski and Julius Schoeps, 255–269. Berlin: be.bra, 2004.

Brehl, Medardus. "Rassenmischung als Indiskretion: Textliche Re-Präsentationen des 'Mischlings' in der Deutschen Kolonialliteratur über den Hererokrieg." In *Rassenmischehen, Mischlinge, Rassentrennung: Zur Politik der Rasse im deutschen Kolonialreich*, edited by Frank Becker, 254–268. Stuttgart, Germany: Franz Steiner, 2004.

Bridgeman, Jo, and Daniel Monk. "Introduction: Reflections on the Relationship between Feminism and Child Law." In *Feminist Perspectives on Child Law*, edited by Jo Bridgeman and Daniel Monk, 1–18. London: Cavendish, 2000.

Briggs, Julia. *Virginia Woolf: An Inner Life.* Orlando, FL: Harcourt, 2005.

Briggs, Laura. *Reproducing Empire: Sex, Science and U.S. Imperialism in Puerto Rico.* Berkeley: University of California Press, 2002.

Bristow, Joseph. "Introduction." In *Wilde Discoveries: Traditions, Histories, Archives*, edited by Joseph Bristow, 1–45. Toronto: University of Toronto Press, 2013.

———, ed. *Oscar Wilde and Modern Culture: The Making of a Legend.* Athens: University of Ohio Press, 2008

———. *Sexuality.* 2nd ed. New York: Routledge 2011.

———, ed. *Wilde Discoveries: Traditions, Histories, Archives.* Toronto: University of Toronto Press, 2013.

———. "Wilde, *Dorian Gray* and Gross Indecency." In *Sexual Sameness: Textual Difference in Lesbian and Gay Writing*, edited by Joseph Bristow, 44–62. Abingdon, UK: Routledge, 2014.

Brown, Jennifer, and Sandra L. Walklate, eds. *Handbook on Sexual Violence.* Abingdon, UK: Routledge, 2012.

Brown, Ron. *Art of Suicide.* London: Reaktion Books, 2001.

Brunton, Deborah, ed. *Health, Disease and Society in Europe, 1800–1930: A Source Book.* Manchester, UK: Manchester University Press, 2004.

Bullough, Vern L., ed., *Before Stonewall: Activists for Gay and Lesbian Rights in Historical Context.* Binghampton, UK: Haworth, 2002.

Bülow, Franz Josef von. *Deutsch-Südwestafrika: Drei Jahre im Lande Henrik Witboois.* Berlin: Mittler and Sohn, 1897.

"The Bülow Libel Case." *The Times* (London), November 8, 1907, p. 7.

Butler, Judith. *Frames of War: When Is Life Grievable?* London: Verso, 2009.
———. *Parting Ways: Jewishness and the Critique of Zionism.* New York: Columbia University Press, 2013.
———. *Precarious Life: The Power of Mourning and Violence.* London: Verso, 2006.
———. *Undoing Gender.* New York: Routledge, 2004.
Cain, Roy. "Disclosure and Secrecy among Gay Men in the United States and Canada: A Shift in Views." In *American Sexual Politics: Sex, Gender, and Race since the Civil War*, edited by John C. Fout and Maura Shaw Tantillo, 289–309. Chicago: University of Chicago Press, 1993.
Canguilhem, George. *On the Normal and the Pathological*, translated by Carolyn R. Fawcett. London: Reidel, 1978.
Canning, Kathleen. "Gender and the Imaginary of Revolution in Germany." In *Germany 1916–23: A Revolution in Context*, edited by Klaus Weinhauer, Anthony McElligott, and Kirsten Heinsohn, 103–126. Bielefeld, Germany: Transcript, 2015.
Caramagno, Thomas. *The Flight of the Mind: Virginia Woolf's Art and Manic-Depressive Illness.* Berkeley: University of California Press, 1992.
Carano, Carol Lorraine. "Mad Lords and Irishmen: Representations of Lord Byron and Oscar Wilde since 1967." Ph.D. diss., University of Missouri–Kansas City, 2008.
Carter, Julian. "Normality, Whiteness, Authorship: Evolutionary Sexology and the Primitive Pervert." In *Science and Homosexualities*, edited by Vernon Rosario, 155–176. New York: Routledge, 1997.
Caruth, Cathy, ed. *Trauma: Explorations in Memory.* Baltimore: Johns Hopkins University Press, 1995.
Chakrabarti, Pratik. *Medicine and Empire: 1600–1960.* Basingstoke, UK: Palgrave Macmillan, 2014.
Chatterjee, Partha, and Pradeep Jeganathan, eds. *Community, Gender and Violence.* London: Hurst, 2000.
Chiang, Howard, ed. *Transgender China.* New York: Palgrave, 2012.
Chiang, Howard, and Ari Larissa Heinrich, eds. *Queer Sinophone Cultures.* New York: Routledge, 2014.
Chisholm, Dianne. "Benjamin's Gender, Sex, and Eros." In *A Companion to the Work of Walter Benjamin*, edited by Rolf G. Goebel, 246–272. Rochester, NY: Camden House, 2009.
Ciarlo, David. *Advertising Empire: Race and Visual Culture in Imperial Germany.* Cambridge, MA: Harvard University Press, 2011.
Cohen, Ed. *Talk on the Wilde Side.* New York: Routledge, 1993.
Conradt, Sebastian. *German Colonialism: A Short History.* Cambridge: Cambridge University Press, 2012.
Cook, Matt. *London and the Culture of Homosexuality, 1885–1914.* Cambridge: University of Cambridge Press, 2003.
Cook, Matt, and Jennifer Evans, eds. *Queer Cities, Queer Cultures: Europe since 1945.* London: Bloomsbury, 2014.
Cooks, Bridget R. "Fixing Race: Visual Representations of African Americans at the World's Columbian Exposition, Chicago, 1893." *Patterns of Prejudice* 41, no. 5 (2007): 435–465.
Correa, Silvio Marcus de Souza. "'Combatting' Tropical Diseases in the German Colonial Press." Translated by Derrick Guy Phillips. *História, Ciêncas, Saúde—Manguinhos,*

March 2012. Available at http://www.scielo.br/pdf/hcsm/v20n1/en_ahop0313.pdf.

Cory, William. *Ionica*. London: George Allen, 1905.

Cox, Rosie. *The Servant Question: The Home Life of a Global Economy*. London: Tauris, 2006.

Craig, Layne Parish. *When Sex Changed: Birth Control and Literature between the World Wars*. New Brunswick, NJ: Rutgers, 2013.

Cramer, Elizabeth. *Addressing Homophobia and Heterosexism on College Campuses*. New York: Routledge, 2014.

Creighton, S., J. Alderson, S. Brown, and C. L. Minto. "Medical Photography: Ethics, Consent, and the Intersex Patient." *BJU International* 89, no. 1 (2002): 67–71.

Crenshaw, Kimberlé. "Mapping the Margins: Intersectionality, Identity Politics, and Violence against Women of Color." *Stanford Law Review* 43, no. 6 (1991): 1241–1299.

Crespi, Leo P., and Edmund A. Stanley Jr. "Youth Looks at the Kinsey Report." *Public Opinion* 12, no. 4 (1948–1949): 687–696.

Crozier, Ivan. "All the Appearances Were Perfectly Normal: The Anus and the Sodomite in Nineteenth-Century Medical Discourse." In *Body Parts: Critical Explorations in Corporeality*, edited by Christopher E. Forth and Ivan Crozier, 65–84. Lanham, MD: Lexington, 2005.

Cryle, Peter. *The Telling of the Act: Sexuality as Narrative in Eighteenth- and Nineteenth-Century France*. London: Associated University Press, 2001.

Cryle, Peter, and Lisa Downing, eds. "Feminine Sexual Pathologies." Special issue, *Journal of the History of Sexuality* 18, no. 1 (2009).

———, eds. "Nature and Normality in the History of Sexuality." Special issue, *Psychology and Sexuality* 1, no. 3 (2010).

Cvetkovich, Ann. *An Archive of Feelings: Trauma, Sexuality and Lesbian Public Cultures*. Durham, NC: Duke University Press, 2003.

———. *Depression: A Public Feeling*. Durham, NC: Duke University Press, 2012.

Damousi, Joy, Birgit Lang, and Katie Sutton, eds. *Case Studies and the Dissemination of Knowledge*. New York: Routledge, 2015.

Dave, Naisargi N. *Queer Activism in India: A Story in the Anthropology of Ethics*. Durham, NC: Duke University Press, 2012.

Davies, Margrit. *Public Health and Colonialism: The Case of German New Guinea, 1884–1914*. Wiesbaden, Germany: Otto Harrassowitz, 2002.

Davis, Georgiann. *Contesting Intersex: The Dubious Diagnosis*. New York: New York University Press, 2015.

D'Cruze, Shani. "Sexual Violence since 1750." In *The Routledge History of Sex and the Body*, edited by Kate Fisher and Sarah Toulahan, 444–460. Abingdon, UK: Routledge, 2013.

Dean, Carolyn J. *The Fragility of Empathy after the Holocaust*. Ithaca, NY: Cornell University Press, 2004.

———. *The Frail Social Body: Pornography, Homosexuality and Other Fantasies in Interwar France*. Berkeley: University of California Press, 2000.

———. *Sexuality and Modern Western Culture*. New York: Twayne, 1996.

Dehner, George. *Influenza*. Pittsburgh, PA: University of Pittsburgh Press, 2012.

D'Emilio, John, and Estelle B. Freedman. *Intimate Matters: A History of Sexuality in America*. New York: Harper and Row, 1988.

"Deny Professor Hirschfeld Is Dead." *New York Times*, October 15, 1920, p. 4.

DeTora, Lisa. "Recognizing the Trauma: Battering and the Discourse of Domestic Violence." In *Gender Scripts in Medicine and Narrative*, edited by Marcelline Block and Angela Laflen, 238–268. Cambridge: Cambridge Scholars, 2010.

Deutsches Historisches Museum. "11. Treptow: Die Deutsche Colonial-Ausstellung von 1896 im Treptower Park." Available at https://www.dhm.de/ausstellungen/namibia/stadtspaziergang/treptow.htm#59 (accessed October 8, 2016).

Deutsches Institut für Japanstudien. "Gakken Bunko (Dohi Keizō)." Available at http://tksosa.dijtokyo.org/?page=collection_detail.php&p_id=311 (accessed October 10, 2016).

Dever, Maryanne. "Papered Over." In *Out of the Closet, Into the Archives: Researching Sexual Histories*, edited by Amy L. Stone and Jaime Cantrell, 65–95. New York: State University of New York Press, 2015.

Dickinson, Edward Ross. *The Politics of German Child Welfare from the Empire to the Federal Republic*. Cambridge, MA: Harvard University Press, 1996.

"Die Befreiung des Menschen von Leiden, Not und Schaden ist Dr Magnus Hirschfelds Bestimmung." *New Yorker Volkszeitung*, December 5, 1930.

Die Geprügelte Generation. "Die Rolle der Justiz." Available at http://gepruegelte-generation.de/hintergrundinformationen/die-rolle-der-justiz (accessed October 10, 2016).

"Die Kinderhölle in Mariaquell." *Die Unzufriedene: Eine unabhängige Wochenschrift für alle Frauen* 7, no. 12 (1929): 1–12.

Dierkes-Thrun, Petra. *Salome's Modernity: Oscar Wilde and the Aesthetics of Transgression*. Ann Arbor: University of Michigan Press, 2011.

Dinshaw, Carolyn. *Getting Medieval: Sexualities and Communities, Pre- and Postmodern*. Durham, NC: Duke University Press, 1999.

Doan, Laura. *Disturbing Practices: History, Sexuality, and Women's Experiences of Modern War*. Chicago: University of Chicago Press, 2013.

———. *Fashioning Sapphism: The Origins of a Modern English Lesbian Culture*. New York: Columbia University Press, 2001.

Dohi, Keizō. *Beiträge zur Geschichte der Syphilis in Ostasien*. Leipzig, Germany: Akademische Verlagsgesellschaft, 1923.

Dose, Ralf. *Magnus Hirschfeld: Deutscher—Jude—Weltbürger*. Berlin: Hentrich and Hentrich, 2005.

———. *Magnus Hirschfeld: The Origins of the Gay Liberation Movement*. New York: Monthly Review Press, 2014.

———. "Vorbemerkungen." In *Testament: Heft II*, by Magnus Hirschfeld, edited by Ralf Dose, 4–12. Berlin: Hentrich and Hentrich, 2013.

Dowling, Linda. *Hellenism and Homosexuality in Victorian Oxford*. Ithaca, NY: Cornell University Press, 1994.

Downing, Lisa. *The Subject of Murder: Gender, Exceptionality, and the Modern Killer*. Chicago: University of Chicago Press, 2013.

Downing, Lisa, and Robert Gillett, eds. *Queer in Europe: Contemporary Case Studies*. Farnham, UK: Ashgate, 2011.

Dreesback, Anne. *Gezähmte Wilde: Die Zurschaustellung "exotischer" Menschen in Deutschland, 1870–1940*. Frankfurt, Germany: Campus, 2005.

Dreger, Alice. *Hermaphrodites and the Medical Invention of Sex*. Cambridge, MA: Harvard University Press, 2009.

"Dr Magnus Hirschfeld am Sonntag im Labor Temple." *New Yorker Volkszeitung*, December 16, 1930.

"Dr Magnus Hirschfeld Spricht am Sonntag über 'Naturgesetze der Liebe.'" *New Yorker Volkszeitung*, December 25, 1930.

Drucker, Donna J. *The Classification of Sex: Alfred Kinsey and the Organization of Knowledge*. Pittsburgh: Pittsburgh University Press, 2013.

Duggan, Lisa. *Sapphic Slashers: Sex, Violence, and American Modernity*. Durham, NC: Duke University Press, 2000.

Durkheim, Émile. *Le Suicide*. Paris, 1897.

———. *Suicide: A Study in Sociology*. Edited by George Simpson. Translated by John A. Spaulding and George Simpson. New York: Free Press, 1979.

Eckert, Lina. "Intersexualization and Queer-Anarchist Futures." In *Queer Futures: Reconsidering Ethics, Activism, and the Political*, edited by Elahe Hashemi Yekani, Eveline Killian, and Beatrice Michaelis, 51–66. London: Routledge, 2013.

Egan, R. Danielle, and Gail Hawkes. *Theorizing the Sexual Child in Modernity*. Basingstoke, UK: Palgrave Macmillan, 2010.

Ellis, Edith. *Attainment*. London: Alston Rivers, 1909.

Ellis, Havelock. "Die Bedeutung der Schwangerschaft." *Mutterschutz* 1 (1905): 213–216.

———. Preface to *The Sexual Life of Savages in North-Western Melanesia*, by Bronislaw Malinowski, vii–xiii. New York: Harvest, 1929.

———. *Studies in the Psychology of Sex*. Vol. 7, *Eonism and Other Supplementary Studies*. Philadelphia: F. A. Davies, 1928.

———. "Ursprung and Entwicklung der Prostitution," *Mutterschutz* 3 (1907): 13–23.

Ellis, Robert. "People-Watching: *Völkerschau* Viewing Practices and *The Indian Tomb* (1921)." In *"Es ist seit Rahel uns erlaubt, Gedanken zu haben": Essays in Honor of Heidi Thomann Tewarson*, edited by Steven R. Huff and Dorothea Kaufmann, 187–206. Würzburg, Germany: Königshausen and Neumann, 2012.

Ellmann, Richard. *Oscar Wilde*. London: Vintage, 1988.

El-Tayeb, Fatima. "Dangerous Liaisons: Race, Nation and German Identity." In *Not So Plain as Black and White: Afro-German Culture and History, 1890–2000*, edited by Patrizia Mazón and Richard Steingrover, 27–60. Rochester, NY: University of Rochester Press, 2005.

"Employment of Homosexuals and Other Sex Perverts in the U.S. Government: Interim Report Submitted to the Committee on Expenditures in the Executive Departments." 81st Congress, no. 241, December 15 (legislative day November 27), 1950. Available at https://ecf.cand.uscourts.gov/cand/09cv2292/evidence/PX2337.pdf.

Eng, David L. *Racial Castration: Managing Masculinity in Asian America*. Durham, NC: Duke University Press, 2001.

Engels, Friedrich, letter to Karl Marx, June 22, 1869. In *Marx and Engels Collected Works*, vol. 43, edited by Jack Cohen et al., 295. London: Lawrence and Wishard, 2010.

Erber, Nancy. "The French Trials of Oscar Wilde." *Journal of the History of Sexuality* 6, no. 4 (1996): 549–588.

Ernst, Morris Leopold. "Reflections on the *Ulysses* Trial and Censorship. *James Joyce Quarterly* 3, no. 1 (1965), 3–11.
Ernst, Morris Leopold, and David Loth. *Sexual Behaviour and the Kinsey Report*. London: Falcon Press, 1949.
Evangelista, Stefano. "'Lovers and Philosophers at Once': Aesthetic Platonism in the Victorian Fin de Siècle." *Yearbook of English Studies* 36, no. 2 (2006): 203–244.
———, ed. *The Reception of Oscar Wilde in Europe*. New York: Continuum, 2010.
Faderman, Lillian. *Odd Girls and Twilight Lovers: A History of Lesbian Life in Twentieth-Century America*. New York: Penguin, 1992.
Fauve-Chamoux, Antoinette, ed. *Domestic Service and the Formation of European Identity: Understanding the Globalization of Domestic Work, 16th–21st Centuries*. Bern, Switzerland: Peter Lang, 2004.
Fedden, Henry Romilly. *Suicide: A Social and Historical Study*. London: Peter Davies, 1938.
Ferguson, Roderick. *Aberrations in Black: Toward a Queer of Color Critique*. Minneapolis: University of Minnesota Press, 2004.
Fishburn, Matthew. "Books Are Weapons: Wartime Responses to the Nazi Bookfires of 1933." *Book History* 10 (2007): 223–251.
———. *Burning Books*. Basingstoke, UK: Palgrave Macmillan, 2008.
Flegel, Monika. *Conceptualizing Cruelty to Children in Nineteenth-Century England: Literature, Representation and the NSPCC*. Farnham, UK: Ashgate, 2009.
Forbes, Geraldine. *Women in Modern India*. Cambridge: Cambridge University Press, 2004.
Foucault, Michel. *The History of Sexuality*. Vol. 1, *An Introduction*, translated by Robert Hurley. London: Penguin Books, 1990.
Fout, John C. "Sexual Politics in Wilhelmine Germany: The Male Gender Crisis and Moral Purity and Homophobia." In *Forbidden History: The State, Society, and the Regulation of Sexuality in Modern Europe*, edited by John C. Fout, 259–292. Chicago: University of Chicago Press, 1992.
Franks, Angela. *Margaret Sanger's Eugenics Legacy: The Control of Female Fertility*. Jefferson, NC: McFarland, 2005.
Freccero, Carla. *Queer/Early/Modern*. Durham, NC: Duke University Press, 2006.
———. "Queer Spectrality: Haunting the Past." In *A Companion to Lesbian, Gay, Bisexual, Transgender, and Queer Studies*, edited by George E. Haggerty and Molly McGarty, 194–213. Oxford: Blackwell, 2007.
Freeman, Elizabeth. "Time Binds; or, Erotohistoriography." *Social Text* 23, nos. 3–4 (2005): 57–68.
———. *Time Binds: Queer Temporalities, Queer Histories*. Durham, NC: Duke University Press, 2010.
Freud, Sigmund. "The Aetiology of Hysteria." In *The Standard Edition of the Complete Psychological Works of Sigmund Freud*. Vol. 3, *Early Psycho-Analytic Publications*, translated and edited by James Strachey, 187–221. London: Hogarth, 1978.
———. "Femininity." In *The Standard Edition of the Complete Psychological Works of Sigmund Freud*. Vol. 22, *"New Introductory Lectures on Psycho-Analysis" and Other Works*, translated and edited by James Strachey, 111–135. London: Hogarth, 1933.
———. *The Freud/Jung Letters: The Correspondence between Sigmund Freud and C. G. Jung*, edited by William McGuire, translated by Ralph Mannheim and R.F.C. Hull. London: Hogarth, 1974.

———. "Totem and Taboo." In *The Standard Edition of the Complete Psychological Works of Sigmund Freud*. Vol. 13, *"Totem and Taboo" and Other Works*, translated and edited by James Strachey, 1–161. London: Hogarth, 1933.

Friedrichsmeyer, Sara, Sara Lennox, and Susanne Zantop, eds. *The Imperialist Imagination: German Colonialism and Its Legacy*. Ann Arbor: University of Michigan Press, 1998.

Frühstück, Sabine. *Colonizing Sex: Sexology and Social Control in Modern Japan*. Berkeley: University of California Press, 2003.

Fuchs, Rachel. *Abandoned Children: Foundlings and Child Welfare in Nineteenth-Century France*. Albany: State University of New York Press, 1984.

———. *Gender and Poverty in Nineteenth-Century Europe*. Cambridge: Cambridge University Press, 2005.

Fuechtner, Veronika. "Indians, Jews, and Sex: Magnus Hirschfeld and Indian Sexology." In *Imagining Germany Imagining Asia: Essays in Asian-German Studies*, edited by Veronika Fuechtner and Mary Riehl, 111–130. Rochester, NY: Camden House, 2013.

Fuechtner, Veronika, Douglas Haynes, and Ryan Jones, eds. *Towards a Global History of Sexual Science, 1880–1950*. Berkeley: University of California Press, forthcoming.

Funding Universe. "The New York Times Company History." Available at http://www.fundinguniverse.com/company-histories/the-new-york-times-company-history (accessed October 10, 2016).

Funke, Jana. "Navigating the Past: Sexuality, Race, and the Uses of the Primitive in Magnus Hirschfeld's *The World Journey of a Sexologist*." In *Sex, Knowledge, and Receptions of the Past*, ed. Kate Fisher and Rebecca Langlands, 111–134. Oxford: Oxford University Press, 2015.

———. "'We Cannot Be Greek Now': Age Difference, Corruption of Youth and the Making of *Sexual Inversion*." *English Studies* 94, no. 2 (2013): 139–153.

Gates, Barbara. *Victorian Suicide: Mad Crimes and Sad Histories*. Princeton, NJ: Princeton University Press, 1988.

Gellately, Robert. *Backing Hitler: Consent and Coercion in Nazi Germany*. Oxford: Oxford University Press, 2001.

"German Expert, 62, Will Study Marriage Here." *New York Times*, November 23, 1930.

"In Germany Today." *Palestine Post*, October 26, 1934, p. 5.

Giffney, Noreen, Michelle Sauer, and Diane Watt, eds. *The Lesbian Premodern*. New York: Palgrave Macmillan, 2011.

Giles, Geoffrey J. "'The Most Unkindest Cut of All': Castration, Homosexuality, and Nazi Justice." *Journal of Contemporary History* 27, no. 1 (1992): 41–61.

Gilman, Sander. *The Jew's Body*. New York: Routledge, 1992.

Gilmour, Rachel. *Grammars of Colonialism: Representing Languages in Colonial South Africa*. Basingstoke, UK: Palgrave Macmillan, 2006.

Goldie, Terry. *The Man Who Invented Gender: Engaging the Ideas of John Money*. Vancouver, British Columbia: UCB Press, 2014.

Goldney, Robert D., Johann A. Schioldann, and Kirsten I. Dunn. "Suicide before Durkheim." *Health and History* 10 no. 2 (2008): 73–93.

Gopinath, Gayatri. *Impossible Desires: Queer Diasporas and South Asian Cultures*. Durham, NC: Duke University Press, 2005.

Grau, Günter, and Claudia Schoppmann, eds. *Hidden Holocaust: Gay and Lesbian Persecution in Germany, 1933–45*. New York: Routledge, 1995.
Grauke, Kevin. "'I Cannot Bear to Be Hurted Anymore': Suicide as Dialectical Ideological Sin in Nineteenth-Century American Realism." In *Representations of Death in Nineteenth-Century US Writing and Culture*, edited by Lucy Frank, 77–88. Aldershot, UK: Ashgate, 2007.
Gross, Babette. *Willi Münzenberg: Eine Politische Biographie*. Stuttgart, Germany: Deutsche Verlags-Anstalt, 1967.
Grossmann, Atina. "Magnus Hirschfeld, Sexualreform und die Neue Frau: Das Institut für Sexualwissenschaften und das Weimarer Berlin." In *Magnus Hirschfeld: Ein Leben im Spannungsfeld von Wissenschaft, Politik und Gesellschaft*, edited by Elke-Vera Kotowski and Julius Schoeps, 201–216. Berlin: be.bra, 2004.
———. *Reforming Sex: The German Movement for Birth Control and Abortion Reform, 1920–1950*. Oxford: Oxford University Press, 1995.
———. "'Satisfaction Is Domestic Happiness': Mass Working-Class Sex Reform Organizations in Weimar Germany." In *Towards the Holocaust: Anti-Semitism and German Fascism in Weimar Germany*, edited by Michael Dobowski and Isidor Wallimann, 265–293. Westport, CT: Greenwood, 1983.
Guma, Prince Karakire. "Revisiting Homophobia in Times of Solidarity and Visibility in Uganda." *Rupkatha Journal on Interdisciplinary Studies in Humanities* 6, no. 1 (2014): 97–107.
Haeberle, Erwin J. "A Movement of Inverts: An Early Plan for an Organisation of Inverts in the United States." In *Journal of Homosexuality* 10, nos. 1–2 (1984): 127–135.
———. "Swastika, Pink Triangle, and Yellow Star: The Destruction of Sexology in Nazi Germany." In *Hidden from History: Reclaiming the Gay and Lesbian Past*, edited by Martin Duberman, Martha Vicinus, and George Chauncey Jr., 365–379. London: Penguin, 1991.
Halberstam, Judith (Jack). *Female Masculinity*. Durham, NC: Duke University Press, 1998.
———. *In a Queer Time and Place: Transgender Bodies, Subcultural Lives*. New York: New York University Press, 2005.
———. *The Queer Art of Failure*. Durham, NC: Duke University Press, 2011.
Halle, Felix. *Geschlechtsleben und Strafrecht*. Berlin: Mopr, 1931.
Hamilton, Lisa. "Oscar Wilde, New Women and the Rhetoric of Effeminacy." In *Wilde Writings: Contextual Conditions*, edited by Joseph Bristow, 230–253. Toronto: University of Toronto Press, 2003.
Haritaworn, Jin, Adi Kunstman, and Silvia Posocco. Introduction to *Queer Necropolitics*, edited by Jin Haritaworn, Adi Kunstman, and Silvia Posocco, 1–28. New York: Routledge, 2014.
Harper, Fowler V. "The Cases of Mooney and Billings." *Oregon Law Review* 8, no. 4 (1929): 374–376.
Harvey, Andy. "Regulating Homophobic Hate Speech: Back to the Basics about Language and Politics?" *Sexualities* 15, no. 2 (2012): 191–206.
Haskins, Victoria K., and Claire Lowrie, eds. *Colonization and Domestic Service: Historical and Contemporary Perspectives*. New York: Routledge, 2015.
"Hatred of the Hun: The Pathology of It Explained." *Manchester Courier*, July 5, 1915, p. 8.

Hegarty, Peter. *A Gentleman's Disagreement: Alfred Kinsey, Lewis Terman, and the Sexual Politics of Smart Men*. Chicago: University of Chicago Press, 2013.

Heineman, Elizabeth D. "Sexuality and Nazism: The Doubly Unspeakable?" In *Sexuality and German Fascism*, edited by Dagmar Herzog, 22–66. Oxford: Berghahn, 2005.

Herrn, Rainer. *Schnittmuster des Geschlechts: Transvestitismus und Transsexualität in der frühen Sexualwissenschaft*. Giessen, Germany: Psychosozial, 2005.

———. "Sex brennt: Magnus Hirschfeld, sein Institut für Sexualwissenschaft und die Bücherverbrennung." Available at https://gedenkort.charite.de/fileadmin/user_upload/microsites/ohne_AZ/sonstige/gedenkort/ausstellung_sex-brennt/Sex-brennt_Hirschfeld.pdf (accessed December 30, 2016).

———. "Vom Traum zum Trauma: Das Institut für Sexualwissenschaft." In *Magnus Hirschfeld: Ein Leben im Spannungsfeld von Wissenschaft, Politik und Gesellschaft*, edited by Elke-Vera Kotowski and Julius Schoeps, 173–199. Berlin: be.bra, 2004.

Herzer, Manfred. "Communists, Social Democrats, and the Homosexual Movement in the Weimar Republic." In *Gay Men and the Sexual History of the Political Left*, edited by Gert Hekma, Harry Oosterhuis, and James Steakley, 197–226. Binghampton, UK: Haworth, 1995.

Herzog, Dagmar, ed. *Brutality and Desire: War and Sexuality in Europe's Twentieth Century*. Basingstoke, UK: Palgrave Macmillan, 2009.

———. "Hubris and Hypocrisy, Incitement and Disavowal: Sexuality and German Fascism." In *Sexuality and German Fascism*, edited by Dagmar Herzog, 1–21. Oxford: Berghahn, 2005.

———. *Sex after Fascism: Memory and Mortality in Twentieth-Century Germany*. Princeton, NJ: Princeton University Press, 2005.

———, ed. *Sexuality and German Fascism*. London: Berghahn, 2005.

Hewitt, Andrew. *Political Inversions, Homosexuality, Fascism and the Modernist Imaginary*. Stanford, CA: Stanford University Press, 1996.

Hill, Darryl B. "Sexuality and Gender in Hirschfeld's *Die Transvestiten:* A Case of the 'Elusive Evidence of the Ordinary.'" *Journal for the History of Sexuality* 14, no. 3 (2005): 316–332.

Hill, Leonidas E. "The Nazi Attack on 'Un-German' Literature, 1933–1945." In *The Holocaust and the Book*, edited by Jonathan Rose, 9–46. Amherst: University of Massachusetts Press, 2001.

Hirschfeld, Magnus. *Alkohol im Familienleben*. Berlin: Fritz Stolt, 1906.

———. "Aus Amerika." *Die Aufklärung* 1, no. 4 (1929): 128.

———. "Aus der Bewegung." *Jahrbuch für sexuelle Zwischenstufen* 20 (1920–1921): 106–142.

———. "Aus England." *Die Aufklärung* 1, no. 3 (1929): 3.

———. "Autobiographical Sketch." In *Encyclopedia Sexualis: A Comprehensive Encyclopedia-Dictionary of Sexual Sciences*, edited by Victor Robinson, 317–321. New York: Dingwall-Rock, 1936.

———. *Berlins Drittes Geschlecht*. Leipzig, Germany: Seeman, 1904.

———. *Berlins Drittes Geschlecht*, edited by Manfred Herzer. Berlin: Rosa Winkel, 1991.

———. "Choosing Mate a Science under Guidance of German 'Love Clinic.'" Interview by George Viereck. *Milwaukee Sentinel*, November 30, 1930, p. 1.

———. "Das Russische Strafrecht." *Die Aufklärung* 1, no. 8 (1929): 225–227.
———. *Das urnische Kind*. Berlin: Urban and Schwarzenberg, 1903.
———. "Die Bestrafung sexueller Triebabweichungen." In *Zur Reform des Sexualstrafrechts*, 158–176. Bern, Switzerland: Bircher, 1926.
———. "Die Gründung des WHK und seine ersten Mitglieder." In *Von Einst bis Jetzt: Geschichte einer homosexuellen Bewegung 1897–1922*, edited by Manfred Herzer and James Steakley, 47–64. Berlin: Rosa Winkel, 1986.
———. *Die Gurgel Berlins*. Berlin: Seemann, 1907.
———. *Die Gurgel Berlins*. 2nd ed. Berlin: Seemann, 1908.
———. *Die Homosexualität des Mannes und des Weibes*. Berlin: de Gruyter, 1984. First published 1914.
———. "Die Intersexuelle Konstitution." *Jahrbuch für sexuelle Zwischenstufen* no. 23 (1923): 3–27.
———. *Die Transvestiten: Eine Untersuchung über den erotischen Verkleidungstrieb*. Berlin: Medicinischer, 1910.
———. *Die Weltreise eines Sexualforschers*. Brugg, Switzerland: Böyzberg, 1933.
———. "'Dr Einstein of Sex' Not So Favourably Impressed by U.S." Interview by George Viereck. *Milwaukee Sentinel*, February 2, 1931, p. 1.
———. "Geleitwort." In *Liebe im Orient: Anangaranga, Die Bühne des Liebesgottes*, by Ferdinand Leiter and Hans H. Thal, ix–xiii. Vienna, Austria: Schneider, 1929.
———. "Geleitwort." In *Liebe im Orient: Das Kamasutram des Vatsyayana*, by Ferdinand Leiter and Hans H. Thal, v–vii. Lindau, Germany: Rudolph, 1929.
———. *Geschlechts-Übergänge*. Leipzig, Germany: Malende, 1905.
———. *Kriegspsychologisches*. Bonn, Germany: Marcus and Webers, 1916.
———. *Men and Women: The World Journey of a Sexologist*. Translated by Oliver P. Green. New York: G. P. Putnam's, 1935.
———. *Naturgesetze der Liebe: Eine gemeinverständliche Untersuchung über den Liebes-Eindruck, Liebes-Drang und Liebes-Ausdruck*. Berlin: Pulvermacher, 1912.
———. "New Morals for Old in Soviet Russia." *Illustrated London News*, April 6, 1929, p. 586.
———. "Oscar Wilde." In *Von Einst bis Jetzt: Geschichte einer homosexuellen Bewegung 1897–1922*," edited by Manfred Herzer and James Steakley, 64–74. Berlin: Rosa Winkel, 1986.
———. "Prügelpädagogen." *Die Aufklärung* 1, no. 4 (1929): 96–98.
———. *Racism* Translated by Eden and Cedar Paul. London: Victor Gollancz, 1938.
——— [Th. Ramien, pseud.]. *Sappho und Sokrates, oder Wie erklärt sich die Liebe der Männer und Frauen zu Personen des eigenen Geschlechts?* Leipzig: Max Spohr, 1896.
———. "Sexualeingriffe." *Die Aufklärung* 1, no. 7 (1929): 201–202.
———. "Sexual Hypochondria and Morbid Scrupulousness." In *Sexual Truths*, edited by William J. Robinson, 207–226. Hoboken, NJ: American Biological Society, 1919.
———. *Sexualität und Kriminalität*. Berlin: Renaissance, 1924.
———. *Sexualpathologie: Ein Lehrbuch für Ärzte und Studierende*. Vol. 2, *Sexuelle Zwischenstufen*. Bonn: Marcus and Webers, 1922.
———. *Sexualpsychologie und Volkspsychologie: Eine epikritische Studie zum Harden-Prozess*. Leipzig, Germany: Georg H. Wigand, 1908.

———, ed. *Sittengeschichte des Weltkriegs*. Leipzig, Germany: Sexualwissenschaft Schneider, 1930.

———. *Testament: Heft II*, edited by Ralf Dose. Berlin: Hentrich and Hentrich, 2013.

———. "Über Erkrankungen des Nervensystems im Gefolge der Influenza." Ph.D. diss., Friedrich-Wilhelms-Universität, Berlin, 1892.

———. *Übergänge zwischen dem männlichen und weiblichen Geschlecht*. Leipzig, Germany: Malende, 1904.

———. *Verstaatlichung des Gesundheitswesens*. Berlin: Neues Vaterland, 1919.

———. Vorwort [Foreword] to *Geschlechtsleben und Strafrecht*, by Felix Halle, ix–xii. Berlin: Mopr, 1931.

———. *Warum Hassen uns die Völker? Eine Kriegspsychologische Betrachtung*. Bonn, Germany: Marcus and Webers, 1915.

———. "Was eint und trennt das Menschengeschlecht?" *Die Aufklärung* 1, nos. 11–12 (1929): 321–322.

———. *Weltreise eines Sexualforschers im Jahre 1931/32*. Edited by Hans Christoph Buch. Frankfurt, Germany: Eichborn, 2006.

———. *Women East and West: Impressions of a Sex Expert*. Translated by Oliver P. Green. London: William Heinemann, 1935.

Hirschfeld, Magnus, and Ewald Bohm. *Sexualerziehung: Der Weg durch Natürlichkeit zur neuen Moral*. Berlin: Universitas, 1930.

Hirschfeld, Magnus, and Richard Linsert. *Empfängnisverhütung: Mittel and Methoden*. Berlin: Neuer Deutscher, 1928.

Hirschfeld, Magnus, and Franziska Mann. *Was jede Frau vom Wahlrecht wissen muß!* Berlin: A. Pulvermacher, 1918.

"Hirschfeld, Magnus, *Jahrbuch für sexuelle Zwischenstufen, Heft 5*." *Mutterschutz* 3 (1907): 217.

Hoechstetter, Sophie. "Dr Magnus Hirschfeld." In *Vierteljahresberichte des Wissenschaftlich-humanitäres Kommitees während der Kriegszeit: Zum 50: Geburtstag von Dr Magnus Hirschfeld, 14 Mai 1818* 18, nos. 2–3 (1918): 11–12.

Holland, Sharon Patricia. *The Erotic Life of Racism*. Durham, NC: Duke University Press, 2012.

Holmes, Morgan, ed. *Critical Intersex*. Farnham, UK: Ashgate, 2012.

Hommen, Tanja. *Sittlichkeitsverbrechen: Sexuelle Gewalt im Kaiserreich*. Frankfurt, Germany: Campus, 1999.

Hoyer, Niels, ed. *Man into Woman: An Authentic Record of a Change of Sex*. London: Jarrolds, 1933.

Hull, Isabel. *Absolute Destruction: Military Culture and the Practices of War in Imperial Germany*. Ithaca, NY: Cornell University Press, 2005.

———. *The Entourage of Kaiser Wilhelm II, 1888–1918*. Cambridge: Cambridge University Press, 1982.

Hund, Wulf D. "Advertising White Supremacy: Capitalism, Colonialism and Commodity Racism." In *Colonial Advertising and Commodity Racism*, edited by Wulf D. Hund, Michael Pickering, and Anandi Ramamurthy, 31–67. Vienna, Austria: Lit, 2013.

Hund, Wulf D., Michael Pickering, and Anandi Ramamurthy, eds. *Colonial Advertising and Commodity Racism*. Vienna, Austria: Lit, 2013.

Hyde, Montgomery. *The Other Love: A Historical and Contemporary Survey of Homosexuality in Britain.* London: Mayflower, 1972.
Irvine, Janice. *Disorders of Desire: Sexuality and Gender in Modern American Sexology.* Philadelphia: Temple University Press, 2005.
Isherwood, Christopher. *Christopher and His Kind.* London: Vintage, 1976.
Ivory, Yvonne. "The Trouble with Oscar Wilde's Legacy for the Early Homosexual Rights Movement in Germany." In *Oscar Wilde and Modern Culture: The Making of a Legend,* edited by Joseph Bristow, 133–153. Athens: Ohio University Press, 2008.
———. "The Urning and His Own: Individualism and the Fin-de-Siècle Invert." *German Studies Review* 26, no. 2 (2003): 333–352.
Iwaya, Suyewo. "Nan sho 'k: Päderastie in Japan." *Jahrbuch für sexuelle Zwischenstufen* 5 (1902): 265–271.
Jackson, Louise. *Child Sexual Abuse in Victorian England.* London: Routledge, 2000.
Jackson, Zakkiyah. "Animal: New Theorizations of Race and Posthumanism." *Feminist Studies* 39, no. 3 (2014): 669–685.
Jacob, Wilson Chacko. *Working Out Egypt: Effendi Masculinity and Subject Formation in Colonial Modernity, 1870–1940.* Durham, NC: Duke University Press, 2011.
Janoff, Douglas. *Pink Blood: Homophobic Violence in Canada.* Toronto: University of Toronto Press, 2005.
Jaworski, Katrina. "The Author, Agency and Suicide." *Social Identities* 16, no. 5 (2010): 675–687.
Joff, Annette. "Iwaya Sazanami: Berliner Tagebuch, November–Dezember 1900." Master's thesis, Humboldt University, Berlin, 2007.
Johnson, David K. *The Lavender Scare: The Cold War Persecution of Gays and Lesbians in the Federal Government.* Chicago: University of Chicago Press, 2004.
Johnson, Mark. "Transgression and the Making of a 'Western' Sexual Science." In *Transgressive Sex: Subversion and Control in Erotic Encounters,* edited by Hastings Donnan and Fiona Magowan, 167–189. New York: Berghahn, 2009.
Joiner, Thomas. *Myths about Suicide.* Boston: Harvard University Press, 2010.
Josipovic, Andrea. "Secret Things and the Confinement of Walls: 'The Private Sphere' in Crimes of Child Sexual Abuse Perpetrated by Women." *Australian Feminist Studies* 30, no. 85 (2015): 252–272.
Jütte, Robert. "Einleitung." In *Handwörterbuch der Sexualwissenschaft,* by Max Marcuse, ii–viii. Berlin: de Gruyter, 2001.
Kam, Lucetta Yip Lo. "Desiring T, Desiring Self: 'T-Style' Pop Singers and Lesbian Culture in China." *Journal of Lesbian Studies* 18, no. 3 (2014): 252–265.
Kaplan, Ann E. *Trauma Culture: The Politics of Loss and Terror in Media and Literature.* New York: Rutgers University Press, 2005.
Karkazis, Katarina. *Fixing Sex: Intersex, Medical Authority, and Lived Experience.* Durham, NC: Duke University Press, 2008.
Karsch, F. "Uranismus und Tribadismus under den Naturvölkern." *Jahrbuch für sexuelle Zwischenstufen* 3 (1901): 72–202.
Katz, Jonathan. *The Invention of Heterosexuality.* Chicago: University of Chicago Press, 1995.
Kempf, Edward. "The Psychopathology of the Acute Homosexual Panic: Acute Pernicious Dissociation Neuroses." In *Psychopathology,* by Edward Kempf, 477–515. St. Louis, MO: C. V. Mosby, 1920.

Kennedy, Hubert. "Johann Baptist von Schweitzer: The Queer Marx Loved to Hate." *Journal of Homosexuality* 29, nos. 2–3 (1995): 69–96.

Khalidi, Rashid. *Palestinian Identity: The Construction of Modern National Consciousness.* New York: Columbia University Press, 2010.

Kholoussy, Hanan. "Monitoring and Medicalising Male Sexuality in Semi-colonial Egypt." *Gender and History* 22, no. 2 (2010): 677–691.

"Kill Dr. M. Hirschfeld: Well-Known German Scientist Victim of a Munich Mob." *New York Times*, October 12, 1920, p. 14.

King, Joyce E. "Dysconscious Racism: Ideology, Identity, and the Miseducation of Teachers." *Journal of Negro Education* 60, no. 2 (1991): 133–146.

Kinsey, Alfred C., Wardell B. Pomeroy, and Clyde E. Martin. *Sexual Behavior in the Human Male.* Philadelphia: W. B. Saunders, 1948.

Kinsey, Alfred C., Wardell B. Pomeroy, Clyde E. Martin, and Paul H. Gebhard. *Sexual Behavior in the Human Female.* Philadelphia: W. B. Saunders, 1953.

Kissack, Terence, ed. "Alfred Kinsey and Homosexuality in the '50s: Recollections of Samuel Morris Steward as Told to Len Evans." *Journal of the History of Sexuality* 9, no. 4 (2000): 472–491.

Knox, Melissa. *A Long and Lovely Suicide.* New Haven, CT: Yale University Press, 1996.

Knuth, Rebecca. *Burning Books and Leveling Libraries: Extremist Violence and Cultural Destruction.* Westport, CT: Praeger, 2006.

Kopf, Jennifer. "Picturing Difference: Writing the Races in the 1896 Berlin Trade Exposition's Souvenir Album." *Historical Geography* 36 (2008): 112–138.

Kozma, Liat. *Policing Egyptian Women: Sex, Law, and Medicine in Khedival Egypt.* New York: Syracuse University Press, 2011.

———. "The Silence of the Pregnant Bride: Non-marital Sex in Middle Eastern Societies." In *Untold Histories of the Middle East: Recovering Voices from the 19th and 20th Centuries*, edited by Amy Singer, Christoph K. Neumann, and Selçuk Akşin Somel, 71–88. London: Routledge, 2011.

———. "Translating Sexology, Writing the Nation: Sexual Discourse and Practice in Hebrew and Arabic in the 1930s." In *Sexology and Translation: Cultural and Scientific Encounters across the Modern World*, edited by Heike Bauer, 135–153. Philadelphia: Temple University Press, 2015.

———. "'We, the Sexologists . . .': Arabic Medical Writing on Sexuality, 1879–1943." *Journal of the History of Sexuality* 22, no. 3 (2013): 426–445.

Krafft-Ebing, Richard von. *Psychopathia Sexualis with Especial Reference to the Antipathic Sexual Instinct: A Medico-Legal Study.* Translated by F. J. Rebman. New York: Eugenics, 1934.

Krämer, Gudrun. *A History of Palestine: From the Ottoman Empire to the Founding of the State of Israel.* Translated by Graham Harman and Gudrun Krämer. Princeton, NJ: Princeton University Press 2011.

Kreuschner, Curt Rudolf. "Die Herero." *Freiburger Zeitung*, January 17, 1904, p. 1.

Kulpa, Robert, and Joanna Mizielińska, eds. *De-Centring Western Sexualities: Central and Eastern European Perspectives.* Farnham, UK: Ashgate, 2011.

Kunzel, Regina. *Criminal Intimacy: Prison and the Uneven History of Modern American Sexuality.* Chicago: Chicago University Press, 2008.

Kushner, Howard. *American Suicide.* New Brunswick, NJ: Rutgers University Press, 1991.

Lababidi, Lesley Kitchen, with Nadia El-Arabi. *Silent No More: Special Needs People in Egypt.* Cairo: American University Press, 2002.

Labbé, Jean. "Ambroise Tardieu: The Man and His Work on Child Maltreatment a Century before Kempe." *Child Abuse and Neglect* 29 (2005): 311–324.

Lamberti, Marjory. "Radical Schoolteachers and the Origins of the Progressive Education Movement in Germany, 1900–1914." *History of Education Quarterly* 40, no. 1 (2000): 22–48.

Lanfranchi, Sania Sharawi. *Casting Off the Veil: The Life of Huda Shaarawi, Egypt's First Feminist.* London: I. B. Tauris, 2012.

Lang, Birgit. "Sexualwissenschaft auf Reisen: Zur antikolonialen Mimikry in Magnus Hirschfeld's *Die Weltreise eines Sexualforschers* (1933)." *Österreichische Zeitschrift für Geschichtswissenschaften* 22, no. 1 (2011): 199–213.

Langbehn, Volker, ed. *German Colonialism, Visual Culture, and Modern Memory.* New York: Routledge, 2010.

Langbehn, Volker, and Mohammad Salama, eds. *German Colonialism: Race, the Holocaust, and Postwar Germany.* New York: Columbia University Press, 2011.

Lautmann, Rüdiger. "The Pink Triangle: The Persecution of Homosexual Males in Concentration Camps in Nazi Germany." In *The Gay Past: A Collection of Historical Essays*, edited by Salvatore J. Licata and Robert P. Petersen, 141–160. New York: Routledge, 2013.

Lawson, Kate, and Lynn Shakinovsky. *The Marked Body: Domestic Violence in Mid-Nineteenth-Century Literature.* Albany: State University of New York Press, 2002.

Leng, Kirsten. "Culture, Difference, and Sexual Progress in Turn-of-the-Century Europe: Cultural Othering and the German League for the Protection of Mothers and Sexual Reform, 1905–1914." *Journal of the History of Sexuality* 25, no. 1 (2016): 62–82.

———. "The Personal Is Scientific: Women, Gender, and the Production of Sexological Knowledge in Germany and Austria, 1900–1931." *History of Psychology* 18, no. 3 (2015): 238–251.

Leslie, Esther. *Hollywood Flatlands: Animation, Critical Theory and the Avant-Garde.* London: Verso, 2002.

———. *Walter Benjamin.* London: Reaktion, 2007.

Light, Alison. *Mrs. Woolf and the Servants.* London: Penguin, 2008.

Lim, Adelyn. *Transnational Feminism and Women's Movements in Post-1997 Hong Kong: Solidarity beyond the State.* Hong Kong: Hong Kong University Press, 2015.

Linge, Ina. "Gender and Agency between 'Sexualwissenschaft' and Autobiography: The Case of N.O. Body's *Aus eines Mannes Mädchenjahren*." *German Life and Letters* 68, no. 3 (2015): 387–404.

Littauer, Amanda. *Bad Girls: Young Women, Sex, and Rebellion before the Sixties.* Chapel Hill: University of North Carolina Press, 2015.

Lochrie, Karma. *Heterosyncracies: Female Sexuality When Normal Wasn't.* Minneapolis: University of Minnesota Press, 2005.

Logan, Cheryl A. *Hormones, Heredity, and Race: Spectacular Failure in Interwar Vienna.* New Brunswick, NJ: Rutgers University Press, 2013.

Love, Heather. *Feeling Backward: Loss and the Politics of Queer History.* Cambridge, MA: Harvard University Press, 2007.

———. "Forced Exile: Walter Pater's Queer Modernism." In *Bad Modernisms*, edited by Douglas Mao and Rebecca L. Walkowitz, 19–43. Durham, NC: Duke University Press, 2006.

Madley, Benjamin. "From Africa to Auschwitz: How German South West Africa Incubated Ideas and Methods Adopted and Developed by the Nazis in Eastern Europe." *European History Quarterly* 35, no. 3 (2005): 429–464.

Magnus Hirschfeld Society. "Founders of the Institute." Available at http://www.magnus-hirschfeld.de/institute-for-sexual-science-1919-1933/personnel/founders-of-the-institute (accessed October 10, 2016).

———. "Institute Employees and Domestic Personnel." Available at http://www.magnus-hirschfeld.de/institute-for-sexual-science-1919-1933/personnel/institute-employees-and-domestic-personnel (accessed October 10, 2016).

Mak, Geertje. *Doubting Sex: Inscriptions, Bodies, Selves in Nineteenth-Century Case Histories.* Manchester, UK: Manchester University Press, 2012.

———. "'Passing Women': Im Sprechzimmer von Magnus Hirschfeld. Warum der Begriff 'Transvestit' nicht für Frauen in Männerkleidern eingeführ wurde." Translated by Mirjam Hausmann. *Österreichische Zeitschrift für Geschichtswissenschaften* 9, no. 3 (1998): 383–399.

Malinowski, Bronislaw. *Sex and Repression in Savage Society.* London: Routledge and Kegan Paul, 1927.

———. *The Sexual Life of Savages in North-Western Melanesia.* New York: Eugenics, 1929.

Mancini, Elena. *Magnus Hirschfeld and the Quest for Sexual Freedom: A History of the First International Sexual Freedom Movement.* New York: Palgrave Macmillan, 2010.

Mann, Franziska. *Der Schäfer: Eine Geschichte aus der Stille.* Berlin: Axel Juncker, 1919.

———. *Die Stufe: Fragment einer Liebe.* Berlin: Mosaik, 1922.

Marhoefer, Laurie. *Sex and the Weimar Republic: German Homosexual Emancipation and the Rise of the Nazis.* Toronto: University of Toronto Press, 2015.

Marsh, Ian. *Suicide: Foucault, History and Truth.* Cambridge: Cambridge University Press, 2010.

Marshall, Daniel, Kevin P. Murphy, and Zeb Tortorici. "Editors' Introduction." In "Queering Archives: Intimate Tracings." Special issue, *Radical History Review* 2015, no. 122 (2015): 1–10.

Marx, Karl. "Peuchet on Suicide," translated by Eric A. Plaut, Gabrielle Edgcomb, and Kevin Anderson. In *Marx on Suicide*, edited by Eric A. Plaut and Kevin Anderson, 45–75. Evanston, IL: Northwestern University Press, 1999.

Mason, Gail. *The Spectacle of Violence: Homophobia, Gender and Knowledge.* New York: Routledge, 2002.

Masson, Jeffrey. *The Assault on Truth: Freud's Suppression of the Seduction Theory.* New York: Farrar, Straus, and Giroux, 1984.

Matte, Nicholas. "International Sexual Reform and Sexology in Europe, 1897–1933." *Canadian Bulletin of Medical History/Bulletin canadien d'histoire de la medecine* 22, no. 2 (2005): 253–270.

Matysik, Tracie. "In the Name of the Law: The 'Female Homosexual' and the Criminal Code in Fin de Siècle Germany." *Journal of the History of Sexuality* 13, no. 1 (2004): 26–48.

McClintock, Anne. *Imperial Leather: Race, Gender and Sexuality in the Colonial Contest.* New York: Routledge 1995.

Mendelssohn, Michèle. *Henry James, Oscar Wilde and Aesthetic Culture.* Edinburgh: Edinburgh University Press, 2007.

Metropolitan Museum of Art. "One Who Understands." Available at http://www.metmuseum.org/art/collection/search/489986 (accessed October 7, 2016).

Meyer, Sabine. *"Wie Lili zu einem richtigen Mädchen wurde": Lili Elbe; Zur Konstruktion von Geschlecht und Identität zwischen Medialisierung, Regulierung und Subjektivierung.* Bielefeld, Germany: Transcript, 2015.

Meyerowitz, Joanne. *How Sex Changed: A History of Transsexuality in the United States.* Cambridge, MA: Harvard University Press, 2002.

———. "Sex Change and the Popular Press: Historical Notes on Transsexuality in the United States, 1930–1955." *GLQ: A Journal of Lesbian and Gay Studies* 4, no. 2 (1998): 159–187.

Micheler, Stefan. "Homophobic Propaganda and the Denunciation of Same-Sex Desiring Men under National Socialism," translated by Patricia Szobar. In *Sexuality and German Fascism*, edited by Dagmar Herzog, 95–130. London: Berghahn, 2005.

Miles, Robert. "Apropos the Idea of 'Race' . . . Again." In *Theories of Race and Racism: A Reader.* 2nd ed., edited by Les Back and Jon Solomos, 180–198. London: Routledge, 2009.

Mischlich, Adam. *Lehrbuch der Hausasprache.* Berlin: Georg Reimer, 1911.

———. *Wörterbuch der Hausasprache.* Berlin: Georg Reimer, 1906.

Mizejewski, Linda. *Divine Decadence: Fascism, Female Spectacle, and the Makings of Sally Bowles.* Princeton, NJ: Princeton University Press, 1992.

Moll, Albert. *Das Sexualleben des Kindes.* Leipzig, Germany: Vogel, 1908.

———. *The Sexual Life of the Child.* Translated by Eden Paul. New York: Macmillan, 1912.

———. *The Sexual Life of the Child.* Translated by Eden Paul. New York: Macmillan, 1919.

"Monkeyana." *Punch*, May 18, 1861, p. 206.

Morantz, Regina Markell. "The Scientist as Sex Crusader: Alfred C. Kinsey and American Culture." *American Quarterly* 29, no. 5 (1977): 563–589.

Morland, Iain, ed. "Intersex and After." Special issue, *GLQ: Journal of Lesbian and Gay Studies* 15, no. 2 (2009).

Morris-Reich, Amos. *Race and Photography: Racial Photography as Scientific Evidence, 1876–1980.* Cambridge, MA: Harvard University Press, 2016.

Morton, Marsha. *Max Klinger and Wilhelmine Culture: On the Threshold of German Modernism.* Farnham, UK: Ashgate, 2014.

Mosse, Georg, and James Jones. "Bookburning and the Betrayal of German Intellectuals." *New German Critique*, no. 31 (1984): 143–155.

Mowrer, Harriet. "Sex and Marital Adjustment: A Critique of Kinsey's Approach." *Social Problems* 1, no. 4 (1954): 147.

Moyd, Michelle R. *Violent Intermediaries: African Soldiers, Conquest, and Everyday Colonialism in German East Africa.* Athens: University of Ohio Press, 2014.

Mühsam, Richard. "Chirurgische Eingriffe bei Anomalien des Sexuallebens." *Therapie der Gegenwart* 67 (1926): 451–455.

Muñoz, Jose. *Cruising Utopia: The Then and There of Queer Futurity.* New York: New York University Press, 2009.

Murray, David B. A., ed. *Homophobias: Lust and Loathing across Time and Space.* Durham, NC: Duke University Press, 2009.

Myers, John E. B. "A Short History of Child Protection in America." *Family Law Quarterly* 42, no. 3 (2008): 449–463.
Narain, Vrinda. *Reclaiming the Nation: Muslim Women and the Law in India*. Toronto: University of Toronto Press, 2008.
Naranch, Bradley. "Introduction: Colonialism Made Simple." In *German Colonialism in a Global Age*, edited by Geoff Ely and Bradley Naranch, 1–18. Durham, NC: Duke University Press, 2014.
Naranch, Bradley, and Geoff Ely. *German Colonialism in a Global Age*. Durham, NC: Duke University Press, 2014.
Nehru, Jawaharlal. *The Essential Writings of Jawaharlal Nehru*. Edited by Sarvepalli Gopal and Uma Iyengar. Oxford: Oxford University Press, 2003.
Neill, Deborah J. "Germans and the Transnational Community of Tropical Medicine." In *German Colonialism in a Global Age*, edited by Bradley Naranch and Geoff Ely, 74–92. Durham, NC: Duke University Press, 2015.
"Neuer Magnus Hirschfeld Vortrag am Sonntag." *New Yorker Volkszeitung*, December 15, 1930.
Ngai, Sianne. *Ugly Feelings*. Cambridge, MA: Harvard University Press, 2005.
Nietzsche, Friedrich. *Also Sprach Zarathustra? Ein Buch für Alle und Keinen*. Chemnitz, Germany: Ernst Schmeitzner, 1883.
Nur, Ofer. *Eros and Tragedy: Jewish Male Fantasies and the Masculine Revolution of Zionism*. Boston: Academic Studies Press, 2013.
Olusoga, David, and Casper Erichsen. *The Kaiser's Holocaust: Germany's Forgotten Genocide and the Colonial Roots of Nazism*. London: Faber and Faber, 2011.
Oosterhuis, Harry, and Hubert Kennedy, eds. *Homosexuality and Male Bonding in Pre-Nazi Germany: The Youth Movement, the Gay Movement and Male Bonding before Hitler's Rise; Original Transcripts from "Der Eigene," the First Gay Journal in the World*. Binghampton, UK: Haworth, 2011.
O'Riley, Michael F. "Postcolonial Haunting: Anxiety, Affect, and the Situated Encounter." *Postcolonial Text* 3, no. 4 (2007). Available at http://www.postcolonial.org/index.php/pct/article/view/728/496.
Palmore, Erdman. "Published Reactions to the Kinsey Reports." *Social Forces* 31, no. 2 (1952): 165–172.
Paperno, Irina. *Suicide as a Cultural Institution in Dostoevsky's Russia*. Ithaca, NY: Cornell University Press, 1997.
Patton, Cindy, and Benigno Sánchez-Eppler, eds. *Queer Diaspora*. Durham, NC: Duke University Press, 2000.
Pfaefflin, Friedemann. "The Surgical Castration of Detained Sex Offenders Amounts to Degrading Treatment." *Sexual Offender Treatment* 5, no. 2 (2010). Available at http://www.sexual-offender-treatment.org/86.html.
Pick, Daniel. *Faces of Degeneration: A European Disorder, c.1848–c.1918*. Cambridge: Cambridge University Press, 1989.
Piper, Maria. *Die Schaukunst der Japaner*. Berlin: de Gruyter, 1927.
Plant, Richard. *The Pink Triangle: The Nazi War against Homosexuals*. New York: Holt, 1986.
Ploss, Hermann Heinrich, Max Bartels, and Paul Bartels. *Woman: An Historical, Gynæcological and Anthropological Compendium*. Edited by Eric John Dingwall. London: W. Heinemann, 1935.

Poignant, Roslyn. *Professional Savages: Captive Lives and Western Spectacle.* New Haven, CT: Yale University Press, 2004.
Pomeroy, Wardell B. *Dr. Kinsey and the Institute for Sex Research.* London: Thomas Nelson and Sons, 1972.
Powell, Kerry. *Acting Wilde: Victorian Sexuality, Theatre, and Oscar Wilde.* Cambridge: Cambridge University Press, 2011.
Prasad, Srirupa. *Cultural Politics of Hygiene in India, 1890–1940: Contagions of Feeling.* Basingstoke, UK: Palgrave Macmillan, 2015.
Price, Matthew Burroughs. "A Genealogy of Queer Detachment." *PMLA* 130, no. 3 (2015): 648–665.
Prickett, David James. "Magnus Hirschfeld and the Photographic (Re)Invention of the 'Third Sex.'" In *Visual Culture in Twentieth-Century Germany: Text as Spectacle*, edited by Gail Finney, 103–119. Bloomington: Indiana University Press, 2006.
Pross, Christian. "Nazi Doctors, German Medicine, and Historical Truth." In *The Nazi Doctors and the Nuremberg Code: Human Rights in Human Experimentation*, edited by George J. Annas and Michael A. Grodin, 32–52. Oxford: University of Oxford Press, 1992.
"The Prussian Court Scandals: Count Moltke and Herr Harden." *The Times* (London), October 26, 1907, p. 5.
"Psychology of War: Notable German Statement." *Hawera and Normanby Star* (New Zealand), May 1, 1917, p. 2.
Puar, Jasbir. "Rethinking Homonationalism." *International Middle Eastern Studies* 45 (2013): 336–339.
———. *Terrorist Assemblages: Homonationalism in Queer Times.* Durham, NC: Duke University Press, 2010.
Puar, Jasbir, and Maya Mikdashi. "Pinkwatching and Pinkwashing: Interpenetration and Its Discontents." *Jadaliyya*, August 9, 2012. Available at http://www.jadaliyya.com/pages/index/6774/pinkwatching-and-pinkwashing_interpenetration-and.
Qureshi, Sadiah. *Peoples on Parade: Exhibitions, Empire, and Anthropology in Nineteenth-Century Britain.* Chicago: University of Chicago Press, 2011.
Ralston, John C. *Fremont Older and the 1916 San Francisco Bombing: A Tireless Crusade for Justice.* Charleston, SC: History Press, 2013.
Ransome, Arthur. *Oscar Wilde: A Critical Study.* New York: Mitchell Kennerly, 1912.
"Rassenfragen." *Deutsche Kolonialzeitung*, September 4, 1909, pp. 593–594.
Rauch, Thilo. *Die Ferienkoloniebwegung: Zur Geschichte der privaten Fürsorge im Kaiserreich.* Wiesbaden, Germany: Springer, 1992.
Rawson, J. K. "Introduction: An Inevitable Political Craft." *Transgender Studies Quarterly* 2, no. 4 (2015): 544–552.
Reddy, Chandan. *Freedom with Violence: Race, Sexuality, and the U.S. State.* Durham, NC: Duke University Press, 2011.
Reich, Wilhelm. *Die Sexualität im Kulturkampf: Zur sozialistischen Umstrukturieung des Menschen.* 2nd ed. Berlin: Sexualpolitik, 1936.
Reid, Victoria. "André Gide's 'Hommage à Oscar Wilde' or 'The Tale of Judas.'" In *The Reception of Oscar Wilde in Europe*, edited by Stefano Evangelista, 96–107. New York: Continuum, 2010.
Reis, Elizabeth. *Bodies in Doubt: An American History of Intersex.* Baltimore: Johns Hopkins University Press, 2010.

Reumann, Miriam G. *Sexual Character: Sex, Gender, and National Identity in the Kinsey Reports.* Berkeley: University of California Press, 2005.

"Review of 'The Journey of a Sexologist.'" *Canadian Jewish Chronicle*, May 17, 1935, p. 13.

Rich, Adrienne. "Compulsory Heterosexuality and Lesbian Existence." *Signs* 5, no. 4 (1980): 631–660.

Ripa, Alexandra. "Hirschfeld privat: Seine Haushaelterin erinnert sich." In *Magnus Hirschfeld: Ein Leben im Spannungsfeld von Wissenschaft, Politik und Gesellschaft*, edited by Elke-Vera Kotowski and Julius Schoeps, 65–70. Berlin: be.bra, 2004.

Ritchie, J. M. "The Nazi Book-Burning." *Modern Language Review* 83, no. 3 (1988): 627–643.

Robins, Ashley H., and Sean L. Sellars. "Oscar Wilde's Terminal Illness: Reappraisal after a Century." *The Lancet* 356 (November 2000): 1841–1843.

Robinson, Victor. *The Story of Medicine.* New York: New Home Library, 1943.

Roen, Katrina. "Queer Kids: Toward Ethical Clinical Interactions with Intersex People." In *Ethics of the Body: Postconventional Challenges*, edited by Margrit Shildrick and Roxanne Mykitiuk, 259–278. Cambridge, MA: MIT Press, 2005.

Rogers, Molly. *Delia's Tears: Race, Science and Photography in Nineteenth-Century America.* New Haven, CT: Yale University Press, 2010.

Rohy, Valerie. *Anachronism and Its Others: Sexuality, Race, Temporality.* Albany: State University of New York Press, 2009.

Rolnik, Eran. *Freud in Zion: Psychoanalysis and the Making of Modern Jewish Identity.* London: Karnac, 2012.

Romesburg, Don. "Making Adolescence More or Less Modern." In *The Routledge History of Childhood in the Western World*, edited by Paula S. Fass, 229–248. New York: Routledge, 2013.

Rosario, Vernon A. *The Erotic Imagination: French Histories of Perversity.* Oxford: Oxford University Press, 1997.

———, ed. *Science and Homosexualities.* New York: Routledge, 1997.

———. "Studs, Stems and Fishy Boys: Adolescent Latino Gender Variance and the Slippery Diagnosis of Transsexuality." In *Transgender Experience: Place, Ethnicity and Visibility*, edited by Chantal Zabus and David Coab, 51–67. New York: Routledge, 2014.

Rose, Jacqueline. *The Question of Zionism.* Princeton, NJ: Princeton University Press, 2005.

Rothblum, Esther D., and Lynne A. Bond, eds. *Preventing Heterosexism and Homophobia.* Thousand Oaks, CA: Sage, 1996.

Rothfels, Nigel. *Savages and Beasts: The Birth of the Modern Zoo.* Baltimore: Johns Hopkins University Press, 2002.

Rubin, Henry. "The Logic of Treatment." In *The Transgender Reader*, edited by Susan Stryker and Stephen Whittle, 482–498. New York: Routledge, 2006.

Rudwick, Elliott, and August Meier. "Black Man in the 'White City': Negroes and the Columbian Exposition 1893." *Phylon* 26, no. 4 (1965): 354–361.

Rupp, Leila. *Sapphistries: A Global History of Love between Women.* New York: New York University Press, 2009.

Sa'di, Ahmad H., and Lila Abu-Lughod, eds. *Nakba: Palestine, 1948, and the Claims of Memory.* New York: Columbia University Press, 2007.

Sang, Tse-Lan D. *The Emerging Lesbian: Female Same-Sex Desire in Modern China.* Chicago: University of Chicago Press, 2003.
Sanger, Margaret. *An Autobiography.* New York: Norton, 1938.
———. *The Pivot of Civilization.* New York: Brentano's, 1922.
Sauerteig, Lutz D. H. "Loss of Innocence: Albert Moll, Sigmund Freud, and the Invention of Childhood around 1900." *Medical History* 56, no. 2 (2012): 156–183.
Schaffner, Anna Katharina. *Modernism and Perversion: Sexual Deviance in Sexology and Literature, 1850–1930.* Basingstoke, UK: Palgrave Macmillan, 2011.
Schaffner, Anna Katharina, and Shane Weller, eds. *Modernist Eroticisms: European Literature after Sexology.* Basingstoke, UK: Palgrave Macmillan, 2012.
Schaller, Dominic J. "Genocide in Colonial South-West Africa: The German War against the Herero and Nama, 1904–1907." In *Genocide of Indigenous Peoples: A Critical Bibliographic Review*, edited by Samuel Totten and Robert K. Hitchcock, 37–60. New Brunswick, NJ: Transaction, 2011.
Scheper-Hughes, Nancy, and Philippe Bourgois. "Introduction: Making Sense of Violence." In *Violence in War and Peace*, edited by Nancy Scheper-Hughes and Philippe Bourgois, 1–32. Oxford: Blackwell, 2004.
Schiebinger, Londa. *The Mind Has No Sex? Women in the Origins of Modern Science.* Cambridge, MA: Harvard University Press, 1991.
Schilling, Britta. "Imperial Heirlooms: The Private Memory of Colonialism in Germany." *Journal of Imperial and Commonwealth History* 41, no. 4 (2013): 663–682.
Schmidt, Norbert. *Kolonialmetropole Berlin: Zur Funktion der Völkerschau im Rahmen der ersten deutschen Kolonialaustellung in Berlin 1896.* Berlin: GRIN, 2005.
Schneider, Dorothee. *Trade Unions and Community: The German Working Class in New York, 1870–1900.* Urbana: University of Illinois Press, 1994.
Schücking, Walter, Helene Stöcker, and Elisabeth Rotten. *Durch zum Rechtsfrieden.* Berlin: Neues Vaterland, 1919.
Schwarz, Christa. "Europe and the Harlem Renaissance: 2—Berlin." In *Encyclopedia of the Harlem Renaissance, A–J*, edited by Cary D. Wintz and Paul Finkelman, 344–347. New York: Routledge, 2004.
Scull, Andrew. *Social Order/Mental Disorder: Anglo-American Psychiatry in Historical Perspective.* Berkeley: University of California Press, 1989.
Sedgwick, Eve Kosofsky. *Between Men: English Literature and Male Homosocial Desire.* New York: Columbia University Press, 1985.
———. *Epistemology of the Closet.* Berkeley: University of California Press, 1990.
Seitler, Dana. *Atavistic Tendencies: The Culture of Science in American Modernity.* Minneapolis: University of Minnesota Press, 2008.
Sengoopta, Chandak. *The Most Secret Quintessence of Life: Sex, Glands, and Hormones, 1850–1950.* Chicago: University of Chicago Press, 2006.
"Sex Behaviour of the Human Male: Discussion on the Kinsey Report." *British Medical Journal* 2, no. 4584 (1948): 872.
Shahani, Nishant. *Queer Retrosexualities: The Politics of Reparative Return.* Bethlehem, PA: Lehigh University Press, 2012.
Sigel, Lisa Z. *Making Modern Love: Sexual Narratives in Interwar Britain.* Philadelphia: Temple University Press, 2012.
Sigusch, Volkmar, ed. *Personenlexikon der Sexualforschung.* Frankfurt, Germany: Campus, 2009.

Sinha, Mrinalini. Introduction to *Mother India*, by Katherine Mayo, edited by Mrinalini Sinha, 1–41. Ann Arbor: University of Michigan Press, 2000.
Smith, Helmut Walser. *The Continuities of German History: Nation, Religion, and Race across the Long Nineteenth Century.* Cambridge: Cambridge University Press, 2008.
Smith, Jill Suzanne. *Berlin Coquette: Prostitution and the New Woman, 1890–1930.* Ithaca, NY: Cornell University Press, 2013.
Somerville, Siobhan B. *Queering the Color Line: Race and the Invention of Homosexuality in American Culture.* Durham, NC: Duke University Press, 2000.
———. "Scientific Racism and the Emergence of the Homosexual Body." *Journal for the History of Sexuality* 5, no. 2 (1994): 243–266.
Soreinen, Antu. "Cross-Generational Relationships before "the Lesbian": Female Same-Sex Sexuality in 1950s Rural Finland." In *Queer 1950s: Rethinking Sexuality in the Postwar Years*, edited by Heike Bauer and Matt Cook, 77–93. Basingstoke: Palgrave Macmillan, 2012.
Spanger, Tade Matthias. *Medical Law in Germany.* Alphen, Netherlands: Kluger, 2011.
Spector, Scott, Helmut Puff, and Dagmar Herzog, eds. *After "The History of Sexuality": German Genealogies with and beyond Foucault.* New York: Berghahn, 2012.
Spiro, Mia. *Anti-Nazi Modernism: Challenges of Resistance in 1930s Fiction.* Evanston, IL: Northwestern University Press, 2012.
Spivak, Gayatri Chakravorty. "Can the Subaltern Speak?" In *Marxism and the Interpretation of Culture*, edited by Cary Nelson and Lawrence Grossberg, 271–316. Basingstoke, UK: Macmillan, 1988.
Stanley, Liz. *Sex Surveyed, 1949–1994: From Mass-Observation's "Little Kinsey" to the National Survey and the Hite Reports.* London: Taylor and Francis, 1995.
Steakley, James. "Cinema and Censorship in the Weimar Republic: The Case of *Anders als die Andern*." *Film History* 11, no. 2 (1999): 181–203.
———. *The Homosexual Emancipation Movement in Germany.* Salem, NH: Ayer, 1975.
———. *Per scientiam ad justitiam*, Magnus Hirschfeld and the Sexual Politics of Innate Homosexuality." In *Science and Homosexualities*, edited by Vernon A. Rosario, 133–154. New York: Routledge, 1997.
Steinbacher, Sybille. *Wie der Sex nach Deutschland kam: Der Kampf um Sittlichkeit und Anstand in der frühen Bundesrepublik.* Munich, Germany: Siedler, 2011.
Stekel, Wilhelm. *Die Geschlechtskälte der Frau.* Berlin: Urban and Schwarzenberg, 1921.
———. *Peculiarities of Behaviour: Wandering Mania, Dipsomania, Cleptomania, Pyromania and Allied Impulsive Acts.* Vol. 1, translated by James S. van Teslaar. London: Williams Norgate, 1925.
Stephens, Elizabeth. "Bad Feelings." *Australian Feminist Studies* 30, no. 85 (2015): 273–282.
Stern, Guy. "The Burning of the Books in Nazi Germany, 1933: The American Response." *Simon Wiesenthal Center Annual* 2. Available at http://motlc.wiesenthal.com/site/pp.asp?c=gvKVLcMVIuG&b=395007 (accessed October 10, 2016).
Stevens, Hugh, and Caroline Howlett, eds. *Modernist Sexualities.* Manchester, UK: Manchester University Press, 2000.
St. John-Stevas, Norman. *Life, Death and the Law: Law and Christian Morals in England and the United States.* Washington, DC: Beard Books, 2002.

Stöcker, Helene. *Verkünder und Verwirklicher: Beiträge zum Gewaltproblem nebst einem zum erstem Male in deutschen Sprache veröffentlichten Briefe Tolstois*. Berlin: Neue Generation, 1928.

Stoler, Ann Laura. *Along the Archival Grain: Epistemic Anxieties and Colonial Common Sense*. Princeton, NJ: Princeton University Library, 2010.

———. *Carnal Knowledge and Imperial Power: Race and the Intimate in Colonial Rule*. Berkeley: University of California Press, 2002.

———. *Race and the Education of Desire: Foucault's "History of Sexuality" and the Colonial Order of Things*. Durham, NC: Duke University Press, 2005.

Stone, Amy L., and Jaime Cantrell. "Introduction: Something Queer at the Archive." In *Out of the Closet, Into the Archives: Researching Sexual Histories*, edited by Amy L. Stone and Jaime Cantrell, 1–22. New York: SUNY Press, 2015.

Stryker, Susan. *Transgender History*. Berkeley, CA: Seal Press, 2008.

Stryker, Susan, and Stephen Whittle, eds. *Transgender Studies Reader*. New York: Routledge, 2006.

Sullivan, Shannon. *Revealing Whiteness: The Unconscious Habits of Racial Privilege*. Bloomington: Indiana University Press, 2006.

Sutton, Katie. *The Masculine Woman in Weimar Germany*. New York: Berghahn, 2011.

———. "Representing the 'Third Sex': Cultural Translations of the Sexological Encounter in Early 20th-Century Germany." In *Sexology and Translation: Cultural and Scientific Encounters across the Modern World, 1880–1930*, edited by Heike Bauer, 53–71. Philadelphia: Temple University Press, 2015.

———. "Sexological Cases and the Prehistory of Transgender Identity Politics in Interwar Germany." In *Case Studies and the Dissemination of Knowledge*, edited by Joy Damousi, Birgit Lang, and Katie Sutton, 85–103. New York: Routledge, 2015.

———. "'We Too Deserve a Place in the Sun': The Politics of Transvestite Identity in Weimar Germany." *German Studies Review* 35, no. 2 (2012): 335–354.

Suzuki, Michiko. *Becoming Modern Women: Love and Female Identity in Prewar Japanese Literature and Culture*. Stanford, CA: Stanford University Press, 2010.

———. "The Translation of Edward Carpenter's The Intermediate Sex in Early Twentieth-Century Japan." In *Sexology and Translation: Cultural and Scientific Encounters across the Modern World*, edited by Heike Bauer, 197–215. Philadelphia: Temple University Press, 2015.

Sweeney, Fionnghuala. *Frederick Douglass and the Atlantic World*. Liverpool, UK: University of Liverpool Press, 2006.

Symonds, John Addington. *The Memoirs of John Addington Symonds*. Edited by Phyllis Grosskurth. London: Hutchinson, 1984.

Tamagne, Florence. *A History of Homosexuality in Europe*. Vols. 1 and 2, *Berlin, London, Paris, 1919–1939*. New York: Algora, 2005.

Tardieu, Auguste Ambroise. *Etude Médico-Légale sur les Attentats aux Mœurs*. Paris: Charpentier, 1857.

———. "Etude médico-légale sur les sévices et mauvais traitements exercés sur des enfants." *Annales d'hygiène publique et de médecine légale* 12 (1860): 361–398.

Taxil, Léo. *La Corruption Fin-de-Siècle*. Paris: Librairie Nilsson, 1894.

Taylor, Lesley A. "'I Made up My Mind to Get It': The American Trial of *The Well of Loneliness*, New York City, 1928–1929." *Journal of the History of Sexuality* 10, no. 2 (2001): 250–286.

Terry, Jennifer. *An American Obsession: Science, Homosexuality and Medicine in Modern Society.* Chicago: University of Chicago Press, 1999.

Thome, Helmut. "Violent Crime (and Suicide) in Imperial Germany, 1883–1902." *International Criminal Justice Review* 20, no. 1 (2010): 5–34.

Thyen, Ute, and Irene Johns. "Recognition and Prevention of Child Sexual Abuse in Germany." In *Child Abuse in Europe*, edited by Corinne May-Chahal and Maria Herzog, 79–100. Strasbourg, France: Council of Europe, 2003.

Tinsley, Omise'eke Natasha. *Thiefing Sugar: Eroticism between Women in Caribbean Literature.* Durham, NC: Duke University Press, 2010.

Tobin, Robert Deam. *Peripheral Desires: The German Discovery of Sex.* Philadelphia: University of Pennsylvania Press, 2015.

———. *Warm Brothers: Queer Theory and the Age of Goethe.* Philadelphia: University of Pennsylvania Press, 2000.

———. "Widernatürliche Unzucht! Paragraph 175 in Deutsch-Südwestafrika." In *Crimes of Passion: Repräsentationen der Sexualpathologie im frühen 20. Jahrhundert*, edited by Oliver Böni and Jasper Johnstone, 277–300. Berlin: de Gruyter, 2015.

Toulahan, Sarah, and Kate Fisher, eds. *The Routledge History of Sex and the Body, 1500 to the Present.* New York: Routledge, 2013.

Tréhel, Gilles. "Magnus Hirschfeld (1868–1935) et la femme soldat." *L'Esprit du Temps*, no. 125 (2013–2014): 125–137.

———. "Magnus Hirschfeld, Helene Deutsch, Sigmund Freud et les trois femmes combatants." *Psychothérapies* 35, no. 4 (2015): 267–274.

Turville-Petre, Francis. "Excavations in the Mugharet El-Kebarah." *Journal of the Royal Anthropological Institute of Great Britain and Ireland* 62 (1932): 271–276.

Ulrichs, Karl Heinrich. *Forschungen über das Rätsel der mannmänlichen Liebe.* Leipzig, Germany: Selbstverlag des Verfassers, 1864.

———. *Gladius furens: Das Naturräthsel der Urningsliebe und der Irrtum des Gesetzgebers*, edited by Wolfram Setz. 1868. Reprint, Munich: Forum Homosexualität, 2000.

———. *Memnon: Die Geschlechtsnatur des mannliebenden Urnings.* Schleiz, Germany: Hugo Benn, 1868.

UN Human Rights. "Convention on the Rights of the Child." 1990. Available at http://www.ohchr.org/en/professionalinterest/pages/crc.aspx.

Usborne, Cornelie. *Cultures of Abortion in Weimar Germany.* New York: Berghahn, 2007.

Vanita, Ruth, ed. *Queering India: Same-Sex Love and Eroticism in Indian Culture and Society.* New York: Routledge, 2002.

Vicinus, Martha. "The Adolescent Boy: Fin-de-Siècle Femme Fatale?" In *Victorian Sexual Dissidence*, edited by Richard Dellamora, 83–108. Chicago: University of Chicago Press, 1999.

———. *Intimate Friends: Women Who Love Women, 1778–1928.* Chicago: University of Chicago Press, 2004.

Volcano, Del LaGrace. "The Herm Portfolio." *GLQ: A Journal of Lesbian and Gay Studies* 15, no. 2 (2009): 261–265.

Walkowitz, Judith. *City of Dreadful Delight: Narratives of Sexual Danger in Late-Victorian London.* Chicago: University of Chicago Press, 1992.

Wallis, W. Allen. "Statistics of the Kinsey Report." *Journal of the American Statistical Association* 44, no. 248 (1949): 463–484.

Waters, Chris. "Sexology." In *Palgrave Advances in the Modern History of Sexuality*, edited by H. G. Cocks and Matt Houlbrook, 41–63. Basingstoke, UK: Palgrave, 2005.
Weber, Cynthia. *Queer International Relations*. Oxford: Oxford University Press, 2016.
Weedon, Chris. *Gender, Feminism, and Fiction in Germany, 1840–1914*. New York: Peter Lang, 2006.
Weeks, Jeffrey. *Sex, Politics and Society: The Regulations of Sexuality since 1800*. London: Pearson, 1981.
Weinberg, George. *Society and the Healthy Homosexual*. New York: St. Martin's Press, 1992.
Weinberg, Sonja. *Pogroms and Riots: German Press Responses to Anti-Jewish Violence in Germany*. Frankfurt, Germany: Peter Lang, 2010.
Weindling, Paul. *Health, Race and German Politics between National Unification and Nazism, 1870–1945*. Cambridge: Cambridge University Press, 1989.
Weiss, Richard. "Modern Rejuvenation." *Malayan Saturday Post*, April 13, 1929, p. 30.
Weiss, Volker. *. . . mit ärztlicher Hilfe zum richtigen Geschlecht?* Hamburg, Germany: Männerschwarm, 2009.
Wells, Karen, and Heather Montgomery. "Everyday Violence and Social Recognition." In *Childhood, Youth and Violence in Global Context: Research and Practice in Dialogue*, edited by Karen Wells, Erica Burman, Heather Montgomery, and Alison Watson, 1–20. Basingstoke, UK: Palgrave Macmillan, 2014.
Wesling, Meg. "Why Queer Diaspora?" *Feminist Review* 90 (2008): 30–47.
White, Chris, ed. *Nineteenth-Century Writings on Homosexuality: A Sourcebook*. London: Routledge, 1999.
Wieringa, Saskia, and Horacio Sivori, eds. *The Sexual History of the Global South: Sexual Politics and Postcolonialism in Africa, Asia and Latin America*. London: Zed Books, 2013.
Wildenthal, Lora. *German Women for Empire, 1884–1945*. Durham, NC: Duke University Press, 2001.
Wilke, Christiane. "Remembering Complexity? Memorials for Nazi Victims in Berlin." *International Journal of Transitional Justice* 7, no. 1 (2013): 136–156.
Wolff, Charlotte. *Magnus Hirschfeld: A Portrait of a Pioneer in Sexology*. London: Quartet Books, 1986.
Woods, Gregory. *Homintern: How Gay Culture Liberated the Modern World*. New Haven, CT: Yale University Press, 2016.
World Committee for the Victims of Fascism. *The Brown Book of the Hitler Terror*. New York: Alfred A. Knopf, 1938.
Zabus, Chantal, and David Coab, eds. *Transgender Experience: Place, Ethnicity, and Visibility*. New York: Routledge, 2014.

Index

Abortion, 65, 68, 72, 80
Abraham, Felix, 87, 92, 103–104
Abuse: critique of, 73–74; and law, 73; terminology of, 58
Activism, 24, 33–36, 46, 56, 76–77, 124, 134
Age of consent, 59, 62–63
Ahmed, Sara, 7, 13, 17, 102–103, 117, 125
Ammon, Therese, 72–73
Anders als die Andern (1919), 50, 108
Antisemitism, 7, 15, 16, 25–26, 64, 92, 96, 100
Archive: of the Institute of Sexual Science, 88–91, 93–94; of sexual science, 3; theorization of, 4–6
Arondekar, Anjali, 4–5, 109

Bartlett, Neil, 133
Benjamin, Harry, 90, 104
Benjamin, Walter, 9, 22, 38, 47, 81, 93
Birth control, 79, 80, 105
Blackmail, 26, 47, 50
Bloch, Ernst, 81
Bloch, Iwan, 80
Bohm, Ewald, 67–68
Bose, Girindrashekhar, 113, 114
Bourgeois, Philippe, 6
Boy love, 60–61

Brand, Adolf, 43, 63
Bülow, Franz Josef von, 24–25
Bund für männliche Kultur (League for Manly Culture), 43
Butler, Judith, 7, 10, 16, 56, 88, 94

Cantrell, Jaime, 4
Caruth, Cathy, 43
Castration, 69, 71–72
Chicago World's Fair, 19–20
Children: prostitution of, 59, 62–63; protection of, 63–64, 65–66; sexual abuse of, 60, 63, 69, 70–71, 74–75 (*see also* Pedophilia)
Chisholm, Dianne, 81
Class: and feminism, 82–83; and homosexuality, 83; and transgender people, 85–86
Colonialism (German), 17–20, 31–32
Corporeal punishment, 72–74
Cox, Rosie, 82
Crenshaw, Kimberlé, 10
Cross-dressing, 33, 48, 84, 86, 87, 90
Cvetkovich, Ann, 5, 7, 14, 37, 41

Darwin, Charles, 14, 20
D'Cruze, Shani, 58
Die Aufklärung (journal), 74–75

Die Homosexualität des Mannes und Weibes (Hirschfeld), 23, 30, 47, 62
Die Sittengeschichte des Weltkriegs (Hirschfeld), 34–35
Die Weltreise eines Sexualforschers (Hirschfeld), 108–110
Dohi, Keizō, 111
Domestic labor, 82–83
Dorchen (Rudolph Richter), 86–87
Dose, Ralf, 4
Douglass, Frederick, 20
Downing, Lisa, 71
Durkheim, Émile, 45

Elkan, Edward, 123
Ellis, Edith Lees, 83
Ellis, Havelock, 80, 83, 116, 130
El-Tayeb, Fatima, 21
Engels, Friedrich, 46–47
Eugenics, 8, 19, 79, 80
Eulenburg affair, 25–27, 131
Exile, 102–103

Fischer, Eugen, 29
Foucault, Michel, 6
Freccero, Carla, 8
Freeman, Elizabeth, 8, 9
Freud, Sigmund, 32, 42, 60, 71
Friedländer, Benedict, 43
Fuechtner, Veronika, 113–114, 115
Funke, Jana, 59, 61, 111

Gemeinschaft der Eigenen (Community of the Autonomous), 43
Giese, Karl, 81, 83, 91, 103–104, 118, 123–124
Gohrbandt, Erwin, 86–87
Gross, Babette, 81–82

Halberstam, Judith (Jack), 5, 85, 169n98
Harden trials, 25–27, 131
Herero genocide, 28–29
Herrn, Reiner, 38, 85, 87
Herzog, Dagmar, 97
Heterosexuality, 16, 105–106
Hirschfeld, Magnus: attacks on, 7, 25–26, 131–132; and colonialism, 28–29, 30–31, 32–34, 114–115; death of, 123; education of, 18–19; in Egypt, 119–120; in France, 98, 123–124; in India, 113–118; in Indonesia, 112, 114; in Japan, 111–113; pacifism of, 35, 80; in Palestine, 120–123; on race, 14–15; reception of, 131–132; on sexuality, 30; socialism of, 25, 81; in the United States, 19–21, 104–108, 112
Hodann, Max, 103
Hoechstetter, Sophie, 33
Holland, Sharon Patricia, 95–96
Homophobia, 16, 27–28, 46, 94, 100–101, 105, 129–132
Homosexuality: persecution of, 28, 48, 51, 54, 92, 131–132; and race, 30–31; subcultures of, 21, 33, 43, 55, 60–62, 90
Homosexual panic, 26
Homosexual rights, 9–10, 24, 26, 33, 35–36, 54, 62–63, 64, 79, 124, 134
Hormone treatment, 86
Hund, Wulf, 22, 23

Institute of Sexual Science, 43, 79–80; and communism, 81–82; as home, 81–83; representation of, 1–2
Intersex, 69–70
Isherwood, Christopher, 83, 85, 91
Ivory, Yvonne, 54

Jackson, Louise, 58, 59
Jackson, Zakkiyah, 20
Jahrbuch für sexuelle Zwischenstufen (journal), 24–25, 42, 80, 112
Jaworski, Katrina, 41

Kinsey, Alfred, 126–129, 130
Klee, Paul, 9
Kopf, Jennifer, 22
Kozma, Liat, 109, 118–119
Krafft-Ebing, Richard von, 59–60
Kriegspsychologisches (Hirschfeld), 34
Krupp, Friedrich, 50
Kunzel, Regina, 6

Labouchère amendment, 59
Leng, Kirsten, 81
Lesbianism, 27, 30–31, 49–50, 52
Levy-Lenz, Ludwig, 74, 85–86, 92, 103
Linsert, Richard, 80, 106
Lochrie, Karma, 44
Love, Heather, 7, 8, 39, 102, 105, 129

Mak, Geertje, 84–85
Malinowski, Bronislaw, 116

INDEX 213

Mancini, Elena, 33
Mann, Franziska, 80
Marhoefer, Laurie, 35
Marx, Karl, 45–46
Mayo, Katherine, 115
Moll, Albert, 68, 145n80
Muñoz, Jose, 38
Münzenberg, Willi, 81–82

Naturgesetze der Liebe (Hirschfeld), 15
Nazism: and attacks against Hirschfeld, 7, 93–94; and homosexuality, 92, 94–96, 97, 98–99, 131; and the Institute of Sexual Science, 92–94; racial ideology of, 14–15, 97

Panhumanism, 122
Pansexuality, 16
Paragraph 175, 25–26, 47, 80, 90, 97
Paranoia, 27
Patel, Geeta, 109
Paul, Cedar, 14, 124
Paul, Eden, 14, 68, 124
Pedophilia, 59–60, 68, 69. *See also* Children: sexual abuse of
Poignant, Roslyn, 22
Pomeroy, Wardell, 128
"The Priest and the Acolyte" (Bloxham), 61–62
Puar, Jasbir, 36, 134

Queer, definition of, 10
Qureshi, Sadiah, 22

Racial displays, 20, 22–23
Racial mixing, 23
Racial theory, 15–16
Racism, 20–21, 25, 30, 35, 95, 114, 116–117, 124
Racism (Hirschfeld), 13, 14–17
Rawson, K. J., 84
Reich, Wilhelm, 65
Robins, Ashley, 53

Sanger, Margaret, 79, 90–91, 105
Sappho und Sokrates (Hirschfeld), 24, 54
Scheper-Hughes, Nancy, 6
Sedgwick, Eve Kosofsky, 26
Sellars, Sean, 53
Sex education, 67–68

Sexology, emergence of, 6
The Sexual History of the World War (Hirschfeld), 34–35
Sexual intermediaries (sexuelle Zwischenstufen), 30, 81, 87–90, 91, 121, 127
Sexualpsychologie und Volkspsychologie (Hirschfeld), 27–28
Shahani, Nishant, 118
Shapiro, Bernard, 86, 103–104
Soldiers, 19, 29, 33
Somerville, Siobhan, 13
Soviet Russia, 65–66, 67, 81
Spivak, Gayatri, 116
Spohr, Max, 24
Stead, W. T., 59, 115
Stekel, Wilhelm, 60
Stephens, Elizabeth, 7
Stöcker, Helene, 80–81
Stoler, Ann Laura, 36
Stone, Amy L., 4
Stryker, Susan, 84
Suicide, 39–41, 42–44; lesbian, 49–50; in prison, 48; statistics on, 45–47, 49; terminology of, 40–41; of young officer, 39–41
Sullivan, Shannon, 19
Sutton, Katie, 85–86, 90
Symonds, John Addington, 61–62

Tao Li, 4, 110–111, 118, 123, 124
Tardieu, Auguste Ambroise, 60
Taxil, Léo, 27
Third sex, 90
Titus Pearls, 107, 119
Tobias, Recha, 81
Tobin, Robert Deam, 19, 24, 29
Transgender people, 1–2, 70, 76, 84–87, 88–90, 100
Transparent (TV series), 1–2
Transvestites, 33, 84–83, 85, 103, 112. *See also* Transgender people
Tribadism, 25, 27, 29–31
Turville-Petre, Francis, 83

Ulrichs, Karl Heinrich, 46, 64

Veidt, Conrad, 50–51, 108
Vicinus, Martha, 61
Viereck, George, 105–107
Violence, definition of, 6–7, 66
Virchow, Rudolf, 18, 64

Warum Hassen uns die Völker? (Hirschfeld), 31–33
Weinberg, George, 28
Wilde, Oscar, 52–53, 54–56, 62, 133
Wissenschaftlich-humanitäres Kommittee (WhK; Scientific Humanitarian Committee), 24–25, 33, 42–43, 80, 106

Wolff, Charlotte, 32, 93
Woolf, Virginia, 38, 83

Yearbook for Sexual Intermediaries (journal), 24–25, 42, 80, 112

Zionism, 120, 122

Heike Bauer is a Senior Lecturer in English and Gender Studies at Birkbeck College, University of London. She is the author of *English Literary Sexology: Translations of Inversion, 1860–1930*, the editor of *Women and Cross-Dressing, 1800–1939* and *Sexology and Translation: Cultural and Scientific Encounters across the Modern World* (Temple), and the coeditor (with Matt Cook) of *Queer 1950s: Rethinking Sexuality in the Postwar Years*.

www.ingramcontent.com/pod-product-compliance
Lightning Source LLC
Chambersburg PA
CBHW020653230426

43665CB00008B/418